The Wooden Horse

'Tony Winyard.'

'What's he going to do?'

John was examining his reflection for any unblackened patches. 'He's going to crawl out of the bottom hut to attract the dogs up to that end of the compound.'

'Sooner him than me,' Pomfret said.

'Or me,' Peter said. 'He's done it several times. He carries a bag of pepper and reckons that if the worst comes to the worst he can throw it in the dog's face. It'll be useful if he can keep the dogs up that end. They stage it rather like a bullfight. Tony's the matador. The others each have a hole in the floor of their room and shout to distract the dog's attention. The poor bloody animal doesn't know which way to go.' I hope, he thought. He looked again at the watch. 'OK, John. Off we go.'

He crossed to the trapdoor and lowered himself into the space under the hut. The sand felt cool to his hands and the air was musty and full of the odour of pinewood. He crawled towards the edge of the hut and lay waiting until John joined him. 'After the next beam,' he whispered. 'Then we'll make a dash for the sand pit.'

Running, bent double, they reached the sand pit and crouched in its welcome darkness, gasping for breath, reluctant to begin the long crawl to the bathhouse. Peter looked up at the sky. It was the first time he had been out-of-doors at night since he was captured. There were no clouds and the heavens were trembling with a myriad stars. The moon, past its zenith, would rise later. They must be safely back in the hut by then.

'Better get going.'

It took them several minutes to wriggle under the coiled wire round the bathhouse; easing themselves through, stopping to free their clothes from the rusty spikes. But once inside, with the wire replaced behind them, they were free from the dogs and the sweeping searchlights. They took a few minutes' rest while their eyes adjusted to the gloom. Then they worked fast, in silence. Peter selected offcut lengths of rafter, and John scoured the floor for nails and any tools that might have been left lying around. He struck luck with a bricklayer's trowel –

ideal for the tunnel – and a handful of long nails.

'Ready, Pete?'

'Just need two long ones for the bearers,' Peter whispered. 'You go ahead and I'll pass it through the wire.'

'Don't be long.'

Between them they dragged the awkward lengths of timber back to the sand pit, trying to churn up the surface as little as they could. Three times they had to lie flat while the blinding beam of the searchlight raked the compound. It's just like being over Berlin, Peter thought. Just the same feeling of naked vulnerability.

They heard a dog bark; a short sharp yelp of rage that made them grin nervously in the darkness as they squirmed under the hut. There was more than the usual noise coming from the hut; a carefully orchestrated background, arranged by Phil, to divert the attention of the guards. They knew that every blackout shutter in the hut was unfastened, that men were waiting in every room to drag them inside if they had to bolt for it.

They reached their own room without being discovered, and buried the timber and the trowel in the sand beneath it.

•   •   •

The next morning Peter went along to the camp theatre to borrow some tools, while John canvassed the compound for prisoners who would be willing to vault.

The theatre was a large room formed by removing two of the partition walls in one of the centre huts. A low stage had been erected at one end of the room. Behind the stage was a small dark recess used as dressing-room, property-room and carpenter's shop.

Before going to Liverpool Peter had worked with his father creating sets for the West End theatre. Now he was painting the scenery for Robbie's next production, *Private Lives*. The scenery was made up of narrow 'flats' – wooden frames covered with thin brown paper. If the covering of the frame was done on a damp day the paper contracted when the weather changed, and split. If the covering was done on a dry day the paper expanded and sagged. It was a usual thing to paint an entire 'flat' one evening and return the following morning to find it useless.

McIntyre, the stage carpenter, was making easy chairs from the plywood chests in which the Red Cross supplies arrived from England. He was a typical stage carpenter, taciturn, pessimistic, and a genius at improvization.

'Morning, Mac. How's it going?'

'All right.'

'I wonder if I could borrow a hammer and a saw?'

'Aye. If you take care of 'em.'

Peter sat in one of the finished armchairs and looked round. Mac's retreat. The bulwark he had built himself against the boredom of prison life. Pieces of furniture, machines for 'noises off', props. All Mac's. He leaned back in the chair.

'This is a damned comfortable chair, Mac.'

'Aye.' (Hammering at an unfinished chair.)

'We could do with one of these in our room.'

'Aye,' Mac said. 'I daresay.'

Peter sat up. 'Mac – could you spare me any of this plywood?'

'What for?'

'I want to make a vaulting-horse.'

'A what did ye say?'

'A vaulting-horse. You know – one of those box horses. I want to cover the sides with plywood.'

McIntyre straightened up. 'Aye. You'll need quite a few boxes for that. I'm having a load sent in from the Kommandantur. I'll have some extra ones put in for you.'

'Thanks a lot . . . Could you spare any three-inch nails? I'll get on with making the framework this morning and then I'll be ready for the plywood when it arrives.'

'Aye.' McIntyre was silent for a moment. 'Why the sudden interest in gymnastics?'

Peter lowered his voice. 'Camouflage for a hole.'

'Sorry, Pete.' McIntyre's attitude became at once cold and antagonistic. 'I can't let you use these tools for escape purposes. You know that as well as I do. They're on parole. Why

47

the hell don't you give it a rest?'

'Sorry, Mac.' He understood McIntyre's jealousy for his tools, his reliance on the parole for everything that made prison life tolerable for him. 'It's all right, I shouldn't have asked you really.' He started to move towards the door.

'Why not go along and see Wings Cameron?' McIntyre said. 'He's got a few illicit tools and he'll lend a hand in making it.'

'I'll go along now,' Peter said. 'Thanks all the same, Mac.' As he walked away from the theatre he wondered why McIntyre had suggested that. Just to get rid of him, or with a genuine desire to help? How little I know of him, he thought. How little I know of any of them. Old Mac, completely absorbed in his carpentry, proud of his resourcefulness in making something out of nothing, making a vocation out of imprisonment.

Wings Cameron lived in a small room at the end of Hut 64. As a wing commander he enjoyed the privilege of a room to himself. He needed it. He was another enthusiast, and enthusiasts are not easy to live with in a prison camp. Like Mac he loved making things. Give him a piece of string, some bent nails, a few empty Klim tins – leave him alone for a while – and he would produce a lamp, a cooking stove, a patent device for digging tunnels – whatever you had asked him for.

As Peter walked down the corridor of Hut 64 he could hear the sounds of hammering coming from the room at the end. Good show, he thought, he's in the mood for some heavy work. He stopped at the wing commander's door. Stuck to the centre panel was a cartoon cut from an American magazine. It showed a convict digging a hole in the floor of his cell. He was using a pickaxe. Outside the barred door, over which the convict had draped a blanket, stood two warders. 'I don't know what he's making,' one of them was saying, 'but it's keeping him very quiet.'

Peter knocked on the door, waited a moment and went in.

The room was twelve feet by six feet. Across the narrowness of it, at the end farthest from the door, stood a two-tier bunk. The bottom bunk was made up for sleeping. The top bunk was a confusion of old Klim tins, bits of wire, bed-boards, the pieces of a broken-down cast-iron range, and the remains of a wooden bicycle that Wings had started to make and never finished. Klim tins stood in rows on wooden shelves fixed to the walls. Klim tins stood on the table and on the chairs. Klim tins overflowed all these and stood in serried rows under the bunks. The tins were filled with nails, lengths of string, screws, nuts and bolts, small pieces of glass, odds and ends of paint from the theatre; everything that Wings had acquired from years of diligent scrounging.

Along the wall under the window were a drawing board and a work bench. On the drawing board was pinned a scale drawing of a sailing yacht. On the work bench lay another confusion of odds and ends, a vice made by Wings out of the parts of an old bed and a model steam engine constructed from Klim tins and a German water bottle.

He was a small man with a large moustache. A plumber's moustache, hiding his upper lip. He was wearing a pair of Egyptian sandals, rose-coloured socks, paint-splashed grey flannel trousers and a bright yellow shirt with a large red handkerchief of Paisley design knotted loosely round his neck. He had been shot down wearing these clothes. 'Thought I'd dress like a foreigner,' he explained later. 'Then I shouldn't be noticed if I had to bale out. But I think I must have dressed as the wrong sort of foreigner because I was arrested quite soon.'

The wing commander was on his knees nailing a wooden batten to the floor. The batten formed a frame round a large square hole.

'What's that for?' Peter asked.

'To stop me falling down the hole.' The wing commander replied without looking up from his work.

'No, I don't mean the piece of wood. I mean the hole.'

'Oh, that!' He straightened up. 'That's part of an air-conditioning plant I'm fitting.'

'How will it work?'

'I'm fitting a fan under the floor. I've got the parts for it here.' He pointed to a wheel with propeller-like blades cut

49

from plywood. 'The fan is driven by a belt and pulley from a large wheel under the floor. A shaft runs from the wheel up through the floor to the top of the work bench. I shall have this old gramophone turntable mounted on top of the shaft. The winding handle of the gramophone will be fixed to the turntable as a crank. When the room gets too hot I merely turn the handle and cold air is driven up through the hole in the floor. The hot air leaves through another hole I'm going to cut near the ceiling.'

'Why don't you use the gramophone motor to drive the fan?'

'Oh, the motor's broken. I used the parts to make a clock.'

'Wait till the goons see it. They'll be after you for damage to Reich property.'

'They have.' The wing commander said it with satisfaction. 'The Feldwebel came round this morning and started screaming at me. I told him to push off and bring someone who spoke English. Then a Gefreiter came crawling under the hut and tried to nail the hole up from underneath. I pranced around stamping on his fingers. He went away after a bit and came back with the Lager Offizier. I'm going to the cooler for fourteen days – when there's a cell free.'

'It's a wonder they don't take your tools away.'

Wings looked cunning. 'Look at this.' He pointed to a tool-rack fixed to the wall over the work bench. 'Have a look at these tools.'

Peter examined them. Every one was phoney. It must have taken Wings weeks to fashion the hacksaw blades and wicked-looking knives from pieces of rolled-out Klim tins. There were chisels too, made of wood and painted to look like steel.

'They do a swoop now and again, but all they find is this. All my real tools are hidden behind the panelling of the wall. They think I'm mad, but quite harmless really.'

Peter laughed. 'I expect they think most of us are round the bend. I want to make a vaulting-horse and I came along to ask your advice and see if you could let me have a bit of plywood and the loan of some tools.'

'Yes, I think so.' To him a vaulting-horse was a problem

50

in terms of materials available.

Peter explained that the horse was to conceal the entrance to a tunnel.

Wings was at once enthusiastic. 'We must set it out first.' He unpinned the drawing of the sailing yacht and replaced it with a clean sheet of paper. 'It will have to be light and strong,' he said. 'Strong both ways. Both for vaulting and for carrying you inside it.' He took up a scale rule and bent over the drawing board.

3

Between them they had built the vaulting-horse. It stood four feet six inches high, the base covering an area of five feet by three feet. The sides were covered with two-feet square plywood sheets from Red Cross packing cases, generously donated by Wings from his secret store. The sides tapered up to the top which was of wood bed-boards padded with their bedding and covered with white canvas from the bales in which cigarettes arrived from England. There were four slots, four inches long by three inches wide, cut in the plywood sides. When pieces of rafter six feet long and three inches by two inches thick were pushed through these holes the horse could be carried by four men in the manner of a sedan chair.

Vaulting horse showing one lifting bar in position

The horse was kept in the canteen. This was a canteen in name only, a long low extension to the camp kitchen and it housed the barber's shop and a large empty room used by the camp orchestra and choir. Like all the other buildings in the compound it was raised above the surface of the ground, but it had brick foundations and was more solidly built than the living-huts. The entrance was by double doors at the top of a short flight of wide wooden steps. To the left of the entrance was the camp notice board where German standing orders and notices were pinned.

While the horse was being built John, with some help from Phil, had been recruiting prisoners for the vaulting. He had made posters which he stuck up round the compound, advertising gym classes to be held every afternoon. Special prisoners were detailed by the Escape Committee to talk to the German guards, remarking on this typically British craze for exercising and telling them, casually, about the vaulting-horse.

•　　•　　•

The doors of the canteen were flung open and a team of prisoners dressed only in shorts marched down the steps. The four strongest members brought up the rear, carrying a box-like object slung on wooden poles. At a likely spot, not too far from the canteen and behind the goal-posts at one end of the football pitch, they placed it carefully on the ground and withdrew the poles.

The team formed up in line. Under the direction of the captain of the team they began to vault over the box. The guards, bored with watching the prisoners walking the endless circuit of the wire, turned towards the unusual spectacle. They did not give their whole attention to the vaulting. A boxing match or a faked spontaneous fight was a well-known kriegie method of distracting their attention while an attempt was being made on the wire. So the guards watched the vaulting but cast frequent glances along the stretch of wire for which they were responsible.

The standard of vaulting was high. The captain of the team led his men in a complicated series of jumps. But one of the men was clumsy and his vaulting inept. The guards soon singled him out as the butt of the party and grinned whenever he failed to clear the horse. The vaulting had drawn a crowd of amused prisoners, who jeered and catcalled when he made his run up to the box. Every time he failed to clear the horse he drew a guffaw of laughter from an appreciative audience.

Soon the guards in the watch-towers were leaning on their elbows waiting for him to make his run. It was not often that they had the chance to laugh at the prisoners. The boot was usually on the other foot. The more the spectators laughed the more determined this man appeared to be to clear the obstacle. He took a final desperate leap and, missing his foot-step, crashed into the horse and knocked it over on its side, so that the interior was in full view of the guards.

The horse was empty. The vaulters righted the box and went on with their sport. Soon they carried the horse back into the canteen, where it would remain until the following afternoon. Before they left the canteen they tied pieces of black cotton across the doorway and from the edge of the horse to the skirting-board.

In the morning the cotton was broken. The ferrets were taking no chances. During the night the vaulting-horse had been carefully examined.

* * *

It was a week since the vaulting had first started. *Appell* over, Peter and John were walking round the circuit.

'I think we ought to start digging tomorrow,' John said. 'The goons have got used to the vaulting now. We've knocked the horse over often enough for them to see that there's nothing inside.'

Peter paused to light his pipe. 'Did you ever hear the story of the two bulls?'

'No,' John said. 'What was that?'

'There were two bulls in a pen. One was an old bull, the other was a young bull. Suddenly the young bull said to the old bull, "Look! The farmer's left the gate open. There are some cows in the next field. Let's dash down and do a couple." "No," said the old bull, "we'll *walk* down and do the lot." '

John laughed. 'That's all very well if you're a bull with a field full of cud-chewing cows contentedly waiting their turn.

The Wooden Horse

REVISED EDITION

Eric Williams

Collins
St James's Place, London
1979

William Collins Sons & Co Ltd
London · Glasgow · Auckland · Sydney
Toronto · Johannesburg

FIRST IMPRESSION	FEBRUARY, 1949	
SECOND	,, FEBRUARY, 1949	
THIRD	,, MARCH, 1949	
FOURTH	,, MARCH, 1949	
FIFTH	,, MARCH, 1949	
SIXTH	,, APRIL, 1949	
SEVENTH	,, MAY, 1949	
EIGHTH	,, MAY, 1949	
NINTH	,, JUNE, 1949	
TENTH	,, JULY, 1949	
ELEVENTH	,, OCTOBER, 1949	
TWELFTH	,, DECEMBER, 1949	
THIRTEENTH	,, APRIL, 1950	
FOURTEENTH	,, AUGUST, 1950	
FIFTEENTH	,, OCTOBER, 1950	
SIXTEENTH	,, DECEMBER, 1950	
SEVENTEENTH	,, MARCH, 1951	
EIGHTEENTH	,, JUNE, 1951	
NINETEENTH	,, NOVEMBER, 1952	
TWENTIETH	,, JANUARY, 1955	
TWENTY-FIRST	,, MAY, 1956	
TWENTY-SECOND	,, NOVEMBER, 1958	
TWENTY-THIRD	,, JANUARY, 1964	
TWENTY-FOURTH	,, FEBRUARY, 1967	
TWENTY-FIFTH	,, JUNE, 1972	
NEW AND REVISED	,, 1979	

© Eric Williams 1949 and 1979

ISBN 0 00 216875 8

Set in Plantin
Made and printed in Great Britain by
William Collins Sons & Co Ltd, Glasgow

For Sibyl

again – as always

*'There was things which he stretched,
but mainly he told the truth.'*

Mark Twain

Explanation

During the Second World War three British officers escaped from a German prison camp by digging a tunnel whose entrance they concealed beneath a wooden vaulting horse. All three reached home.

I was one of them. I had been captured a year earlier, three days after my Stirling bomber was shot down in a raid on Duisburg in the Ruhr. Although captain of the aircraft, I was not the pilot but the observer, and while I was grounded in Germany observers became redundant. Thanks to the inventions of the boffins, navigating and bomb-aiming could now be done more efficiently by instruments operated by highly trained specialists.

On my return to England I reported to the Air Ministry, but they patently did not know what to do with me. I applied for the pilot's course which I had been too old to take at the beginning of the war. They said they would consider the application and sent me on extended leave. This was broken at intervals by tours of airfields around the country where I lectured the new breed of aircrews on what to expect if shot down over enemy territory. For this I was given an allocation of petrol coupons which enabled me to visit the families of fellow-prisoners who had asked me to take home messages of comfort and reassurance. The parents, wives and sweethearts asked so many questions that I determined to write a book describing the day-to-day life of a prisoner of war.

Military Intelligence had decreed that prison camps were on the Secret List. Even though I might, and did, know what was safe to write about and what was not, *no* factual material was to be published. I well remember the peremptory summons to one of those Home Counties mansions so dear to Military

7

Intelligence, and the fury of the Brigadier when I told him that I intended to publish the book as fiction.

On leave in the 1944 London of buzz-bombs, still waiting word from the Air Ministry about the pilot's course, I sat down and wrote the story of my last raid, capture and life in three German camps. I omitted or deliberately made misleading any mention of escape, and suppressed all information of possible use to the enemy. Writing in the form of a novel I was able to reduce the number of background characters and to select and highlight those incidents which seemed to me most valid. I found it convenient to describe my own actions, thoughts and emotions by writing in the third person and calling myself Peter Howard. My other characters, though typical, were not based on individual prisoners. The description of life in the camps where I had been held was as true as I could make it.

The finished novel was short, about 60,000 words. Its title was *Goon In The Block*, the warning cry with which the P.O.W. broadcast the arrival of a German guard. I sent the typescript to Jonathan Cape. He accepted it within forty-eight hours and published it in the early summer of 1945 when hundreds of thousands of prisoners held in Germany were beginning to stream home. Although the whole print was sold in the first week, wartime paper rationing precluded a reprint.

Inspired by *Goon In The Block*'s modest success and the encouraging reviews, I began to write my escape story. The war in Europe was nearly over but I was serving in the RAF and the Official Secrets Act was still in force. For this reason, and because I liked the freedom it gave me, I again wrote in the form of a novel. Again my alter ego was Peter Howard. My fellow-escapers Michael Codner and Oliver Philpot emerged thinly disguised as John Clinton and Philip Rowe. The other prisoners portrayed are more difficult to identify; but ex-inmates of Stalag-Luft III may recognize Tommy Calnan, Aidan Crawley and a few other originals.

Writing the story as fiction gave me perhaps too much freedom. When faced with the problem of not knowing what had been going on around me – or forgetting exactly what happened when – I was able to take, and happily took, a few liberties with facts. The horse, the tunnel, the break from the camp, the train journey across enemy territory, the stay in Stettin, our contacts with French workers and the escape from Germany itself were, and are today, vivid in my memory. After a night of seasickness in the stinking bilges of a Baltic freighter events became a bit confused. Hidden ashore in Copenhagen as bewildered protégés of a teenage Danish seaman, Mike and I no longer had any say in our destiny. Following the thrill of running our own lives, of being fugitives in the midst of the enemy, the final crossing to neutral Sweden seemed a tame way to end the story. Accordingly I invented a climax which, I thought, matched the preceding pages for excitement.

Fair enough.

The escape story, which I called *The Sagan Horse*, was nearly 200,000 words long. I sent it to Jonathan Cape whose contract for *Goon In The Block* had given him an option on my next book. He turned it down, saying that no one wanted to read about the war. As it incorporated much background material from *Goon In The Block* I retrieved rights, and was free to offer the new book to another publisher.

I offered it, in all, to seven publishers. It was rejected by every one – each time on the grounds that war books were finished. Each time I got it back I worked on it before sending it out again.

I wrote the first version on the various airfields where I trained as a pilot and on board troopships on my way back from the Far East where I had been posted to recover Allied prisoners from the Japanese. On demobilization, in common with a million others, I had to find a way of earning a living. I was the richer by all of £200 from *Goon In The Block* – and Cape had rejected its successor. My pre-war employers were committed to finding good jobs for their ex-Servicemen. Because of my somewhat ephemeral literary experience they offered to make me book-buyer for their seven provincial department stores.

If one had to have a nine-to-five indoor job, book-buying

for a nation-wide organization was a pleasant way of selling one's time. It gave me an office in the West End of London and plunged me into the world of books. My library grew by leaps and bounds; I had only to voice an interest over the telephone and an advance copy, with the publisher's compliments, was on my desk within the hour. I was invited to literary cocktail parties where I met established authors. I gambled the firm's money on personal preferences – and worked evenings and weekends on my own unpublished manuscript.

One day Ronald Politzer, publicity manager of Collins, invited me to a business lunch. He talked of his experiences as an intelligence officer in Cairo, and I told him about my Home Counties Brigadier. He wanted to know how I had escaped from Germany. I said that it was a long story and would send him the typescript.

Ronald was enthusiastic about the book and recommended it for publication. However he felt that the story should start, not with the last raid and capture, but with the idea for the successful escape. He also suggested that the title be changed to *The Wooden Horse*. He was right on both counts.

On the day before publication – in February 1949 – eleven of the thirteen Sunday newspapers carried a feature or a review, and at least one printed a leading article on the escape. The dailies and periodicals followed suit. I was elated at the publicity and the fact that when, as with *Goon In The Block*, the first print sold out immediately Collins, unlike Cape, were able to reprint. I was concerned that the book was being read as straight autobiography and not as a novel. Nevertheless, it seemed carping and pedantic, then, to point out how much of the story was fact and how much fiction.

Now I am not so sure. I believe that one's sense of how to behave is shaped largely by one's childhood reading. Not only does the type of hero, or non-hero, of contemporary literature reflect the thinking of that generation of adults, it shapes the thinking of generations to follow. Over the thirty years since the publication of *The Wooden Horse* I have regretted that children have grown up believing that an escaping British P.O.W. – who had been honourably treated by his captors – had crept up on a German sentry from behind and murdered him in cold blood.

When a children's edition was published in 1956 I did modify this act of mayhem. In this thirtieth anniversary edition I have set the record straight.

* * *

It must be difficult for the reader who was not there to appreciate the strange mixture of chivalry and expediency which governed the Luftwaffe's treatment of its prisoners. We were, generally, treated with politeness and in accordance with the Geneva Convention; the international agreement designed by professional soldiers to protect their kind by codifying the conditions of the prisoner of war and his behaviour in captivity.

We were housed well away from the battle zone, and the fact that we were always hungry was not usually deliberate deprivation. Allied airmen fell into German hands straight from life in a Mess where they were given special rations. The standard diet of the German troops was far below that of any Allied serviceman, even below that of British civilians in their beleaguered and overcrowded islands. What would have been a normal meal for our guards was considered by us to be quite inadequate. Yet at the war's end, when the German nation was practically starving, there was an accumulated supply of some 150,000 Red Cross parcels from Canada full of tinned meat, jam, milk, tea, coffee and chocolate in the storerooms of Stalag-Luft III. There were millions of cigarettes, crates of pipe tobacco and mountains of soap, of all of which the Germans were in dire need. It says much for Luftwaffe discipline that so little of this treasure, hoarded by the prisoners in case supplies failed to get through, found its way on to the German market.

The *kriegsgefangener* (or kriegie as he called himself) was also allowed to receive clothing, books, sports equipment and musical instruments from home. The civilian suit which disguised me as a French worker was sent out to our Air Force camp as a Royal Marine officer's dress uniform. That the

Germans could accept that any prisoner would want to wear mess kit when he sat down to a dinner of boiled swedes, rotten potatoes and a slice of reconstituted meat – which he himself had cooked over a smoking stove – is hard to believe. That they did not suspect that this uniform had been tailored for easy conversion is incomprehensible, especially as an identical uniform had been used by a First World War escaper and described in detail in his book.

Most of us responded to our guards' polite correctness with derision and contempt. We never called the Germans anything but goons. This soubriquet originated in a doggerel dinned into us during operational flying training: *Beware of the hun in the sun – beware of the goon in the moon.* Had we behaved reasonably, and not like a mob of unruly schoolboys, fewer of the enemy would have been needed to guard us, more could have been released for active service; and our morale would not have been so high.

Just occasionally we were embarrassed by our behaviour. One evening the German officers were invited to a camp concert. Courteously they left their sidearms in the cloakroom. A prisoner planning to escape disguised as a guard stole a pistol. The German guests were shocked by this breach of hospitality; their British hosts were dismayed. For weeks afterwards the expressions 'damned bad show' and 'not on, old boy' could be heard rumbling round the huts. The culprit was shamed into returning his loot.

This relationship between prisoner and guard, outdated by the conception of total war in which any skulduggery is permissible, worked well enough in World War I and, up to the time of my escape, in the European theatre of World War II. Then two factors began to affect the situation of the escaper. The Allied Command stepped up aid to resistance movements in the Occupied Countries by dropping arms and experts to train the guerrillas in their use; and the Escape Committees in the prison camps, now able to produce any quantity of forged papers, concentrated on larger and larger tunnels through which hundreds of prisoners might escape together.

It is small wonder that the Gestapo, which was always trying to wrest control of P.O.W. camps from the military, put two and two together to make five and insisted that the object of such highly organized mass breaks was not to escape to Britain but to provide trained officers to encourage and lead a revolt of foreign workers inside the Third Reich. This, they claimed, contravened the Geneva Convention which deemed that a man who had surrendered his arms had thereby become a non-combatant. Prisoners who escaped must be shot on recapture.

It is true that our guards stuck up posters in the camp to warn us of the new danger – but we laughed the whole thing off as a typical example of goon bluff.

Mike, Ollie and I did not realize how near we were to death in front of a firing squad or from a bullet in the back. To us escaping was still a sport; our Luftwaffe guards, opponents in a game which had set rules observed by both sides. Even outside the camp the escaper was the responsibility of the camp commandant and, if caught, had always been returned to him. However, the papers we carried were not, as in earlier years, palpable improvizations but expert forgeries. We did not know that the *Metallhuttenwerke* company whose letter heading was on one of our forged papers was a genuine German company, nor that the original had been stolen by a Jewish employee and, at the risk of her life, passed to a French worker for onward transmission to London. Two prisoners who escaped from Stalag-Luft III soon after us were nearly handed over to the Gestapo by the ordinary police because of the for onward transmission to London. Two prisoners who escaped through the big tunnel in the North compound, fifty were shot by the Gestapo although their status as prisoners of war had been clearly established. I shall never forget my sick feeling of disbelief when I was given the news at M.I.9 in March 1944.

The camp commandant, Colonel von Lindeiner, who had demanded the return of his charges, was himself imprisoned after being courtmartialled for 'tolerance, patience and consideration' towards the enemy.

Now that war has become total and its aim the destruction of as many lives – but not buildings – as possible, there may be no more prisoners. If there are, I doubt we shall see a camp commandant, a gentleman himself, salute a motley gang of bedraggled intransigents with the words 'Good morning, gentlemen'.

*　　*　　*

In this revised edition I have, I hope, made clearer how much Mike and I owed our final escape from Germany to Frenchmen who had been conscripted as forced labour, and to Sigmund Hjelm-Jensen the nineteen-year-old Danish seaman who looked after us from the moment he met us outside Stettin docks and smuggled us aboard his ship. Bravery in the heat of action with the support of your Government is one thing; to risk your neck to assist an escaping prisoner requires a different brand of courage.

Sigmund is now a retired ship's captain, living with his wife Kamma in a house they built themselves on the island of Ibiza. He had remained a good friend, and it is thanks to him and his excellent memory that I have been able to reconstruct what happened to Mike and myself after that night of sea-sickness in the *Norensen*'s bilges; as well as what happened to her ship's company when she was waylaid by the German Navy after a tip-off to the Gestapo that she was carrying escaping prisoners of war.

For details of what went on in the camp after the tunnel was discovered I am grateful to Group Captain R. B. Ward who was the Escape Committee clothing officer and adjutant in charge of the subsequent identity parades; to Group Captain W. S. O. Randle, C.B.E., A.F.C., D.F.M., himself an escaper from Occupied Europe and today Librarian at the Royal Air Force Museum, Hendon; and to Doctor G. M. Bayliss, Keeper of Printed Books at the Imperial War Museum. Like Sigmund, all three responded swiftly and generously to my cry for help.

I refreshed my memory by re-reading *Free As A Running Fox* by T. D. Calnan, *Escape In Germany* by Aidan Crawley, *A Crowd Is Not Company* by Robert Kee, *Stolen Journey* by

14

Oliver Philpot and *Wings Day* by Sidney Smith. These books carried me back over the years to the strange half-life of the prisoner of war, from which I had the luck to escape.

ERIC WILLIAMS

Kara Ağaç, Turkey. 1978

Inside

I

The man in the upper bunk stirred, grunted and turned over on his back. He lay still for a few seconds, then with a jerk that shook the whole structure he sat up, rubbed his eyes and yawned.

In the bunk below, Peter did not open his eyes. A few scraps of wood shavings fell from the mattress above and settled on his face. He brushed them away and pulled the thin grey blanket tightly around his ears. He had seen it all too often. A pair of legs covered with long sandy hair would appear over the side of the bunk, toes wriggling disgustingly as their owner pulled on socks and clogs before landing like an avalanche beside his head. He tensed himself expectantly. Crash! Bang! Ger . . . doyng! The room shook. One of the shrouded figures in the other bunks moved impatiently and swore in an undertone. A stool was sent crashing on its side, skidding over the wooden floor. Heavy footsteps stamped across the room, the door was wrenched open. A moment's silence, then clang! as the lid of the tea-jug standing in the corridor was banged shut. More heavy footsteps, the creak of a swinging cupboard door, the sounds of pouring water, of a spoon being stirred violently inside a pottery mug. A gulping noise, the clatter of the mug on the table, more footsteps. The room shook again as the door was slammed.

Peter relaxed and opened his eyes. He knew exactly what had happened since the first convulsive thrashing of limbs had jolted him from sleep. Bennett had pulled on his socks and his wooden clogs which had spent the night beneath his pillow. Next he had leaped for one of the stools, missed it, kicked it over, and sent it slithering across the floor. He had looked astonished, and stamped out into the corridor to see whether the next-door cook had fetched the hot water and made the tea. Finding the jug still contained only a handful of dry leaves, he had forced another exaggerated look of astonishment, and filled a mug with cold water from the large pottery jug which stood near the stove. He had found an envelope of lemonade powder, stirred its contents into the water, drunk the mixture in three great gulps, and gone out, slamming the door behind him, to walk round the circuit until breakfast-time.

Every morning since he had arrived at Stalag-Luft III earlier in the spring, Peter had wakened to the same abrupt reveille. In the beginning he had opened his eyes at the preliminary upheaval. Now he kept them closed until Bennett left the room.

Not a sound came from the other six occupants of the room. Either they were asleep or enjoying the quiet now that Bennett was out of the way. Peter dug himself deeper into the mattress of wood shavings. The narrow cross-planks of the bunk had gone long ago for shoring in a tunnel or fuel for the stove. Now the mattress rested on a hammock of string saved from Red Cross parcels, and it was much more comfortable.

He looked round the small room he knew so well. Tongued-and-grooved pine walls and ceiling, pine floor. Four wooden two-tier bunks, four tall cupboards, a plank table on trestles, two forms and two stools. In one corner, incongruously, a blue-tiled stove. All German issue. In addition, the roughly carpentered shelves which made each bed-space the prisoner's own.

From the corner on his right came the mumbled refrain of Robbie's morning hymn of hate: 'Christ, what a noisy bugger that fellow Bennett is!' They would quarrel soon, Peter could see it coming. Starting over some small detail it would flare up into a bitter feud. A man would stand the boredom for so long and then, slowly at first, the personal habits of his seven companions would begin to wear him down. The way the man ate, or even his accent. Life with him at close quarters would become unbearable, and the quarrels would erupt more and more frequently, until one of them moved into another room.

Poor old Robbie had been a prisoner for well over three years – and a reverberating wooden hut was not Bennett's ideal background. He couldn't have been silent in a padded

18

cell with a thick cork floor. Peter sighed. The thought of a cork floor reminded him of bathrooms. He hadn't had a real bath since he'd been shot down; and he lay visualizing porcelain baths. Green, yellow, pink, black – no, he didn't like black. He liked a bath that lent its colour to the water. Green was best. A sea-green bath, paler green tiles on the walls. Perhaps a sunken bath – yes, a sunken bath, big enough for two to bathe in together. He thought about this for quite a while.

How the hell was he going to get out?'

The eight long wooden huts were locked from dusk till dawn, while specially trained dogs, occasionally visible in the beams of the searchlights on the watch-towers, ranged the deserted compound. The huts were raised on piles three feet above the ground, to discourage tunnelling. The ground, in dry weather, a carpet of soft grey dust; when wet, a sea of clinging mud. Below the surface the sand was reasonably firm, yellow when damp but drying to a startling whiteness in the sun. Good for tunnelling, but apt to fall when dry; and disposing of the white sand was one of the problems.

The *abort* and the washhouse, both built on solid concrete rafts, were possible starting-places; the canteen perhaps better still. But these were the province of the Escape Committee and reserved for 'mass breaks'. One such scheme, led by Bill White, was in operation now and going quite well. Peter wanted no part in a big tunnel 'dienst'. He'd tried it once in Oflag XXIB. Too many involved, too organized. Chaps got so fascinated by their tunnel that they sometimes forgot why they were digging it. Too far from the wire, anyway.

He thought of the wire, a hundred-and-fifty feet from the nearest hut. Two twelve-feet high fences of heavily-interlaced barbed wire set fifteen feet apart, the ground between covered with more, loosely coiled, wire. At intervals along the fence tall wooden towers, topped by sentry-boxes armed with machine-guns, and connected by telephone to the guardroom at the gate. Under the wire seismographs, sunk six feet into the ground, connected to a listening-post in the same guardroom. Twenty feet inside the fence the trip-wire, a foot above the ground; anyone stepping over this was shot at by the guards in the watch-towers or by the sentries outside the camp.

He imagined crawling between the trip-wire and the fence while a group of prisoners diverted the attention of the guards, then trying to cut his way through the wire in the field of fire of all those guns; and turned his thoughts again to tunnelling.

There might be a starting-place that no one had tried – though at this stage of the war it wasn't likely. Some of the prisoners had been trying to get out since 1939. Trouble was he was a comparative newcomer. John too. Odd that he should have been shot down over Germany the very day that John, the Army officer, had been captured in the desert. The seventeenth of December, 1942. It was one date he'd never forget. Now more than four months of '43 had slipped by already. If he and John were to get out before the winter they'd have to get a scheme going soon.

He looked across at the lower bunk nearest the stove, where John was sleeping, a seraphic smile on his face. Black hair worn longer than most, high cheekbones, point chin framed by a wispy beard. In sleep he seemed even younger than his twenty-one years. A student still, and absorbed in his books, yet determined to get back to the war. They'd met at Dulag-Luft, the transit camp, and soon discovered their common interest in escape. There was no one Peter would rather have at his side in a tricky situation.

Bennett apart, the others were easy enough to get on with. David, for instance, with his blue seaman's eyes and fiery beard. He seemed to have lost all interest in escape, although Peter had heard he'd made several daring attempts. Now he was running a farm on paper and all his books were about farming. At the right time of the year he would sow his crops and in due course he would harvest them. He kept a profit and loss account. Funny how seriously he took it. If it rained on the day when he had decided to reap he would walk about with a face of doom. If during a dry spell one of the others remarked on the fine weather he would mutter something about the oats needing rain. Peter smiled as he remembered the occasion when the lower meadows were flooding and David drove a flock of sheep to the safety of the hillside above the farm. The guards had been alarmed when the whole hut turned out to help him drive the sheep across the compound.

They had reached for their tommy-guns when they saw the throng of hissing, whistling, shouting prisoners driving nothing towards the fence. But the upper meadow was inside the wire, and no shots were fired.

The only man who knew more about farming than David was Bennett. But Bennett knew more about everything. Bennett the bull – full of 'bull'. You couldn't discuss anything with him in the room. No matter what the discussion, he would deliver himself of a categorical, crushing pronouncement which would kill the topic dead. Desultory attempts would be made to revive it but under the weight of authority behind the pronouncement the opposition would languish and finally relapse into a baffled and disgruntled silence.

There were many arguments. Paul caused a lot of the trouble. Tall and thin – so tall that you wondered how he had managed to fit into his Hurricane, he had joined the RAF straight from school and was the youngest member of the mess. His whole world was flying and the wide freedom of the sky; without these, he was lost, and moody. Bennett would pick on him for spending too much time on his bunk, doing nothing. Paul's quick temper would flare up, and Robbie would take his side in the ensuing argument.

Robbie, at 35, was the oldest among them, and the only Regular officer. Forced by engine failure to bale out of his Whitley when dropping leaflets over Germany at the time of the 'phoney war', he had been a prisoner longer than anyone else in the camp. He had come to terms with the knowledge that, now, he was not likely to rise beyond the rank of squadron leader; but he could not come to terms with Bennett.

'What about tea, Pete?'

'OK, Robbie. Bags of time yet.' He stretched and rolled off the bunk. It was his turn to be cook. Of all the chores of prison life cooking was the one he hated most. It had been harder for the early prisoners, who had cooked on wood fires in the open air. He had a cast-iron range – at least, he had a fourteenth share in one housed in a small room of its own at the end of the hut. Fourteen dinners for eight men had to be cooked on its one ring and in the small oven every evening. The Hut Cookery Officer drew up complicated rosters varying the turn of each room; so that no one duty cook always had first turn, gasping with watering eyes in clouds of pungent smoke, and none always the last, when the ration of brown-coal blocks had run out and the dying embers must be fanned into a fitful glow.

'Morning, Pete.' Nigel shared with John the bunks nearest the stove. Like most advantages in prison life this had its disadvantage. Although warmer in winter, the bunks were used as seats by their room-mates during the day. Peter preferred the colder privacy and fresher air of the wall by the window.

Nigel was lying on his back, right arm curled round his head, hand gently stroking his blond moustache. His expression was blissful.

Peter stood watching him. 'Why the hell do you keep doing that?'

'I like it, old boy. Feels as though someone else is doing it.' He winked.

'You're crazy.'

'I know. It's nice.'

Peter leaned on the window-sill. It was late spring. Beyond the wire he could see the pale fronds of a silver birch graceful against the dark background of the pine forest. He was fond of that silver birch. He had tried to paint it as a sharp, fragile silhouette against the winter sky; and as he saw it now, a cascade of delicate green, almost yellow in the morning sun. He had painted it often but had not yet been able to capture its isolated beauty, its aloofness against the darkness of the pines. The sky overhead was clear and still. It was going to be hot. Under the window the sand was moist with dew and dew sparkled on the barbed wire. The long green living huts looked washed and cool, uncluttered as yet by the thousand prisoners who would soon spread their restlessness throughout the camp. He refused to think of the biting flies that would swarm into the hut and plague them as the day warmed up.

'It's a lovely morning.'

'*Gut zeigen*. What about a spot of tea?' Nigel specialized in translating RAF slang literally into German. '*Gut zeigen*' was his way of saying 'Good show'. 'Bad show' became *'Schlecht zeigen'* and 'Fair enough' *'Blond genug'*. When he was depressed he considered himself to be *'gebraunt weg'* or 'browned-off'. He sometimes tried his German on the guards and was disappointed when they didn't understand.

'Coming up.' Peter was watching Bennett stride furiously along the track worn by the prisoners in their endless circuit of the trip-wire. To avoid friction when a thousand frustrated men were milling around trying to work off steam it had become a convention to walk only anti-clockwise round the circuit, and although the compound was deserted at this hour Bennett, predictably, was sticking to the convention.

'Come on, Pete,' Robbie called. 'The tea'll be cold.'

He left the window and fetched the jug from the corridor. The next-door cook had taken it, with his own, to the camp kitchen and made tea for both messes. Tomorrow it would be his turn and he would have to get up earlier, to be sure of finding the water on the boil. He took down seven mugs from the shelf over the stove and filled three, one for Nigel, one for Robbie and one for himself. He would not wake the others yet. There was still plenty of time before *appell*. Better prepare breakfast first.

There were dozens of cardboard Red Cross boxes littering the room. Boxes were piled on top of the cupboards, on the shelves, under the bunks, round the stove; filled with the prisoners' personal possessions, chips of wood and waste paper, rotting potatoes, tins of condensed milk and Klim, tobacco and cigarettes. From one of the boxes he extracted a heavy German loaf; ninety per cent potato and a liberal sprinkling of sawdust. A loaf that, if allowed to dry, would split into great fissures and become as hard as stone.

An eighth of a loaf a day was each man's ration. By cutting very thin slices he could make three for breakfast, three for lunch and one for tea. He cut twenty-four slices, spread them sparingly with margarine from a Red Cross parcel, and hacked open a tin of plum jam with a knife. Breakfast was ready. He wished the dinners were as easy. If he and John peeled the potatoes at tea-time and boiled them while no other cook wanted the ring . . .

He was still in pyjamas. 'What about a cold shower before breakfast, Nig?'

'*Blond genug*, old boy.' Nigel unwound himself from his blankets.

'Let's wake John.'

'What? Wake the child? Have a heart, old boy!' Nigel treated John with a teasing respect; respecting him for his intelligence and courage, teasing him because of his youth and absent-mindedness. John's mind was always on his books or lost in dreams of escape; so far removed from his surroundings that Nigel often had to go and find him and bring him to his meals. Nigel loved John and hid his affection behind a veil of chaffing and elaborate practical jokes.

'Yes, go on! Wake him up, it'll do him good.'

'Shall I?'

'Yes, go on!' Peter waited for the joke that had amused him every morning for days.

Nigel reached for his latest invention, a cocoa-tin suspended by a harness of string just above John's head. Through a hole in the top of the tin ran another string holding a bunch of bent and rusty nails. By pulling on the centre string Nigel could conjure forth a most satisfactory rattle. He pulled the string.

John did not wake.

'I think the loose bed-boards were a better idea,' Peter said.

'Yes, but a bit dangerous.' Nigel beamed as he remembered the previous waking device, an arrangement which had effectively removed the one remaining board which had held John's shaking bed together and had deposited him, complete with mattress, on the floor.

'Come on,' Peter said. 'Once round the compound and then a shower.'

Leaving John asleep they clambered out of the window. It was quicker than going via the door and corridor, and gave a sense of satisfaction in that they were not supposed to leave the hut that way.

Once more the room was quiet. Robbie lay lazily flapping at the flies that were already doing circuits and bumps inside his bed-space. There was the whole room for them to fly in and they had to come and buzz round him.

'Robbie – can't you do something about those two noisy blighters?' Pomfret, pale and indignant, was leaning over the side of the upper bunk opposite his. 'They're so horribly hearty. That damn' tin can thing. And why do they want to take a cold shower at this time of the morning? Besides, it's against regulations to climb out of the windows. They'll give the hut a bad name.'

'Keeps them happy, I suppose.'

'Well, it shouldn't. They've no right to be happy in a prison camp. It's not decent . . . and talking of decency, I suppose they're going to sunbathe in the nude again. The S.B.O. ought to stop it. It shouldn't be allowed.'

'Why in heaven not?' Robbie asked. 'There are no women for miles around – and even if there were they couldn't see inside the camp. If they want to get brown all over, why shouldn't they?'

'It's not decent,' Pomfret repeated. He selected a book from the shelf by his head, to show that he meant to have the last word.

'Oh, don't be so bloody lily-livered. I shall sunbathe myself when the weather gets really hot.' Robbie had been brought up in Kenya and suffered from the cold. He lay thinking of the play he was producing. As usual, the feminine lead was the trouble. Young Matthews had played it in the last four shows and the audience was too used to him. He might ask Black; but he'd just taught Matthews to walk properly and to sit without opening his knees. It was the devil, this feminine lead. So many chaps were shy of taking it on. It wasn't so bad until they came to the love passages – then they balked. He'd go round and see Black later on and try to persuade him to do it. He'd have Latimer for the male lead. He was developing into a damned good actor. He wondered how soon Peter would finish the backdrops. No use prodding him this week, while he was cook.

'Come on, show a leg!' Peter was back, followed by a limping Nigel. 'Breakfast up, *appell* up! *Appell* in ten minutes. Who wants breakfast in bed?'

25

Pomfret replaced his book and climbed out of his bunk, muttering under his breath. Putting on a Polish army great-coat over his pyjamas he picked up a Red Cross box containing his washing materials and shuffled off to the washroom.

'What's the matter with her this morning?' Peter asked.

'Oh – Nig woke her with his infernal machine.'

'That's more than I did to the child. Hey, John, wake up! *On appell bitty, mein Herr!*'

'Goon in the block! Goon in the block!'

The shouted warning came from the far end of the corridor. There were booted footsteps, the door was flung open and a German guard stood in the doorway. '*Raus! Raus! Ausgehen! Alle rausgehen!*'

'Goon in the room!' Paul stood by his bunk, trousers in his hand, hair on end. '*Deutschland kaputt!*'

The guard shouted at him.

'Fuck off!' Paul said. 'We don't understand German here.'

The guard shouted a long sentence which ended with the English word 'cooler'.

'You're for it,' Robbie said. 'It's the cooler for you.'

The guard shouted again. He was nearly screaming now.

'Fuck off!' Paul made his stock retort.

The guard began to unsling his rifle; the bayonet was fixed.

'Better be careful, Paul,' Robbie said.

A Feldwebel appeared in the corridor. The guard sprang to attention and made a long complaint in German. The Feldwebel turned to Paul.

'You have been impertinent again, yes?' He spoke in English.

'I object to being shouted at.'

'Come!'

Paul finished pulling on his trousers, gathered up his blankets and toilet things, and accompanied the Feldwebel down the corridor.

'*Ausgehen, alle rausgehen!*' the guard shouted, unmoved by his victory.

'*Gut zeigen*, Joe.' Nigel said it quietly. 'Hey, John! On

appell bitty! Come on, you'll be late for *appell*.'

John opened his eyes. He looked blank. Suddenly he realized what it was all about. 'For Christ's sake, give me a cup of tea, somebody!'

Peter poured a mug of tea and handed it to him. John swallowed deeply and put it down on the floor. He rolled out of his bunk and pushed his feet into clogs. His blue-striped pyjama trousers had been cut short above the knee, the faded pink jacket had no sleeves. He took another gulp of tea, hurled a blanket round his shoulders, snatched up a book and clattered off to roll-call, a slice of bread-and-jam in one hand and his book in the other.

• • •

The prisoners formed up raggedly in fives. Peter stood next to David who, pipe jutting from the depths of his red beard, puffed clouds of smoke into the cool morning air.

'Why do we always stand in fives?' Peter said. 'It used to be threes in XXIB.'

'These are Luftwaffe goons,' David said. 'The others were army goons. Army goons can only count in threes.'

The guards walked down the rows of prisoners; the guards in grey-blue uniform, the prisoners huddled in blankets or defying the cool morning air in pyjamas or shorts. The guards counted slowly: *Vierzig . . . fünf-und-fierzig . . . fünfzig . . . fünf-und-fünfzig . . . sechzig . . .*

The British adjutant called the prisoners to attention. The Lager Offizier, tall and immaculately uniformed, was crossing the square towards the Senior British Officer. After returning the S.B.O.'s salute, the Hauptmann turned to face the assembled prisoners. He bowed from the waist and saluted again as he raised his voice in greeting: *'Guten Morgen, meinen Herren!'*

The kriegies replied with an incoherent roar; the more prudent returning, *'Guten Morgen, mein Herr,'* the wilder spirits shouting their single-syllabled derisive insult. The two replies merged together in an enthusiastic response which made the Lager Offizier beam with pleasure.

The morning *appell* was over. The prisoners dispersed to their huts.

*　　*　　*

Peter sat at the table, waiting for John to finish his breakfast. 'Parcels tomorrow.'

'Good show.' John spoke through a mouthful of bread-and-jam. 'We can have the last tin of salmon for dinner. What about rissoles?'

'No,' Peter said, 'you have to fry those. Better make a shepherd's pie and stick it in the oven.'

'Don't burn it this time,' Bennett said. 'If you'd only do it the way I told you. You want to cover the top with greased paper.'

Peter ignored him. 'If we can get any raisins we'll swop them for biscuits. Then we can make a cake tomorrow.'

'We'll bake it in the afternoon,' John agreed. 'Then if it turns out to be a pudding we can have it for dinner.'

'And if it turns out to be porridge we'll have it for breakfast,' Bennett said. He looked at his watch and left for the *abort*.

'Perhaps I'll run a restaurant after the war.' Nigel was lying on his bunk, plotting a new post-war career. Although in his heart he knew that he would return to his old job at the local Bank, knew too that his thigh wound would bar anything more active, he dreamed of becoming a flying doctor, a game warden, a gold prospector or a deep-sea diver. He took one course of study after another, dropping each one as a more attractive career caught his fancy. 'Yes, that's it, a restaurant. I must study French cooking – '

'How?' Robbie said. 'What'll you practise on?'

'Got to get the theory buttoned up first, old boy. Anyway, once I've got the restaurant making a profit I'll put a manager in and start a pig farm. The waste food from the restaurant will feed the pigs, and the pigs will supply the bacon and pork pies for the restaurant . . .'

'Sort of perpetual motion,' John said.

'Farming's a job for the expert,' David said earnestly. 'You

28

can lose a lot of money. I've got a pedigree bull that's doing very badly. It's a Friesian. I wish I'd decided on Herefords.'

'Friesians look nicer.' Peter said it to cheer him up.

'No, it was a mistake. Herefords give richer milk and make better beef.'

Peter collected the eight knives and mugs – they had no plates – and took them over to the washhouse. The entrance was blocked by a group of men carrying empty water-jugs. Water, food and brown-coal blocks – the three essentials – were always in short supply; sometimes they were withheld by the Germans as a collective punishment. The water for nearly a thousand men came from six taps distributed between the canteen and the washhouse.

Squeezing his way in he found the small square room already crowded with prisoners. Some were washing dirty clothes – dipping them in a bucket of water, slapping them on a bench, soaping them and scrubbing them with nail-brushes. Others were there to rinse their breakfast utensils under one of the taps. In the far corner several naked figures were jostling for position under the meagre trickle of water from a punctured cocoa tin. He was glad that he and Nig had had an early shower.

A silent, absorbed prisoner was standing on the wash-bench, face pressed to the window, oblivious of the surrounding frenzy of cleanliness. Behind him a man shoulder-deep in an open square hole in the concrete floor was handing up small sacks full of sand to two others, who were busily emptying them into water-jugs for the waiting prisoners to take away and disperse.

The bricks which had formed the surface of the floor over the hole had been carefully fitted into a wooden frame to make a trap. The hole itself was cut through the six-inch concrete foundation raft of the building.

Bill White stood by the trap, resting after an hour's digging, on his head a sweat-soaked handkerchief knotted at four corners.

'Hullo, Bill,' Peter said, 'how's it going?'

'Piece of cake!' He lifted his hand, palm open, forefinger

touching the tip of his thumb, and made a clicking noise with his tongue. 'Home by Christmas.'

'How far have you got?'

'About sixty feet.'

'Ferret approaching!' It was the stooge calling urgently from his position by the window.

The man in the hole disappeared in a flash and White scrambled after him. The sand-pourers fitted the trap over the hole, the bathers and clothes-washers surged across the floor, hiding the gaps round the wooden frame.

Peter set to and washed the mugs and knives while a running commentary on the ferret's progress came from the watching stooge. The ferret passed without entering the washhouse. The trap was lifted from the hole, Bill White reappeared, and in seconds the tunnelling was in full swing.

Back in the mess, Bennett was 'tin-bashing'. No cooking utensils were provided by the Germans and the prisoners made their own. The usual thing was a flat dish about twelve inches long by eight wide and two-and-a-half deep. It was made by taking both ends off a Klim tin and rolling the cylinder into a flat sheet. When a number of these sheets had been collected they were joined together by folding the edges one over the other and filling the joint with silver paper salvaged from cigarette packets. With a blunt nail a narrow groove was punched along the double thickness of tin. The edges of the flat sheet thus formed were turned up and the four corners folded to form a dish.

Bennett, surrounded by pieces of rolled-out tin, was bashing them with a personal vindictiveness that made the floor shake and windows rattle.

'It's a lovely day,' Peter offered.

Bennett grunted.

'Wouldn't you rather do that outside in the sun, old boy?'

Bennett grunted again.

Peter sighed. He returned the mugs and knives to the shelves and went to walk round the circuit until it was time to prepare the lunch. He overtook Robbie mooching around clad in an old pullover and khaki slacks cut down to make shorts.

30

The fraying ends of the shorts flapped round his thin brown legs.

'Mail come in yet, Pete?'

'Not yet, Robbie – it's late this morning.'

'Is that bastard Bennett still bashing?'

'Yes.'

'God! I wish that chap would move to another mess. Y'know, he's not like an ordinary man. If he wants to open a door he doesn't just turn the handle. He throws himself at it with all his strength and when he finds the lock won't break he turns the handle.'

'I know,' Peter said. 'Pity his wife on their wedding night.'

They walked several circuits in silence.

'This is a helluva life, Pete.'

'Yes. Pretty foul . . . What wouldn't I give to walk on grass again.' He scraped at the sand with his bare feet. 'There's a place in Warwickshire I'd like to be now, on the Avon. There's a deep pool where I used to swim, and a steep bank to dive from.' He remembered the sun dappling through the trees on to the water, and the earthy smell of the brown river, the warm grass under his feet. 'I'm going there as soon as I get back.'

'I'll put in for some leave and take the wife and kids to Devon,' Robbie said.

Peter kicked at a stone that lay in the path in front of him. His life before the war seemed long ago – a different life, softer and less real than the life he was living now. 'I often wonder whether it's better or worse for you chaps with a wife and family – imprisonment, I mean. At least you've got someone waiting for you. This is just an interlude. I sometimes feel that when I get back it will be too late.'

'Too late for what?' Robbie asked.

Peter kicked another stone. 'Oh, too late to begin again . . . It's this awful feeling of time passing. I'm not getting anywhere – not even fighting. It's such a bloody waste of time.'

'I'm wasting time, too, you know,' Robbie said gently. 'My youngest will be three next month and I haven't seen her yet.'

31

'That's just what I mean, you've got something to look forward to. Something behind you too, to look back on.'

'Well, you can build for the future. Lots of chaps are taking degrees in all sorts of subjects.'

'Yes, I know. I can't settle down to that sort of thing. I want to escape and get back to England.'

'Bah, escape! How many people have made it from this camp so far? None!'

'There's no harm in trying,' Peter said. 'You're not just sitting back waiting for the end of the war.'

'How long has Bill White's crowd been on the washhouse *dienst*?'

'Just over two months.'

'And how far have they got?'

'About sixty feet.'

'There you are. They've another three or four months' tunnelling yet before they're even under the wire. They haven't an earthly, Pete, not an earthly. The goons are bound to tumble to it before then.'

'Oh, I don't know. People have got out before now.'

'Yes, but what percentage? Out of every thirty tunnels started I suppose one gets finished. Once you're outside the camp your difficulties have only just begun. Do you speak German?'

'No,' Peter said. 'I'm no good at languages.'

'There you are. It's no good, Pete, you'd never make it. It's a waste of time.' Robbie walked on, hands in the pockets of his shorts, head lowered. A fresh breeze ruffled his greying hair and blew dust from the circuit across the trip-wire. It brought with it the sound of gramophone music from one of the living-huts, and the smell of burning brown-coal blocks.

'What *is* the time?' Peter asked.

Robbie looked at his watch. 'Just on twelve.'

'Hell. Time I went for the soup.' Two orderlies, other rank volunteers, would soon stagger into the compound from the Kommandantur, carrying between them a dustbin full of an unappetizing watery liquid. There would be some coarse root vegetables floating in it, perhaps a few lumps of gristly meat. This 'stew', together with a loaf of *ersatz* bread per room and a ration of rotting potatoes, formed the prisoners' basic diet. Thank God for the Red Cross, Peter thought.

'You can do another circuit,' Robbie said. 'It's always late. Anyway, there are more bits to chew on at the bottom.'

They walked on past the under-size football pitch in one corner of the compound; across the front of the canteen; under the strings of laundry hanging outside the washhouse; across the miniature golf course whose dirt 'greens' were constantly being kicked up by the feet of passing prisoners, and where a few enthusiasts were hitting home-made balls with clubs cast from melted-down water-jugs; behind the living-huts and the occasional patch of cultivated ground – sprinkled with water, fertilized by primitive means – each bearing its sparse crop of lettuces or tomato plants; past the coiled wire surrounding the unfinished bathhouse which the Germans had agreed to build a year ago after reports by the Protecting Power that the washing facilities did not measure up to the Geneva Convention; behind more huts; and back to the football pitch . . .

'I want to get out,' Peter said. 'I want to ride a horse over the horizon – go rock-climbing in North Wales and see for miles . . . There's a pub called Carrolls in Liverpool where you can feast for a few bob on oysters and draught Guinness – I'd like to take a girl there again.'

'I thought you were a Londoner,' Robbie said.

'I was born there. But I got a job in Liverpool when my father's business packed up.'

'What were you doing?'

'Designing furniture. Gutting old houses and doing them up. It was a good life, not routine. I had a free hand, could make my own decisions. Not like here. I haven't made a decision since I was shot down. Except to escape, and that hasn't got me very far.'

'You can make a decision now,' Robbie said. 'What to have for dinner tonight.'

Peter laughed. 'Not even that. Parcels come tomorrow. We've only a tin of salmon left. That reminds me – I'm off to collect the soup and start dishing up lunch.' With a mug of soup each, they'd have three thin slices of bread and a small square of processed cheese. Oysters and Guinness! he thought.

'There you are,' Robbie said, 'that's a decision. See if there's a letter for me as you go by, will you? I'll wait here and you can chuck it out of the window.'

The room was empty. Bennett had finished his tin-bashing. Lying on the table were some *kriegsgefangener* letter-forms. Peter sorted them out. One for John, two for Nigel, three for Pomfret, one for himself. He crossed over to the window and held out his fist with thumb extended downwards. Robbie shrugged his shoulders and mooched on, hands in pockets.

       •   •   •

Paul is in the cooler in the Kommandantur, in the German compound. It is a narrow cell with one small window just below the ceiling. The window is covered by a metal plate which stands a foot from the wall. A certain amount of light enters the cell round the edges of the plate, but the prisoner cannot see the sky. The light is too dim for reading.

He knows the cell. He has been here before. He knows that shortly after two o'clock, if the sun is shining, a stray beam will creep in through the space between the metal plate and the window-frame. He will watch the beam of light in which specks of dust will be floating, beautiful faerie specks that will dance and swirl as he fans the air with his hand. He will lie looking at them until, with the movement of the sun, the beam of light is there no more.

He hears footsteps in the corridor and the sound of a key in the lock. The door opens and a guard is there with his midday meal. He will have the same meal every day he is in the cooler. A bowl of cabbage water and two potatoes cooked in their jackets. He sits on the bed while the guard places the food on the table. He likes to treat the guard as a waiter. Physically he suffers the hardships of solitary confinement; mentally he wins a battle in the constant war against the enemy.

He spends the long afternoon lying on his bunk and thinking of home. He thinks too of the room he has just left. In a way it is good to be in the cooler again, away from the insistent company of his fellow-prisoners. He is an individualist, a natural fighter pilot. Not for him the dependence and easy comradeship of the bomber crew. He flies far above the clouds in the blue sky, with the sun above him gilding the aircraft's wings and turning the fleecy clouds below him into a carpet of snow. He is the lone hunter, his prey the full-bellied bombers escorted by the waspish fighters. Two three-hundred-miles-an-hour fighters twisting and turning in the sky. The rattle of machine-guns, and the loser plunging on fire into the clouds below.

He imagines himself in the cockpit of his Hurricane (the kick of the controls as you go into a flick roll, the matchless rhythm of a perfectly timed roll off the top, and the way the patchwork quilt of the earth slides over you, the sudden smell of petrol as you pull out of a loop). He remembers the smell of glycol and the way the parachute bangs against the back of your legs as you run out to the waiting aircraft, the bumping over the rough turf, the smoothness as you become airborne, the steep climb through the clouds and the thrill of sighting the enemy below you, silhouetted against them. He remembers the attacking dive when you clench your teeth and press the firing button, and the aircraft judders with the firing of eight guns; the sudden blackout as you pull out of the dive, and the quick look round for the enemy as you recover. The slow roll over the airfield before you come in to land, the peace and quiet when you switch off the engine, the fragrance of the grass as you climb down from the cockpit and the friendly sounds of the countryside as you stand there smoking a cigarette, waiting for the truck to take you back to the dispersal hut.

The cell grows dark. He falls asleep lying on his bunk, the shoddy blanket across his chest, his face young in sleep, untroubled, free.

2

The ferrets in their blue denim boiler-suits were always in the camp. Usually in pairs, they searched every vehicle entering or leaving the compound and were ever-present to watch and listen to any unusual activity among the prisoners. They hid under the floor of the living-huts or in the roof, eavesdropping on the prisoners' conversation; probed the ground with long steel spikes looking for tunnels, and raked it over in search of dispersed white sand. Their sole function was the discovery of escape attempts. Immersed as they were in the routine of camp life they were able to discern at once anything untoward. They sometimes allowed a tunnel to continue weeks after they were aware that it was being dug; prisoners happily digging away underground were out of harm's way so long as they did not get dangerously near the wire.

Inevitably, each ferret had his own stooge who shadowed him whenever he was in the compound, but sometimes the ferret would enter hidden in the rubbish-cart or climb in over the wire at night so that the 'duty pilot' who patiently watched the main gate and made a record of German arrivals and departures for the Escape Committee could not book him in. Some, with a sense of humour, would report to the duty pilot as they came and went. There was politeness between them, and mutual respect.

It was no surprise to Peter when Bill White's tunnel was discovered.

*   *   *

The June sun beat fiercely into the deserted compound. It was early afternoon and most of the prisoners were sleeping on their bunks. Outside the barbed wire fence the sentries paced their beat, rifles slung high across their backs. Beyond them, dark and cool, lay the forest, remote and mysterious from inside the camp where the ground was arid and beaten hard by the feet of the prisoners.

Peter and John were plodding round the circuit, drowsily watched by the guards in the watch-towers.

'Pity about Bill's scheme,' John said. 'I thought they stood a chance.'

'It was too far from the wire.'

'It's as near as anywhere else,' John said. 'It was a good trap too. I would have said they'd be as safe as houses.'

'It had been going on for too long. Every day you spend on it means the risk of discovery's greater. It was too long, too organized. The ferrets were bound to rumble it sooner or later.'

'What happened? I must have been asleep.'

'The goons came in before *appell* and washed the floor down with a hose. It may have been routine or they may have suspected something. The seismographs may have picked up the sound of digging. Anyway a ferret was supervising them and when the hose washed the soap and cement away from the joints he spotted the trap at once. I told Bill the soap wouldn't work.'

'Pity,' John said. 'It was a good scheme.'

'It was too far from the wire. Think of all the sand you've got to hide to dig a tunnel two hundred feet long – especially a big one. The only way to get out is to make the tunnel as narrow and short as possible – start somewhere out here, near the trip-wire.'

'You can't do it. There's nowhere near the wire to start a tunnel from. They chose the nearest building to the wire.'

'Why start from a building at all?' Peter said. 'Why not start out in the open here – camouflage the trap? We could come out to it every day and take it slowly.'

'But that's impossible. It's like the top of a billiard table. Every inch of ground near the trip-wire is in full view of at least three goon-boxes and two outside sentries. You couldn't possibly sink a shaft out here. Besides – How would you get the sand away?'

'It was done once. Ages ago, in another camp. A crowd went out with a chap who played an accordion. While he played they all sat round in a big circle and sang. And while they were singing, the ones in the middle were digging a hole. They passed the sand to the chaps around them who filled their pockets with it. They got the hole as deep as a man's arm, put some boards they'd brought with them over it, and replaced the surface sand. Then they all went back to their barrack block with their pockets full of sand.'

'Did they get away with it?' John asked.

'No – a ferret roaming about the compound that night walked over the trap and fell down the hole. The scheme was too slapdash and hurried.'

They walked on in silence. To John the idea was new and worth considering. 'All we need is something to cover it with, some sort of innocent activity like the accordion.'

'We can't do that again. Must be a classic by now.'

'Might do something like it,' John said.

'Trouble is you've always got to have such a bloody good reason for anything you do. If we start mucking around with the landscape we've got to show it's for some definite purpose, something quite different. Otherwise the ferrets will be on to it like a shot.'

'I sometimes get tired of working out goon reactions,' John said 'All this "we think that they think that we think" stuff.' He shivered and looked up. 'Hallo, look at the trees. There's another of those whirlwind things on the way.'

Peter stopped. Over to the south the tops of the trees were bending and waving while the air in the camp was still. Then sudden gusts of wind blew across the camp, catching at windows left loosely open, stirring up spouts of sand, tugging at the washing hung on lines outside the huts. The swastika over the Kommandantur flared out, then drooped again.

'I'm going in to shut the windows,' Peter said. 'Left some drawings on the table. Coming?'

'I'll stay and watch.'

The whole camp had come to life, prisoners dashing out

38

of the huts and snatching washing from the lines, windows slamming. By now the nearest trees were bowing to the wind and John moved to shelter behind a hut as the fine sand whipped across and stung his legs.

Here she comes, he thought, and quickened his pace, reaching the side of the hut as the whirling column of dust and sand left the trees and swept towards the wire. Twigs and pine needles were caught and flung up into the air, and a large sheet of newspaper whirled skywards, mounting the spiral, up and up, fifty or sixty feet, sliding and somersaulting; crowning the whirlwind as it hit the camp. The nearest goon-box was enveloped in a cloud of sand and he had a sudden impulse to rush the wire while the sentry was blinded.

In a moment it was all over. The fine dust still hung in the air but the sand was gone and the roar in the trees had fallen to a sigh.

Outside the wire the sheet of newspaper was floating downwards and, as he watched, it drifted on to the tops of the pines, hung absurdly for a moment and then slipped out of sight.

Wish that was me, he thought. I could do with a miracle like that. Like old Elijah. Or the Greek tragedies. *Deus ex machina.* When the plot got stuck you lowered him down in a box and he sorted everything out. He pictured a genial old man in a toga and a laurel wreath drifting down into the camp and offering him a lift. 'Any more for the *Skylark*? Penny a ride on Pegasus . . .'

And then he found himself running across the camp, an idea racing through his mind. The god in the box – a box horse – to camouflage the trap . . . must be a classic by now . . . the Trojan horse . . . Peter, he must find Peter.

He found him listening reluctantly to Robbie's latest complaint about Bennett.

John tried to appear calm. 'Pete, the wind's dropped. What about finishing that walk?'

'OK.' Peter was grateful for the interruption. 'Just a minute while I light my pipe.' He took the cigarette from Robbie's hand and held it to the bowl of his pipe. 'I should let it drop, Robbie. You can't do anything about it.'

'I'm getting moved to another mess,' Robbie said, 'if that noisy bastard doesn't – '

'Come on, Pete!' John said.

'I'm with you.' Peter handed the cigarette back to Robbie. 'Come for a walk. It'll do you good.'

'The circuit gives me the willies,' Robbie said.

•   •   •

The windstorm had passed leaving the camp clean, scoured. Prisoners were re-hanging their washing on the lines, gazing despondently at uprooted tomato plants, fetching the tea-water.

John was still tense with excitement but he spoke calmly. 'Pete – that idea of camouflaging the outside trap?'

'Yes?'

'I was thinking, after you'd gone in. You said the accordion effort was a classic by now.'

'Well, it is, in a way.'

'So is this. What about the wooden horse of Troy?'

Peter stared at him. 'The wooden horse of Troy?'

'Yes, but a vaulting horse, a box horse like we had at school. You know, one of those square things with a padded top and sides that go right down to the ground. We'll carry it out every day and vault over it. One of us'll be inside digging while the others vault. We'll have a good strong trap and sink it at least a foot below the surface. It's foolproof.'

'What about the sand?'

'Take it back with us in the horse. Use a kitbag or something. We'll have to keep the horse in one of the huts and get the chaps to carry it out with one of us inside it. We'll take the sand back with us when we go in.'

'It'll have to be a bloody strong horse. But not too heavy . . .' Peter was already working out the size of the timbers.

'Oh, that's your department. You'll be able to knock one up all right.' John could see it, see it clearly and finished. The wooden vaulting horse, the vertical shaft under it and the long straight tunnel. And he could see them going out through the

40

tunnel. 'Let's go and register it with the Escape Committee.'

'It'll have to go through Phil. Have to go through the proper channels, y'know. There's no hurry. Let's get – '

'We'll go and find him now,' John said. 'Someone else might think of it while we're still talking.'

*   *   *

Philip Rowe was one of those men, invaluable in any community, who enjoyed organizing. Shot down at the end of 1941 while on patrol over the North Sea, this was his second spell at Sagan and he knew the ropes. He was the Camp Coal Officer supervising the rationing of brown-coal blocks, Camp Shower Officer assembling the daily parties of prisoners to be marched to the Kommandantur for the weekly hot shower, Hut Cookery Officer and – most importantly – 'Little X', the hut representative on the Escape Committee with the responsibility for rounding up volunteer stooges. Peter and John were thankful that someone else was willing to carry out all these duties, and normally kept out of his way.

They found him translating an article in the *Völkischer Beobachter* for the Committee, bustled him out on to the circuit where they were safe from the ears of the ferrets, and outlined their plan. He was sceptical, but under pressure agreed to take it to Big X, the head of the Committee, right away.

*   *   *

'Well, what did they say?'

'Laughed their heads off.' Phil saw John's expression and relented. 'No – they don't think you stand much chance of getting away with it for long – '

'Oh, we'll have dug the tunnel and be away inside a month,' Peter interrupted.

'Two weeks,' John said.

' – but as there's no other scheme going at the moment in

this compound they're quite keen for you to have a bash.' He lowered his voice, although there was no one within earshot. 'They authorized me to tell you that there's a big tunnel *dienst* under way in the North compound – but it shouldn't affect your effort if a miracle happens and you manage to get out first. That's to go no further of course,' he added hastily, 'I'm only allowed to tell you because you've got a scheme of your own now.'

'Anything else?' John asked.

'Oh yes. If you succeed in producing a vaulting horse they'll give you all the help they can.'

'Decent of them,' Peter said. 'We'll need vaulters. Every day.'

'I wish you luck. It's difficult enough to get chaps to walk as far as the Kommandantur for a hot shower.'

'You'll find them all right,' Peter said; and this time he and John laughed at Phil's expression of dismay.

'I've got quite enough to do already.'

'Come on, Phil,' John said. 'It's your duty.'

'Well, if you two will volunteer to help me with the coal issue – '

'Any time,' Peter said. 'Just give us a shout.'

Phil snorted disbelievingly and went back to his *Völkischer Beobachter*.

They walked on fast round the circuit.

'We'll have to get some strong timbers for the framework,' Peter said. 'Four pieces about three inches square and five feet long would do for the legs. Then we've got to have beams to go round the bottom to tie the legs together – the same round the top . . . And then we've got to cover the sides . . .'

'Why not cover them with canvas?'

Peter considered. 'No, I don't think that would do. The sides will have to be solid otherwise there's no point in covering them at all. And if we do anything pointless the goons will get suspicious and wonder why we're doing it. No – this will have to be an absolutely pukka vaulting horse without anything phoney about it.'

'Why not cover the whole of the four sides with bed-boards?' John suggested.

42

'No, that won't do.'

'Why not? We've plenty of bed-boards. All the chaps will give up one or two each.'

'That's not the point. Do you realize what the thing would weigh if we made the sides of solid wood? It'd be as much as we could do to lift it, let alone carry someone inside it – and then there's the sand. No, we'll have to think of something else.'

They were walking more slowly now, worrying at the problem.

'There are our timbers!' Peter pointed to the abandoned bathhouse. Remembering the watching guards and ferrets he quickly dropped his arm. 'We'll pinch some of the roof-rafters for the frame. Get under that fence easily in the dark.'

'The moon's in its last quarter,' John said. 'Let's do it to-night, before it rises.'

'What about the dogs though?'

'We'll get Tony Winyard to look after the dogs. Let's go and dig a sunbathing pit halfway between the huts so that we can crawl into it without the searchlight picking us up. Then if we get the chaps in the next hut to leave some heaps of stuff out-of-doors this evening we can crawl from one to the other.' John wanted to get on with it.

'OK. That fixes the framework all right. But what about the sides? There's not much point in getting the stuff for the frame until we know what we're going to use on the sides.'

'It'll come,' John said. 'It'll come. Let's go and get organized for tonight.'

*   •   •*

There was no system in the sweeping of the searchlights. While the rest of the mess slept Peter had spent hours sitting at the window watching them. At times it would appear that the men on the lights were following a strict routine – one light following the other in its relentless movement across the camp. There seemed just time to dash quickly from one hut to another in

43

the interval between the beams. Then, with startling abruptness, a beam would stab out in a totally unexpected quarter, confounding the system.

Except when the searchlights ranged it was quite dark in the centre of the compound. Round the perimeter of the camp, covering an area of some sixty feet in width, the ground was brilliantly lit by the floodlights hanging above the wire, a ring of white lights surrounding an area of darkness in which stood the blacked-out wooden huts. In each hut, lifeless from the outside, a hundred prisoners, each with his own private problems, were crowded into family intimacy. Each darkened hut seethed with living cells; loving, hating, chaffing, wrangling.

·   ·   ·

It was eight twenty in the evening. Ten minutes to zero hour. In Peter's room the men sat round the table talking nervously. It was like the crew room before take-off. An air of tension and an eagerness to get it started. To get it over with.

Often, at night, Peter had heard the dogs sniffing and prowling about under the hut. He was thinking of this now as he sat, dressed in an Australian's dark blue battledress, his face blackened with charcoal, waiting to slip out through the trap he had made in the floor.

There was something terrifying to him in the thought of the dogs prowling about in the darkness of the compound. Animals trained by men to hunt men. Men themselves were all right. They knew when to stop. But where would the dogs stop if they caught you? He had seen them being trained, outside the wire. He had seen them set on the masked and padded 'quarry' by the *Hundmeister*; seen them bringing the quarry to earth and stand over him snarling. He rubbed his right hand slowly up and down his left forearm, and glanced impatiently at the watch he had borrowed from Robbie.

John sat, a mirror in front of him, smearing charcoal on his face. 'What time is it, Pete?'

'Twenty twenty-five. Better wait until twenty-thirty. I hope they don't bungle things at the other end.'

'Who's doing it?' Robbie asked.

44

But what about the vaulters? I told them it was a blitz effort. They'll soon get browned-off if we don't get on with it.'

'Yes, I know. I'm rather worried about the vaulters. It's tough going on the little food we get. But it was rushing things that ruined the accordion scheme.'

'Well – how long do you honestly think it will take us?'

'Let's see.' Peter hitched his shorts with his elbows. 'We've got about forty-five feet to go to the trip-wire, and thirty feet across the danger strip. That's seventy-five feet. The wire itself is about ten feet thick so that makes eighty-five feet. We need to break at least thirty feet away from the wire, because of the outside sentries. That would be one hundred and fifteen feet altogether. Allow a bit for going round rocks or tree roots and make it a figure of one hundred and twenty feet.'

'A hundred and twenty feet at five feet a day,' John said. 'That's twenty-four days.'

'We shan't do five feet a day.'

'Oh, I don't know. I could dig five feet in a day. Make it only three feet if you like, that will make it about six weeks.'

'It's not a matter of how much we can dig in a day,' Peter said. 'It's a matter of how much we can carry away in the horse. Do you realize how much sand weighs?'

'Not a clue. You're the construction boss.'

'As far as I can remember a yard of sand weighs about one hundredweight, but I don't know whether that's wet or dry. Ours will be wet, or rather damp. But knowing that wouldn't help us much. What we want to know is how big a pound of sand looks, so that we can figure out how much we can dig in one session. How much do you think we can carry in the horse – with one of us inside as well?'

'What do you weigh?'

'I don't know. I was eleven-three when I was shot down. I reckon I'm not much more than ten-and-a-half now.'

'Then I'm less than ten. Supposing we say we can carry ten stone of sand.'

'That's a hundred and forty pounds. We'll go and weigh a pound of sand and see how much it looks. I think a foot a day seems more reasonable than three.'

'What shall we use as a pound weight?'

'An unopened tin of Klim – that weighs exactly a pound nett. We'll make some scales, put an empty Klim tin on the other side and fill it with damp sand until the scales are even. Then we'll know what a pound of sand looks like.'

'Right,' John said. 'Pity we can't do it now. I'm taking a Latin class in our room in five minutes.'

'I suppose I ought to be going to German classes.'

'Oh, I shouldn't bother. After all, we said we'd travel as French workers. A little knowledge is dangerous. If you start learning German now and try talking outside you'll get us both in the cart. Your best role is dignified silence. I'll do the talking. As long as you can say, *"Ich bin Ausländer – nicht verstehen"*, that should get you through.'

'OK,' Peter said, relieved. *'Ich bin Ausländer – nicht verstehen.* Sounds impressive. What does it mean?'

' "I'm a foreigner – I don't understand." '

'That's a damn good line. I suppose I just keep on saying that until you come along.'

'You can pretend to be deaf and dumb if you like.'

'I know! I'll have a pronounced stutter. I used to stutter as a kid – may be why I was never any good at languages. Then if they ask me anything I'll stutter like hell and you can interrupt and tell them what they want to know.'

'Yes, I'll do that if they speak French – but if they don't you stick to the *nicht verstehen* business. See you later.'

'Ich bin Ausländer,' Peter said. *'Nicht verstehen.'*

He walked on alone round the circuit. *Ich bin Ausländer – nicht verstehen.* What a vocabulary to try to cross Germany with. Apart from a weekend visit to the Paris Exposition in '37 he had never been abroad until the RAF sent him to train in Canada. For him civilization stopped at Dover and the world of Germany outside the wire was an unknown quantity. None of the other kriegies seemed to know much about it either. He had been told that the Germans walked only on the right-hand side of the pavement and that if you walked on the left you'd be spotted at once. But no one really seemed to know.

Even if I spoke fluent German, he thought, how much better off would I be? It's all a matter of luck, this escaping business. Chaps have got through to England without any German at all. And fluent German speakers have been brought back. We're looking too far ahead. We've got to get out of the camp first. Let the morrow take care of itself . . . It'll be good to be back in England though – instead of rotting here waiting for the end of the war. Back on the squadron with the flying and the fear, and the relief, and the parties in the mess and the feeling that it could happen to anyone else, but not to you. And the thankfulness the next morning that it hadn't happened to you and that you could take the crew down to the *King's Head* that night and you wouldn't have to fly again until the night after . . .

•   •   •

That evening Peter made the top section of the shoring for the vertical shaft. He made it with four sides of a plywood packing case reinforced and slotted so that they could be assembled into a rigid four-sided box without top or bottom. The box would stand a considerable inwards pressure.

John stitched twelve bags for the sand. Several prisoners had made themselves shorts by cutting their trousers off above the knee. When John had sewn the bottoms together, roughly hemmed the tops and threaded string through the hem, the trouser-legs had become bags about twelve inches long. As a result of the experiment with Klim tins earlier in the evening, they reckoned that twelve trouser-leg bags full of sand would weigh about the same as one of themselves. With twelve full bags added to the weight of the horse and the tunneller, the vaulters who carried the horse back to the canteen would have to be keen types, and fit.

During the week when they were testing the Germans' reaction to the vaulting they had made two sand pits, one at the side and one at the head of where they positioned the horse near the football pitch. These pits were ostensibly to soften the shock of landing on their bare feet; actually they served as a datum mark, to ensure that the horse was always replaced on the exact spot.

57

The next afternoon they took the horse out with John inside it.

•   •   •

John crouched bent almost double, sitting on one of the removable bearers, a foot braced on each side of the bottom framework. In his arms he cradled a cardboard Red Cross box holding trouser-leg bags, some hooks fashioned from wire, one side of the vertical shoring, and the bricklayer's trowel he had stolen from the bathhouse.

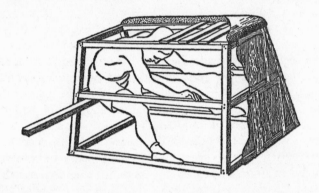

Showing the framework construction of the vaulting horse
with one man in position for being carried.

The horse creaked and groaned as the four men carried it down the steps from the canteen. A smoother ride over the flat ground, more creaking as it was positioned by the sand pits. The vaulting began, with Peter as team captain standing close to the horse.

Inside, John worked quickly. Scraping up the dark grey surface sand he put it into the cardboard box and started to dig a deep trench for one side of the shoring. He put the bright yellow excavated sand into the bags and suspended them from the wire hooks which he had poked up between the boards and canvas padding of the top of the horse.

As the trench got deeper he had difficulty in reaching the

bottom. He made it wider and had to bank the extra sand against one end of the horse. It was hot and stuffy in the confined working space, and he began to sweat.

He finished the trench and dropped the plywood sheet in position, with its upper edge six inches below the surface. He replaced most of the sand, ramming it down with the handle of the trowel, packing the shoring as tight as he could, to prevent any telltale subsidence.

Standing on the framework of the horse he carefully spread some of the remaining sand over the plywood sheet, packing it down hard. He was left with enough surplus sand to fill one trouser-leg bag.

Finally he sprinkled the grey surface sand from the cardboard box over the whole area, obliterating his foot and finger marks.

Calling softly to Peter, he gave the word that he had finished.

The vaulters inserted the bearers and carried the horse back into the canteen.

•   •   •

Working alternately, it took them four afternoons to sink the four walls of the shoring. Then they began to dig out the sand from inside it, covering the hole each time they left it with a trap made from bed-boards and the hoarded surface sand.

Now the vaulters staggered back to the canteen carrying twelve bags of yellow sand inside the horse as well as the digger. Once there, they transferred the sand from the trouser-leg bags into long sausage-like sacks made from the arms and legs of woollen underwear. These they carried away slung round their necks and down inside their trouser-legs.

The sand was dispersed around the compound, some finding its way by devious routes to the *aborts*, some buried under the huts, some sprinkled through special trouser pockets over the tomato patches and dug in by the kriegie gardeners.

When they reached the bottom of the plywood shaft Peter realized they had to dig deeper still; and they made another night sortie to the unfinished bathhouse to get bricks, which

59

they later wedged under the four corners of the shoring to support it. He was not satisfied until they had a shaft five feet deep and two feet six inches square. They had dropped the plywood walls twelve inches as they worked. The tops of the walls were now eighteen inches below the surface of the ground. The eighteen inches of sand above the wooden trap gave them security from the probing-rods of the ferrets and deadened any hollow sound when the trap was walked on. But it was too much sand to remove each time before reaching the trap. To make this easier they filled bags, made from woollen undervests, and placed them on top of the trap before covering them with merely six to eight inches of surface sand. The bags were thin enough not to impede the progress of the ferret's probe, and enabled them to uncover and recover the trap more quickly.

The plywood box stood on four brick piles two feet high. On three sides the shaft below the box was shored with pieces of bed-board. The fourth side was left open for the tunnel.

They found that it was possible to stand in the shaft – with head and shoulders up inside the horse – but it was not possible to kneel; so they removed the bed-boards between the bricks on the side opposite the tunnel entrance and dug a short burrow into which they could thrust their feet.

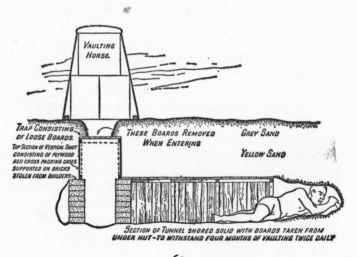

VAULTING HORSE.

TRAP CONSISTING OF LOOSE BOARDS.

TOP SECTION OF VERTICAL SHAFT CONSISTING OF PLYWOOD RED CROSS PACKING CASES SUPPORTED ON BRICKS STOLEN FROM BUILDERS.

THESE BOARDS REMOVED WHEN ENTERING

GREY SAND

YELLOW SAND

SECTION OF TUNNEL SHORED SOLID WITH BOARDS TAKEN FROM UNDER HUT – TO WITHSTAND FOUR MONTHS OF VAULTING TWICE DAILY

60

For the first seven feet the tunnel was lined with bed-boards, to take the force of the impact of the vaulters landing heavily on the surface. Peter made this shoring piecemeal, in the evening, in the security of their room; using as tools a table knife and a red-hot poker. To assemble it he lay on his back in the darkness of the narrow tunnel, scraping away sufficient sand to slide the main bearers into position before inserting the boards. He had to work slowly and carefully and was fearful all the time that a sudden fall of sand might bury him. Even a small fall would be enough to pin him, helpless, on his back in the tunnel.

Once the shoring was in position they had to fill the space between the roof of the tunnel and the wooden ceiling with sand. If this were not done, sand would trickle down and the roof become higher and higher until the subsidence of the ground above would reveal the path of the tunnel.

After the first seven feet the tunnel ran on without any shoring whatever.

The tunnel was very small. They had quickly seen that the progress of the work would be determined by the speed with which they could get the excavated sand away. The smaller the tunnel the less sand they would have to dispose of and the faster the work would go.

While one of them supervised the vaulting the other dug in the tunnel. He worked alone. Once he got into the tunnel with his arms stretched ahead of him he had to stay like that; he could not get his arms behind him again. Nor could he crawl with them doubled up. It was fingers and toes all the way until he got to the end. There, he scraped some sand from the face with the trowel and crawled backwards along the tunnel, dragging the sand with him. When he got back to the vertical shaft he had brought enough sand to fill half a bag. And there were twelve bags to fill.

There was no light in the tunnel and very little air. He spent his spell of digging in a bath of sweat. He worked naked because it was cooler; and if he wore even the lightest clothes he would scrape a certain amount of sand from the sides as he crawled along. Each bag of sand that was scraped from the sides meant one bag fewer taken from the face. As he sweated the sand caked on him. He got sand in his eyes, in his ears, in his nose and under his foreskin.

·   ·   ·

And so they worked until they had dug a tunnel forty feet long. They grew skegs on their elbows and knees and broke their fingernails. As the tunnel grew longer the work became more difficult and the air more foul. They did not put up air holes for fear of the dogs.

After forty feet they could do no more. They were taking two hours to fill the twelve bags, and they had reached the limit of their endurance.

Not only were the tunnellers exhausted by the twenty-four times repeated crawl in both directions along the tunnel, but the vaulters – who had been vaulting every afternoon of the two months that it had taken to dig the forty feet – were exhausted too. The tunnellers were issued with extra rations by the Escape Committee, but the vaulters were not, and they had little energy to spare.

Peter and John had devised games and variations on the theme of vaulting. The whole time one of them was below ground the other would be trying to make the two hours that the horse stood there appear as natural as possible. It was not easy, especially when a ferret was standing within earshot, watching the show.

They organized a medicine-ball and a deck-tennis quoit and the twelve-man team stood in a circle round the horse throwing these to one another. They even organized a run round the circuit – leaving the horse unguarded and vulnerable, with the trap open below it.

It was a considerable physical strain working in the tunnel; yet both of them preferred it to organizing the P.T.

·   ·   ·

The end came one afternoon when John was in the tunnel. It was ten minutes before they were due to take the horse in. Peter had left the vaulters and walked over to the main gate to ask the duty pilot how many Germans were in the compound. There were two ferrets, nowhere near the horse or the canteen. As he walked back he was met by David, pale-faced and running –

'Pete – '

'What's wrong?'

'There's been a fall.'

'Where?'

'Not far from the horse.'

'Is John all right?'

'We called to him but we couldn't get a reply.'

Peter started running. A fall could mean that John was trapped. There were no air-holes. He would be caught in the end of the tunnel; suffocating, trapped by sand.

The vaulting team were grouped round a figure lying on the ground. Peter glanced quickly at the nearest watch-tower. The guard was looking down at them through field-glasses.

'Where *is* the fall?'

'Nig's lying on it,' David said. 'A hole suddenly appeared so Nig fell down on it to stop the guards seeing it. He's pretending he's hurt his leg.'

'How's John?' He bent over Nigel, speaking urgently.

'Can't get a reply.'

Oh God, Peter thought, John's had it. He wanted to overturn the horse and go down, but the thought of the discovery of the tunnel held him back. John would be furious if he panicked for nothing. 'Send someone for a stretcher,' he told David.

Two vaulters went off to the canteen at the double. Peter crouched by Nigel's feet, as near to the horse as possible.

'John,' he called. '*John!*'

No answer.

'Roll over, Nig.'

Nigel rolled over. There was a hole, about as thick as his arm, going down into the darkness of the tunnel.

'John,' he called, projecting his voice down the hole. 'John!'

'That you, Pete?' The answer was weak.

'What happened?'

'There's been a fall but I can clear it. I've taken some of

63

the boards from the shaft. I'll have it fixed in a jiffy. Can you fill-in from the top?'

'OK. Let me know when you've got it fixed.' He pretended to attend to Nigel's leg.

'The goon in the box seems interested,' Nigel said. 'He's still watching.'

'The chaps with the stretcher will be here in a minute,' Peter told him. 'They'll carry you back to the hut. That'll satisfy him.'

Before the stretcher arrived he heard John's voice again; thinly, from inside the tunnel. 'Just putting the shoring in. You can fill-in in about five minutes.'

What a man, Peter thought. Good old John. He poked solicitously at Nigel's leg, and Nigel simulated pain. The two vaulters returned with the stretcher and a first-aid kit. Peter made a business of bandaging Nigel's leg while the others, shuffling round, idly kicked sand towards the hole.

'It'll sink a bit,' Peter said. 'We'll kick some more over it later on . . . What's the time?'

'Three-thirty,' David said.

'Christ – *appell* at four! We must get him up before then.' He got to his feet, and leaned against the horse, kicking it with his heel. 'John!' There was no reply.

The two vaulters bore Nigel away on the stretcher, the rest surged in an untidy group round the hole. The minutes passed. There was no sign from John.

Oh God, we've had it, Peter thought. If we can't get him up before *appell* we've had it. 'Come on, chaps, let's get vaulting again,' he said. 'We can't just stand around.'

They began to vault, with David standing by the hole as though waiting to catch the weaker ones and help them to their feet. Suddenly Peter heard John's voice, tired but triumphant, from inside the horse itself. 'Hey, Pete, what's the time?'

'You've got five minutes.'

'It's a hell of a mess.'

'Don't worry. Get ready.'

At the end of five minutes they carried the horse into the canteen. John could hardly stand. 'It's the hell of a mess,' he repeated. 'There's a bit of tree root there and the vaulting must have shaken it loose. I've jammed it up temporarily but it needs proper shoring.'

'I'll take some down with me tomorrow,' Peter said.

*   *   *

The tunnel was choked with sand, soft shifting sand that continued to fall as he worked. He worked on his back, entirely by feel, and the air was so bad that he panted, gasping for breath. Sand fell into his eyes, his nostrils, his mouth. He worked furiously, clearing the loose sand and fitting the new shoring into position.

When it was securely fitted he managed to pack some of the sand between the shoring and the sides of the tunnel. The rest he spread about the floor, lying flat on his belly and pressing it down with his hands.

When he got back to the horse he could hardly find the strength to climb out of the shaft and replace the trap. Wearily he put it back, placed the woollen sacks filled with sand on top of it, and spread the surface sand. He gave John the signal that he was ready to be taken in. The journey back across the compound was a nightmare and he never knew how he was able to balance on the framework. When they reached the canteen he crawled out from under the horse and fainted.

That evening, after *appell*, he reported to the camp hospital. He knew he had taken too much out of himself with the digging, the vaulting and the worry. The British doctor examined him and ordered a week's complete rest in bed.

4

He woke in the night, sweating. Outside the windows rain was beating down on a corrugated-iron roof somewhere close by, drumming on the roof and sluicing away into the gutter. Occasionally there was a flash of lightning, and thunder rumbled in the distance.

He lay and listened to the rain. It sounded cool and refreshing – summer rain. He imagined it falling on the leaves of the silver birch beyond the wire, pattering on the leaves and then dropping on to the dark earth below. He imagined it, earth-brown, swirling and gurgling as it made a way for itself into the ditch on the forest's edge, eddying but inevitable, with small twigs and leaves like rudderless boats twisting and turning on its surface; the level of the ditch rising until twigs, leaves and rainwater cascaded into the narrow stream that disappeared into the freedom of the forest.

He fell asleep, cool now, soothed by the sound of the rain.

●　　●　　●

When he woke again it was morning. The blackout shutters had been taken from the windows and the sunlight streamed into the room. It seemed more friendly than in the night, more untidy. The other patients were sitting up in bed, washing themselves. Through the open door he could hear the clanging of buckets and the swish of water as the orderlies washed the floor of the corridor.

For a while he lay still, listening to the friendly banter of the other patients. They were ragging the man in the bed next to his own. By his neighbour's lack of repartee, and the noises

66

coming from his bed, it was obvious that he was gargling.

The gargling finished, he was driven to reply. He spoke with a marked Australian accent. 'It was bad luck, that's all. If it hadn't been for that fucking sentry we'd have got away.'

Peter turned his head and looked towards the next bed. The man had a bandage round his temples and his arm was in a sling.

'Morning, cobber. Feeling better?'

'I'm OK,' Peter said. 'What happened to you?'

'Got a bullet through the shoulder. We were just getting a boat at Danzig and a sentry spotted us. Took a pot at me and got me through the shoulder. I cut my head open when I fell down.'

'He's got a sore throat,' one of the other men said. 'There's nothing wrong with him except the sore throat. He got that talking about his escape. He's done nothing but talk about it since he's been here.'

'That joker's arse-ended,' the Australian said. 'Broke his arm jumping off a train. Hadn't been out more than a few hours and he breaks his bloody arm falling off a train. He needs to get some hours in.'

'Where are you from?' Peter asked.

'The North compound. Four of us got out under the wire. I'd have made it if it hadn't been for that bastard of a sentry.'

'How long were you out?'

'Four days. I caught this cold sleeping in a ditch.'

'What happened to the other two?'

'In the cooler. Put their hands up as soon as he started shooting. Wish I'd had the sense to do the same.'

'How did you get to Danzig?' Peter asked.

'Jumped a goods train. Riding the rods, cobber. That's the way for a man to get around.'

'What's Danzig like?'

'Bloody awful. Wouldn't go there again. No future for a joker there. Too many sentries in the docks.'

'Are the docks fenced in?'

'No – but they're stiff with troops. No future there, cobber.'

* * *

That first day in hospital Peter found it impossible to relax, to stop thinking about escape. For two months he had done nothing but build the horse, jump over it, dig beneath it, discuss with John how they would cross Germany, whether they would travel north, south or west from Sagan.

He listened carefully to the experiences of the Australian and the other patients, comparing them with his own; trying to trace a common weakness in their plans. He thought back to his first attempt to get away – from the village *Gasthaus* where the forest keeper who had caught him had stood him sandwiches and beer. The tunnel at Oflag XXIB that had never come to anything because they had been moved to Sagan before it was finished. He had been a prisoner for seven months now and he had never been nearer the fence than the trip-wire. People – Robbie among them – kept telling him it was impossible to get out of Luft III yet here were two men who had done it.

He questioned them about their time outside and tried to analyse the causes of their failure to make it out of Germany. He ran over in his mind all the stories he had heard from prisoners who had been outside the wire. He went over each escape step by step until he came to the moment of recapture. In every case the would-be escaper had been caught on foot and usually within a few days of leaving the camp. Most of them had walked, some of them covering only a few miles before they were recaptured. Of those who had jumped trains only the Australian and his two friends had reached their destination; and they had been caught in the docks in Danzig. They had boarded a train in the goods yard at Sagan and had travelled all the way without a stop.

Personally he would have preferred to walk, to live off the country and use the cover of the forest which ran unbroken for three hundred miles to the Czech border. The ordinary Czech, he'd heard, was pro-British in spite of the betrayal at Munich; and they'd risk their necks to help an escaped airman. But the pooled experience of these chaps who'd been out in the German countryside seemed to be dead against this route. The German villagers had grown suspicious of the stranger who might be a conscripted foreign worker on the loose, a shot-down enemy airman, a deserter from the Russian Front—even a spy. They were liable to report to the police anyone they saw roaming about the countryside. Better to stick to urban areas where strangers were commonplace.

'That seems to be the answer,' he said at the end of a long day on his back, pondering all the alternatives. 'Buy tickets and travel as passengers. There must be hundreds of foreign workers travelling about Germany on the railway.'

'It's not safe,' the Australian said. 'Bound to get caught first time they ask for your papers. The things we make aren't good enough to stand a train check.'

'But you are getting somewhere,' Peter persisted. 'If you do get past the booking office you travel quickly and safely to where you want to go.'

'They have train checks,' the Australian said. 'I had a cobber who tried that. He got past the booking clerk all right but got picked up on the train. Joker came round looking at tickets and asking for papers. When he showed his, they ran him in right away. These jokers are used to looking for forged papers and spot 'em at once.'

'It must have been a fast train,' Peter said. 'You don't want a corridor train. You want to get on a slow local train, one without a corridor. Once you're in, you're in. Nothing can happen until you get to the other end.'

'Unless someone starts talking to you. Jokers are always more talkative on local trains.'

'You can pretend to sleep. Besides, you'd obviously be a foreigner and they'd soon realize it was hopeless.' What was it? he thought, trying to remember. *Ich bin Ausländer* –

'How do you know they allow foreign workers on trains? Probably transport 'em in cattle trucks.'

'We'll have to find that out.'

'I'd rather jump a goods train,' the Australian said. 'Too fucking nerve-racking to sit in the same carriage with a pack of goons for hours. Might fall asleep and start talking in English. Give me the open every time.'

'I'm not so sure,' Peter said. 'I think there's something in this passenger train idea.'

•   •   •

69

He slept badly and when he woke on the second day still physically and mentally exhausted he realized that he must make the most of the week's rest, build up his strength so that when he got back to the compound he would be able to cope with the problems of the tunnel.

It was a relief to lie back and do nothing. It was a queer place, this inner sanctum of captivity; a place remote from barbed wire and goon boxes. The patients were no more prisoners than were the patients in any military hospital. Even the guards were more friendly and, not being closely supervised, were able to come into the wards and chat with the prisoners.

He used this period of enforced idleness to complete his pictorial record of kriegie life. Though he would have to leave the drawings behind when – if – he got away, he wanted to record the untidiness of boxes and old tin cans in which they lived, the bearded figures wrapped in a multitude of sweaters, scarves and greatcoats, hobbling in their wooden clogs out of the barrack huts to attend winter *appell*. The *appell* itself, rows and rows of ragged figures clad in every type and colour of uniform from French horizon blue through RAF blue and British and Polish khaki to the navy blue of the Fleet Air Arm. Khaki balaclava helmets partially hiding every colour of beard – yellow, bright red, black – and feet encased in every form of footwear from wooden clogs to sheepskin-lined flying boots.

He wanted to paint the hospital ward, its bare wooden walls and rows of untidy beds, the rough bedside tables and chairs made from packing-cases; and the pale, angular, cheerful patients.

Above all he wanted to capture the spirit of undefeated humour that was so typical of kriegie life – the humour that inspired the cartoon that hung on the wall of one of the messes in his hut. The drawing showed two unshaven, unwashed prisoners wrapped up like parcels in an assortment of rags, trying to heat a tin of food over a fire made from a smashed-up packing-case, the remains of which lay beside them on the floor. Around them of a chaos of twine, cardboard boxes, bits of wire and sticks of wood, and over all hung the pall of smoke and steam which gathered as soon as the prisoners were locked in for the night. The caption read: 'Not the Berkeley, old boy – wouldn't be seen dead in the place!'

*   *   *

On the Sunday evening the British padre brought a portable gramophone into the ward and played Beethoven's Second Piano Concerto.

Once again Peter was in the studio flat, surrounded by half-finished canvases and the smell of oil and turpentine. There was no war then, no thought of war. The evening sun, filtered by industrial haze, slanted from the rooftops and gilded the white walls and shelves of books. By the high window Pat was trying to put on canvas the magic and beauty of the rooftops and the setting sun. Himself sitting cross-legged on a cushion on the floor, smoking a pipe, playing Beethoven on the paint-spotted radiogram and watching Pat intent against the gold-ness of the sky; learning during the hours spent in watching and loving her how to mix colours, how to paint shadows, how to draw.

Then the war. The first few weeks as a recruit; the square-bashing, the gas-mask in its cardboard box, sentry duty with a pickaxe shaft because there were no rifles. Navigation school in Ontario; flying the Anson over the endless prairie with the shadows of the cumulus clouds moving freely across the disciplined squares of wheat bounded by unnaturally straight highways; swimming in Lake Huron, the water so clear and pure that you drank it as you floated.

And then the squadron.

They were good days, those days on the squadron; crammed to the limit with beauty and experience, living and loving. You glorified in the sunshine on the wide Cambridge countryside and in the soaring flight of the larks as you walked up the chalk road behind the airfield. You glorified in the drinking too, in the crowded bars and smoke-filled hotel lounges. Drinking with men who drank hugely because their time for drinking might be short. And, when the bars closed, piling seven men into a four-seater car and driving back to the mess through the hay-scented darkness. The weekends, too few, when Pat got leave and you came together again, in knowledge and ecstasy. Even now he could not dwell on the stark fact of her death. It was unreal. He had not been there when it happened. Pat . . .

The slow movement began. It was the rustle of the dry ears of barley as you lay drowsing at the field's edge the day after an op, and as the music swelled the wind freshened and the rustling of the barley mingled with the song of the wind in the trees.

The music was driving the Aston Martin fast down the empty Great North Road, with the windscreen down and the early morning sun just warm on your hands as they gripped the wheel; the kick of the wheel as you hit a bump in the tarmac and the long juddering scream of the tyres as you approached a corner fast and came in close to take advantage of the camber of the road.

It was the fear of death.

It was the night he had been shot down. The quiet stooging along miles from the target, the moon and the stars, the flickering searchlights far away on the horizon. The light-hearted conversation of his New Zealander crew. Then with shocking suddenness the hammer and din of machine-gun bullets and the heavier tearing impact of cannon shells as a night fighter closed in from behind them. The wild jinking to avoid the attack, the dry-mouthed sick fear of the smashing, tearing impact of the shells. The smell of cordite, the sudden red mushrooming fire in the cockpit, the fumbling with the parachute harness and the sickening swaying below the flapping parachute as he descended into Germany.

It was his feeling of relief to be safe, unhurt, on the ground. The three days when he was hunted across the German countryside, the capture and handover to the military, solitary confinement, interrogation; being, finally, given up for hopeless and sent to join his fellows in the Dulag-Luft transit camp.

The music was his first real prison camp, Oflag XXIB in Poland. It had been snowing when the new batch of prisoners had arrived and the night had been clear, smelling of fresh snow and pinewoods. Was all of Germany covered by pine forest, he wondered. They had been marched into the barrack block where a hundred prisoners had been locked since dark. After the freshness of the night outside the stench had been appalling. A long low room lit by dozens of home-made goon lamps – tobacco tins filled with rancid animal fat which gave off a feeble red glow and clouds of black evil-smelling smoke. The lamps threw weird distorted shadows on walls which had once been whitewashed but now were grey and smeared by smoke and steam. There were windows in each of the side walls but they were covered from the outside by wooden blackout shutters. The air was thick with tobacco smoke and steam rising from the rows of damp washing which hung at head level from lines strung across the room. Smoke from the goon lamps mingled with the steam and tobacco smoke to form a thick fog which eddied and billowed just below the ceiling.

He remembered his horror at the uncouth appearance of the bearded haggard men who sat huddled round the flickering lamps. Life had been pretty grim in the early days, before the Red Cross parcels had begun to arrive. Then, they had lived on scum-covered turnip or barley soup and rotten potatoes. It seemed almost impossible now, in the heat of the summer, that he had been so cold last winter. He remembered waking in that long, damp, crowded room, fully dressed even to his issue greatcoat, with a woollen skullcap on his head and mittens on his hands. A film of water lay in the grey blanket in which he had wrapped himself from head to toe, and the woodwork of the bunk on which he lay was dripping. He remembered the reveille, the door crashing open and the hoarse baying cry of 'Raus! Raus!' when the guards invaded the room. The equally hoarse shout of 'Fuck off!' with which the prisoners replied.

It was in Oflag XXIB that he had teamed up with John, the lone soldier among so many airmen. At Dulag-Luft transit camp John had seemed aloof, immersed in his books of Latin and ancient Greek; but later, when Peter got to know him, he discovered his eagerness, his consuming desire to escape, to wipe out the disgrace of being captured. It was a disgrace not felt by the airmen because their capture had not involved

73

a surrender of arms.

The music was still playing when a German major with an escort of four guards marched into the ward to conduct a blitz *appell*. The major came to a halt and ordered his men to be silent. When the last notes died away, he waited a moment, then said, 'Ach, Beethoven! A good German.'

'Yes, cobber,' said Peter's neighbour. 'He's dead.'

5

'It's quite obvious that we can't go on as we are,' Peter said. He had been discharged from the hospital only an hour ago, and it felt strange to be back on his feet and out on the circuit after the closer confinement of the ward. 'We've dug forty feet out of the hundred and twenty – only a third – and already we're taking two hours to fill twelve bags. The farther we go the longer it will take.'

'Why not take the horse out twice a day?' After a week of organizing the vaulters John was keen to get digging again. 'Once in the morning and once in the afternoon.'

They walked on in silence while Peter considered. 'We could do that,' he said slowly, 'but we could only take about six bags out at a time. Fewer and fewer the farther we go. It's not the digging, it's getting the blasted sand back from the face to the shaft. It's bad enough at forty feet, but it's going to be impossible to drag it back the whole length of the tunnel. Why, it'll take about half an hour just to crawl up to the face once we get to a hundred feet. It's not like wriggling on the surface. It looks as though we've bitten off more than we can chew.'

'There's always a way,' John said. 'Let's study the problem. It's how to get the sand from the face to the shaft. Why not use a toboggan like we did at Schubin?'

'That was a big tunnel and there were several down there at a session. Here we've no air and no light. Besides, if you took two men out in the horse you couldn't bring any sand back. No room – and it'd be as much as the vaulters could do to carry the two of us, let alone bags of sand as well. And I don't see how a toboggan would help if you were down there alone.'

75

'Then we'll *have* to go down together, that's all.'

Again they walked in silence, worrying at the problem. We *must* finish it, Peter thought. It's too good a scheme to drop. There must be *some* way of getting the sand out of the place . . .

Then he saw it. 'I've got it!' he said. 'It'll be faster than we've been going and I think we'll cope with the whole length of the tunnel.'

'How?'

'We'll go down together, as you suggested. We'll have to crouch head to head, one at each end of the horse. The chaps should be able to carry us both, without sand. We'll have to take thirty-six bags instead of twelve. And we'll have to make a bulge at the end of the tunnel to give the digger room to work. One of us will work in the bulge and the other in the vertical shaft. We'll run a toboggan between us with a rope at each end. We can dig enough in one session to fill the thirty-six bags – it's not the digging that takes the time. When we've filled the thirty-six bags we'll stack them all in the shaft and go back in the horse.'

'You mean, leave all the thirty-six bags in the tunnel?'

'I'm coming to that. We dig in the morning. That afternoon one of us goes out alone in the horse and brings back twelve of the bags. The next morning the other brings back twelve more, and the last twelve that afternoon. On the third morning we go out together again and dig another thirty-six bags of sand.'

'Jolly good idea,' John said. 'Eighteen bags a day instead of twelve. Can't see any snags.'

'There's just one. We'll have to bring someone else in.'

'Why? I thought just we two were going to be in it. I thought we were going to keep it small.'

'We need someone to organize the vaulting – can't be both underground without having someone up there who's in the scheme. It's too much to ask a chap to do all that without giving him the chance to go out with us.'

'I suppose so. Who do you think?'

'What about Tony Winyard?' Peter suggested. 'He's done a

moling *dienst* himself and he might even help with the digging.'

'All right. You go and ask him. I'll organize some more trouser bottoms and get on with the extra bags.'

They separated, but a few seconds later Peter heard John come running after him. 'If I go down this afternoon to clear up, and you make the toboggan this evening, we can get cracking on the new system tomorrow morning.'

'Walk down,' Peter said. 'Do the lot.'

•   •   •

Winyard was in the library, looking for a book on old glass.

'Care for a turn round the circuit?' Peter said. 'There's something I'd like to ask you.'

'Sure. I'm getting bored with glass anyway.' He followed Peter out into the sunshine of the compound. 'How's it going?' He spoke casually.

'That's what I wanted to see you about. We need a third man and we wondered if you'd care to join us.'

Winyard did not answer immediately; he seemed embarrassed. 'Well . . . As a matter of fact, I'm preparing a *dienst* myself. It's a one-man show – under the wire in the Vorlager – but it won't come off until the autumn. I've got to wait for the dark evenings.'

'Oh, we shall break before then,' Peter said. 'We're just starting a new system and we shall go faster from now on.'

Winyard appeared to be thinking it over. 'I'd have liked to,' he said finally, 'but I'll have to turn it down I'm afraid. You see, I've been caught so often that the Kommandant told me I'm for Colditz next time – once you get there you're finished. My next attempt has got to be pretty nearly a dead certainty. Not that yours isn't a good show,' he added quickly, 'but frankly I don't think you stand much chance of getting out.'

'That's all right,' Peter said. 'I can see your point.'

'Don't think I'm knocking your show in any way,' he insisted. 'It's a damn good idea. But it's going to take so long,

77

and I'm afraid the goons are bound to tumble to it before you're finished.'

'Oh, I don't think so. We've got over the worst part – the horse has become a camp institution and the goons are used to it.'

'How much have you done now?'

'About forty feet.'

'How much have you to do in all?'

'A hundred and twenty – at the most.'

'And you've been at it how long? Two months?'

'About. But we've only been digging six weeks.'

'It's halfway through August. That puts you well into November.'

'No, I reckon early October. We'll go more quickly under the new system, and we'll mole the last ten or twenty feet.'

'Well – I wish you luck . . . I've had moling but if you want any tips – '

'Thanks,' Peter said quickly. 'We do. Do we have to put up an airhole as soon as we start to mole?'

'Absolutely. As soon as you begin to bank the sand up behind you you're enclosed in a small pocket of air which soon gets exhausted. What's more, you have to put up another before the first is blocked by the sand behind you. The principle is to move forward inside your pocket of air, pushing up more airholes as you need them.'

'Could three of us do it?'

'Oh yes, if you're all cool types. Not for very long though – hence not very far. With three you'll need a lot of tunnel behind you to take the sand. Get it as far back as possible, making the air pocket as long as you can. That way you'll need fewer airholes. Pass the sand back from man to man. You won't be able to change places so have the best man at the front. I'd only do it half an hour or so before you break. It's risky, because of the airholes and, of course, there's always the danger of the roof falling in on you.'

They walked on in silence for a few minutes, Peter thinking about moling. Probably wouldn't be able to do as much as twenty feet in so narrow a tunnel. Winyard spoke again:

'October, you said?'

'Yes. Must get out before the winter.'

'Christ, you haven't been in the bag long. It's winter then ... How're you travelling?'

'As French workers. By train.'

'Well, if you break before the end of October – I've got a railway timetable valid until then.'

'How on earth – ?'

'Oh I'm one of the types detailed to corrupt the goons.' He grinned. 'Cost a couple of packets of cigarettes – supplied by the Committee, so don't think . . .'

'Thanks,' Peter said. 'Thanks a lot. You've been a great help. I only wish you were joining us.'

'Race you home,' Winyard said.

⁂

Peter found John in the washhouse, canvassing for trouser-leg bottoms; and drew him out on to the circuit.

'How many have you got?'

'Eighteen, I think, so far. I've exhausted all the people who've cut their trousers down already. Now I'm persuading people that shorts are a good thing and getting 'em to cut 'em down while I wait. Nig's hard at work sewing.'

'Winyard doesn't want to come in with us,' Peter said. 'He doesn't think we've an earthly chance of finishing.'

'That's his funeral. I might ask Paul to sew some of them. Time he got off his back.'

'Who do we ask now? To join us I mean. The best chap would be Nig but his leg's so dicky I don't think he'd make it along the tunnel.'

'We shouldn't have let him do so much vaulting,' John said. 'He can hardly walk now and yet he's been coming out every day and hopping round the horse – just to make it look like a crowd.'

'He ought to go into hospital,' Peter said. 'Did he ever tell you how it happened?'

'Doesn't talk about it much, you know Nig. A flak battery shot at him while he was coming down in a parachute.'

'How do you know they shot at *him*? I expect they were

79

just pooping off wildly at everything in general.'

'Why do you always stand up for the Hun, Pete? You've lost more than most people in the war.'

'Oh, I don't know.' He could talk about it now. The last few days in hospital he had faced up to Pat's death. He had realized how lucky he had been to have had those few years with her. No point in grieving when there was nothing he could do. 'Thousands of people have lost their wives or husbands or children in air raids in this war. Germans have too. I've bombed them myself. You can't blame the whole nation. Nig doesn't blame the goons for his leg.'

'Old Phil blames them – makes goon hatred a sort of religion. Chap in his mess says he gets up every morning cursing the goons and keeps it up all day. He's got "Bloody Sagan" written up over his bed.'

'I suppose some chaps work up a hate to keep them going – a useful way of expending surplus energy.'

'He shouldn't have any surplus energy,' John said. 'He's organized practically all the dispersal, as well as vaulting with the best of them.'

'And running the coal and the showers and the stoves,' Peter said. 'But he's not much good at vaulting.'

John laughed. 'I love to see him when he gets really angry. He grits his teeth and charges at the horse with his arms going like piston-rods.'

'The nearer he gets to the horse the slower he runs.'

'Yes, but he does keep at it. He's improved enormously since he started.'

'Let's ask him to come in,' Peter said. 'We'll do the digging and he can organize all the vaulting and the dispersal. I'd rather no one else went down the hole because we know exactly how small we want it and Phil would have grand ideas about enlarging it and putting in an air pump. If he'd look after the vaulting – you know how methodical he is, he'd draw up lists and organize it so that everyone had a certain time on a certain day to vault. It'll look perfectly natural to the ferrets if he takes over, they're used to him running things. And now that we're going to go out twice a day the problem of the vaulters is going to be more difficult than ever.'

'Fine,' John said. 'Let's go and find him right away.'

• • •

They ran him down to earth near the gate leading to the Vorlager. He had a list of names in his hand and was looking worried.

'What's the gen, Phil?' Peter asked. 'Come for a walk round the circuit.'

'I can't at the moment. I'm trying to muster the chaps for their hot showers. But no one seems to want one.'

'Then leave it,' Peter said. 'Come for a walk instead.'

'I can't. It's all right for you – you've no sense of responsibility. I've got a job to do. Someone's got to help run the camp. If we don't use the showers the goons'll withdraw the privilege.'

'Come on, Phil!' John said. They fell in one each side of him and began to walk him towards the circuit.

'All right,' he said, accepting the inevitable. 'But only one round. I've got to find these people for their showers.'

'There are more important things than showers,' Peter said. 'We're going to get you out of the camp and send you home to your wife.'

'You're mad,' Philip said. 'You're both mad. Go away – and find someone else to pester. I've got a job to do.'

'We mean it, Phil,' John said. 'We want you to join us in the *dienst*.'

He stopped in his tracks and looked at them suspiciously. 'Why me?'

'Well,' Peter began, 'knowing your organizing ability –'

'And your almost touching faith in our efficiency –' John continued.

'We thought you'd jump at the idea,' Peter concluded.

'What do you want me to do?'

'We're going to work a new system now. We're both going down together – with a toboggan and rope – and we'll fill thirty-six bags in one session. We spend the next three sessions with one or the other of us fetching twelve bags back at a time. It means taking the horse out twice a day, mornings and afternoons, and we need you to organize the vaulting and the dispersal of the sand.'

'I'm practically doing that already.'

'That's why we think you ought to come in. We can get three out as easily as two.'

'Right,' Philip said with decision. 'I'll come in and help you with the tunnel. But I'll travel alone. I'm not taking the risk of travelling across Germany with you two.'

'Why ever not?' Peter tried to look disappointed.

'You're so – so – ' he groped for the right word – 'disorganized.'

'Are you any good at sewing?' John asked.

6

With the new system of digging the tunnel made progress. They had enlarged the far end to form a 'bulge' large enough to allow the man who was digging at the face to rest on his elbows and draw his knees up under his chest. Instead of using the usual wooden toboggan for transporting the sand down the tunnel they used a metal basin eighteen inches in diameter and eight inches deep. The basin was just small enough to fit into the tunnel. They had drilled two holes in opposite sides of the rim of the basin to take the rope which they had plaited from the string off the Red Cross parcels.

When the bulge was finished – it took them four days to remove the extra sand – the tunnel was driven on. One man worked in the tunnel extension, dragging the sand backwards into the bulge. Once in the bulge he pulled the basin up the tunnel, past his feet and over his legs on to his stomach, where he filled it with the sand he had brought back. Two pulls on the rope was the signal for the man in the shaft to pull back the basin full of sand. He then tipped the basin over and filled his bags while the worker in the bulge crawled up to the end of the tunnel for more sand.

At first they merely threaded the rope through the holes in the rim of the basin. But the holes had been raggedly punched through with a nail and soon cut the rope, leaving the basin stranded – usually halfway along the tunnel. Then there followed a whispered argument as to who was nearer the basin and whose turn it was to crawl up the tunnel and repair the rope. Later they made strong wire hooks with which to attach the basin to the rope.

Up to the time of making the bulge they had been troubled

83

by lack of air in the tunnel. Under the new system they found that sufficient air was pushed up the tunnel by the passage of the basin to supply the man in the bulge. They were now working gradually up towards the surface and it was impossible to remain in the extension beyond the bulge for more than a few minutes. If for any reason the basin was not kept moving the shortage of air became dangerous.

After a time they had driven the tunnel so far beyond the bulge that it became impossible to work in the extension and they made a new bulge at the end of the tunnel, filled in the old bulge, lengthened the rope and carried on as before.

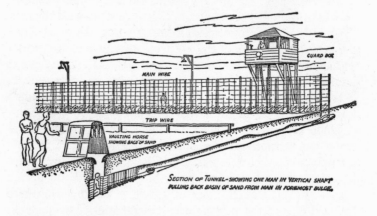

SECTION OF TUNNEL—SHOWING ONE MAN IN VERTICAL SHAFT PULLING BACK BASIN OF SAND FROM MAN IN FOREMOST BULGE.

Try as they might they could not persuade Philip to stay above ground; but he refused to enter the tunnel in the nude, insisting on wearing a shirt, shorts and tennis shoes. They respected his determination to share in the work but did all they could to arrange that he remained in the shaft. It was a feat of some endurance to pull the thirty-odd full basins of sand from the face to the shaft. In addition to this the bags had to be filled and lifted one by one and stacked inside the vaulting horse. So Peter and John pleaded fatigue and persuaded Philip to let one of them work at the face whenever it was his turn to dig.

•   •   •

84

In Peter's mess there was a growing air of tension. They had all been at Sagan now for five months and they knew each other too well. Except for Robbie's departure to another hut — as far as he could get from Bennett without moving to another compound – there had been no changes. Nigel had identified more and more with Peter and John, helping them in every way he could. Immersed in the scheme, the three isolated themselves from the day-to-day preoccupations of the others.

Robbie's bunk remained empty and there were now only seven of them. Once every so often one of the 'ghosts' would come for the night; and there would be new subjects for conversation, more effort made in cooking and serving the evening meal.

There were several such ghosts wandering disconsolately about the camp. At some time in the early days the prisoners had managed to confuse the German nominal roll, so that there were fewer of them on the books than were in the camp. These supernumeraries went into hiding at *appell*, and were kept in reserve to take the place of any prisoner who had escaped or who wanted for some reason to disappear. The life of a ghost was not a happy one. Not being on the roll he could draw no rations, and even his letters from home had to be addressed to a fellow-prisoner.

Although the Germans suspected that ghosts existed they did not know how many there were. At any hour of the day or night the bugle would sound for a blitz *appell*. The prisoners would tumble cursing from their bunks or leave whatever they were doing, and fall in on the parade ground to be counted, while extra guards searched the huts. But no ghosts had yet been found.

Apart from the nights when it was their turn to entertain a ghost, the mess lived in a state of disgruntled apathy.

*   *   *

It was lunch-time. The biscuits had not been buttered. No one had gone for the tea water. Four morose figures sat round a bare table.

85

Pomfret was speaking. '. . . a matter of principle. I've done it every day this week and now it's Friday. Clinton must do it today as a matter of principle.' He advanced his chin obstinately. He was dressed in the full uniform of a flight lieutenant. His collar, ironed with a tin of hot water, was frayed round the edges.

'That's all very well,' Bennett said, 'but it's lunch-time and we're hungry. You and Clinton share the duty of cook and it's up to you to see that the meal is prepared.' Except for his odd assortment of clothing Bennett might have been addressing a board meeting. He delivered his opinion as an ultimatum and glanced round the table for approval. His red hairy arms were crossed upon the table. Having delivered his speech, he sucked his teeth with an air of finality.

'Well, I'm not doing it today.' Pomfret appeared about to cry. 'It's not fair. Just because he's digging a tunnel it doesn't mean he can neglect all his duties in the mess. I'm fed up with doing two people's work. All they think about is their wretched tunnel. I'm sick to death of seeing them sitting in the corner whispering all evening. It was bad enough before they started the tunnel. Clinton was always missing at meal-times. But for more than two months now I've done all the work. It's not right.'

'That's for you and Clinton to settle between yourselves,' said Bennett judicially. 'What about our lunch? It's only a matter of buttering seven biscuits and walking over to the canteen for some hot water.'

'That's not the point! It's a matter of principle.'

'So the whole mess must suffer for the sake of your principles,' David said disgustedly. He was sitting at the head of the table, studying his fingernails.

'It's not my principles that are at fault, it's Clinton's laziness.'

'I don't call it laziness to dig in a tunnel and vault over a horse for several hours a day. Surely you and he can come to some arrangement so that you both do an equal amount of work, but his share doesn't interfere with his tunnelling.'

'You can't come to any arrangement with Clinton,' Pomfret said. 'He always forgets. He hasn't grown up yet. He's got no

86

sense of responsibility.'

'He's not the only one who hasn't grown up,' David said.

'This is all very well,' Bennett interrupted, 'but do we get our lunch?'

'I'm not doing it!' Pomfret said obstinately.

The other three stared at him angrily. The food cupboard was sacred. No one but the cook was allowed to open it. In a life where hunger was the normal condition, food had strict taboos.

'Supposing we split the mess in two,' Pomfret suggested. 'Let them mess together and we four will mess together. They can do what they like then.'

'They always do.' Bennett sucked his teeth again.

'Well, what do you say? I think it would serve them right.'

'Very likely buck them no end.' Paul spoke for the first time.

'I'm in favour,' Bennett said. 'Howard and Clinton can't cook anyway. Let's take a vote.'

'I say yes,' Pomfret said.

David and Paul hesitated, embarrassed, unwilling to make the decision.

'Paul?'

He shrugged. 'I suppose so.'

Bennett looked across at David, who thought of coping with the eccentricities of the absent three. He decided not to risk it; anyway their tunnel would be finished soon.

'I think it's bloody childish,' he said, 'and it'll be damned inconvenient having two messes in one room.'

'Would you rather go in with them? Then you can do all the cooking for four.' Pomfret sounded spiteful.

'No, I'll mess with you. But I don't like the idea of splitting up.'

*   *   *

When they came in they found the biscuits ready buttered and the tea water in the can. John threw himself on his bunk and closed his eyes. He had been working at the face and Peter at the tunnel entrance; Nigel had been hiding the excavated sand under the floor of the canteen.

'Lunch, John?' Peter asked.

'Not for the moment, thanks, old boy.'

'Feeling rotten?' Nigel asked.

'I'm OK. I'll be OK in a minute. I'll wash before I eat.' He lay back with his eyes closed. His body was brown but his face was pale. His hair, matted with sand and sweat, was damp on his forehead. The sand was under his broken fingernails and in his eyelashes, and his nostrils were filled with sand.

Pomfret cleared his throat. 'I prepared the lunch today, Clinton.'

'Thanks, old boy,' John said. 'Was it my turn?'

'It was your turn,' Pomfret replied. 'It has been your turn for the last four days. As a matter of principle I, at first, refused to do it.'

'Thanks for doing it all the same,' John said. 'I'll do the dinner.'

'That will not be necessary. We four have decided to mess separately.'

'After due consideration,' Bennett said, taking the chair, 'we have decided that we four shall mess on our own.'

Pomfret glared at him; after all, it was his idea.

'We are tired of Clinton's impossible attitude,' Bennett continued, 'and we presumed that you three would want to stay together. We have separated the food, and starting with dinner tonight we shall cater for ourselves.'

'OK,' Peter said. 'That suits us. What about you, Nig?'

'*Blond genug*, old boy.'

.   .   .

So the mess was split into two and settled down again. There was still friction between the four, particularly between Paul and Bennett, but the three drifted into an ideal way of living where no one was stooge and yet at the right time, for them, the meals appeared. Most of their waking hours were spent in vaulting, digging and dispersing the sand. When they had nothing to do they lay in the sun. They had dug a sand pit outside the window of the mess and, despite spirited opposition from the 'Purity League' led by Pomfret, lay soaking in the sun that beat back in a shimmering haze from the burning sand. When they got too hot they bathed in the brick fire-water tank, and made fantastic sun-hats from Red Cross cartons. Pomfret hated the sun. He would lie on his bunk cursing the heat and flapping at the flies that buzzed and whined around his head.

The place was thick with flies. Sometimes Peter, John and Nigel would organize a 'daylight sweep'. They closed the door and windows and attacked the flies with tightly rolled copies of the *Völkischer Beobachter*, slashing and cutting at the enemy as he settled on table, stools and bunks. It was glorious while it lasted; a slaughter that relieved the tension of their nerves. Finally, flushed and elated with victory, they would all descend on the sole remaining insect, upsetting table and stools and benches in their mad rush to claim the last of the intruders.

Having cleared the room they would go and swim in the fire-water tank. On their return they would find the room as thick with flies as ever.

Peter had made a refrigerator. He built an open-sided wooden cupboard and stood it on two bricks in a shallow metal tray of water. A loose cover made from a blanket was fitted over the cupboard, its ends falling into the water in the tray. Another metal tray of water was placed on top of the cupboard and 'feeders' – narrow strips of blanket – were led from the upper tray on to the loose cover. By keeping both tins full of water the absorbent loose cover was always moist, and the constant evaporation of this moisture considerably lowered the temperature inside the cupboard. So effective was the refrigerator that tins of food placed inside it soon became coated with beads of moisture.

They filled a canvas kitbag with water and hung it from the ceiling of the room. Water oozing through the canvas and evaporating cooled the atmosphere that would otherwise have been unbearable. The sun blazed down on the wooden huts and turned them into ovens. At intervals the guards came round with hoses and sprayed water over the roofs and under the floors.

In the evenings after dinner the prisoners would sit on the

steps of their huts or stand in groups against the wooden walls, talking desultorily. It reminded Peter of the Liverpool slums. He had pitied the people in those slums in the summer; sitting in rows on their doorsteps and on chairs on the pavement outside their overcrowded tenements, too hot to go inside. Now he too sat in shirt sleeves, smoking his pipe on the doorstep, the dust of the circuit between his toes and the friendly gossip of his neighbours all around him. And sitting there he would feel a quiet contentment, a lazy acceptance of conditions. An acceptance that he knew was laziness and which he banished by concentrating on his plans for the journey outside.

'Well, that's that!' Peter put down his stick of charcoal. 'It's not much like you, I'm afraid, John. But that's about all I can do to it.' He leaned the drawing against a pile of books on the table and stood back. It lacked finish but it had caught something of the character of the sitter. It showed a young man in a creased collarless woollen shirt, sitting with a book in his lap, his back propped up against one of the wooden uprights of the bunk. His right leg was crossed over his left knee, and a wooden-soled sandal hung from his right foot, secured by strips cut from a threadbare RAF greatcoat. The face was in repose. Dark-skinned, with slanting brown eyes and heavily marked eyebrows, it was at once sensitive and mischievous. There was something faunlike in the high cheekbones, the setting of the ears and the long black hair – or Malay, Peter thought. Funny how kids born in the Far East looked oriental in spite of their all-English parentage; was it pre-natal influence on the mother, or spending the formative years in the charge of an ayah? Not too bad an effort though, the drawing. The subject looked as though he were about to speak, and he looked as though what he was about to say would be of interest. 'Sorry I kept you sitting so long.'

'I needed a rest,' John said. 'What about a game of chess?'

'Right.' He knocked out his pipe on the stove and filled it from a tin on his shelf. He lit it with a cigarette end and a piece of paper. 'If you ever see anyone do this after the war, you'll know he's been a kriegie.'

'You won't see anyone do it,' Bennett spoke from the corner by the blacked-out shuttered windows; he was washing his feet in a bowl of water. 'There'll be plenty of matches.'

' "The listening horizon",' Pomfret quoted, looking up from his book. His favourite form of self-torture was to take a book by one of the more popular women novelists and read it slowly, word by word, suffering as much as he could in the process. This evening he was enjoying himself. 'The listening horizon,' he repeated. 'How can a horizon listen?'

'That's poetic licence,' Bennett told him. 'She means it was bloody quiet.'

'Then why doesn't she say "it was bloody quiet"?' Pomfret asked. 'It's bloody nonsense.'

'It gives you a lot of pleasure anyway,' Bennett said, lifting a dripping foot from the bowl and wriggling the toes.

'If I start anything I like to finish it,' Pomfret said happily.

For a few minutes the mess was silent. Through the thin partition wall on one side could be heard the strains of a well-worn jazz record and from the other side the raised voices of two prisoners who were quarrelling.

Nigel sat on his bunk making a golf ball. He had searched the compound for several days before he had found the right stone for the core; smooth, round and not too heavy. Next he had unravelled the top of a pair of woollen socks and carefully wound the wool on to a stick. It was good, resilient wool, resilient enough to give the ball sufficient 'life' to enable him to drive it fifty or sixty yards. He had cut down a pair of issue boots to make shoes and had saved the soft leather of the uppers for the cover of the ball. He had borrowed a paper template and cut two pieces of leather shaped like a solid figure of eight. After winding the wool round the stone until the ball had reached the regulation size, he had soaked the leather in water and was now sewing it together with thread water-proofed with candle grease. Tongue between his teeth, he was gently stretching the damp leather round the ball. Without warning, noisily, he broke wind.

'Good show,' David said, looking up from the chart of next year's crops, which he was printing carefully on a sheet of cardboard to be pinned over his bunk.

Pomfret laid down his book with an expression of exaggerated disgust. 'Really, Wilde, do you think that's necessary?'

'Better out than in, old boy.'

'Well, I think it's disgusting,' Pomfret said. 'Just because we're prisoners is no reason for us to behave like savages. I think it's entirely unnecessary and unpleasant.' He picked up his book, only to drop it again a few seconds later. 'Why can't they play that gramophone more quietly. How can I read!'

'Bet you the next tune's "Boynk, Boynk",' Nigel said.

'Right.' Peter looked up from the chess-board, hopeful that the problem of the next move would resolve itself. 'I'll take you on. Twenty Players it's "Ah, Sweet Mystery of Life".'

'I'm in this,' John said. 'Bet it's "Intermezzo".'

Patiently they waited for the record to be changed.

'There you are!' Nigel said. 'It's "Boynk, Boynk". Twenty Players from both of you.'

'It isn't "Boynk, Boynk" anyway,' Pomfret said. 'It's "Oynk, Oynk".'

'It's not,' Nigel said, 'it's "Boynk, Boynk".'

'It's "Oynk, Oynk" I tell you! Listen!'

'Hell! Are you two at it again?' Peter had returned to the problem of the next move.

There was a knock on the door and Philip came in, kicking it shut behind him. He was carrying a Red Cross carton which he set down carefully on John's bunk. 'Here are your extra rations. I must say neither of you look like invalids after all that sunbathing.' The Red Cross sent Benger's food, Horlicks malted milk, Nestlé's condensed milk and Bemax wheat germ for the hospital; but there was more than was needed and the Escape Committee managed to 'divert' the surplus which they then rationed out to prisoners working in tunnels.

'Thanks,' Peter said. 'Stay for a brew? I can't win. Your game, John.'

'Good idea.' Philip sat down on the vacant bunk. 'Got some news for you. It's OK to talk – the hut's been cleared and we've got stooges out this evening. The radio boffin's trying to get the set to work.'

'I'll brew up.' Nigel abandoned a slightly a-symmetrical golf ball. 'Our jug's on the stove already.' They had found it impracticable to split the tea, coffee and cocoa, and the whole mess

93

still shared the hot drinks.

'What's the gen?' John asked.

'You'll never guess.' Philip began to laugh and seemed unable to stop. 'Gilbert the Gelding went along to the Committee and – ' he doubled up, choking with laughter.

'What the hell is it?'

Philip wiped his eyes. 'He wanted permission to dig a tunnel under the horse! Thought he'd had the idea of the century.'

'How dim can you get,' Peter said. 'I thought the whole compound was in on it already. No real news?'

'Yes – this bit's not so funny. Odell's starting a tunnel from Hut 64. It's an old one that was sealed up some time ago and Odell's getting it going again. It's to be a blitz *dienst* – they'll work the clock round, in shifts, and stuff all the sand in the roof of the hut.'

'But that's bloody silly,' Peter said. 'The goons search the roof once a week.'

'That's just the idea. They'll wait for the next search and start immediately it's finished. They won't disperse the sand at all – just bung it up in the roof – and by working in shifts all day and all night they hope to get out by the next time the roof's searched.'

'How far have they got to go?' John asked.

'About a hundred and fifty feet.'

'They won't get all that sand in the roof. The bloody thing'll collapse with all that weight,' Peter said.

'They'll just put all they can in the roof and then the last few days they'll put it in their bunks and in Red Cross cartons under the beds.'

'How many are going out?' John asked.

'The whole hut.'

'They won't have a chance!' Peter was getting angry now, with the quick prison camp anger that faded as quickly as it came. 'If a hundred men get out at once the goons'll have a nation-wide search and then where will *we* be? There'll be such a flap that it'll completely spoil our show.'

'Oh, it's not as bad as that,' Philip said. 'The whole thing will be over inside a fortnight, and it'll be another month at least before we get out. The flap'll be over by then. Personally

I don't think they'll finish the tunnel. But it's an attempt and they're so few and far between these days that the Committee'll back anything that's put forward.' He grinned. 'The horse is a case in point.'

'They'll be picked up by the seismographs anyway,' John said.

'Yes, particularly if they work day and night,' Peter agreed. He was feeling better now.

'It's a wonder our digging hasn't been picked up,' Philip said.

Peter laughed. 'It's not such a dim scheme, y'know. Anything picked up by the seismographs is blanketed by the vibration of the vaulters landing.'

'God,' Philip said, 'I hadn't thought of that.'

'No – nor did we until the tunnel had been going for some time,' John admitted.

'Oh well.' Philip stood up and yawned. 'Can't wait for that brew I'm afraid – promised to relieve the stooge at the end of the corridor.'

'Wait a minute,' Peter said. 'Did you ask about the money?'

'I did, yes. They're a bit appalled at the idea of first-class train tickets and luxury hotels – '

'Not luxury, you clot. We said, decent hotels.'

' – but they're putting it up to the S.B.O. – he controls the funds. I could do with that coffee – keep me awake. Perhaps one of you would bring me a mug.'

'*Jawohl*,' John said.

When Philip had gone, Peter turned to John. 'It's a bit of luck about Odell, really. The goons haven't found anything for so long they must be getting suspicious. If they come across any of our sand they'll blame it on Odell.'

Nigel came back with the coffee. 'Some silly bastard had taken our hot water,' he said. 'I had to wait for another brew.'

John got to his feet. 'I'll take Phil a mug – '

'Before you go, Clinton,' Pomfret interrupted. 'You're supposed to be a literary type. What's a solid bar of misery?'

'What's that, old boy?'

'That's what I want to know. It says here "a solid bar of

misery seized her by the throat". Now what's a solid bar of misery? Just imagine – ' he made a gesture with his hands indicating a bar – 'a solid bar – ' he seized his throat with both hands and gasped for breath – 'seized her by the throat. I don't get it, do you?'

'No,' John said, moving to the door with Philip's coffee. 'Nig, you tell him what a solid bar of misery is.'

Nigel paused as he poured out the rest of the brew. 'A crowded pub that's run out of beer.'

'Beer,' Peter said, 'beer! He stands there pouring out mud-coloured hot water and talks about beer! What wouldn't I give for a pint of Bass. What wouldn't I give to lean across the bar and say, "Pint of bitter, please"!'

'You were stationed near Cambridge, weren't you, Pete?' Nigel said.

'Yes – round and about.'

'Did you use the Lion much?'

'My spiritual home, the Lion. I think I've drunk more beer in the Lion than any other six pubs put together. We used to go to the Lion before going to the theatre. My whole crew used to book stalls for the theatre once a week, all seven of us.' He sat astride one of the long benches, his mug of coffee forgotten in his hands. 'And every week we went to the Lion for a drink first. I don't remember ever getting to the theatre the whole time we were stationed near Cambridge.'

'What do you expect if you start off with a round of seven?' Nigel said. 'No one could stop drinking and go to the theatre after seven beers. It's too good a start.'

'It didn't stop at seven. My kid brother was on another squadron near Cambridge and he used to bring his crew in. It would be a party of fifteen before we finished.'

Paul closed the book he had been reading with a snap. 'Anyone want a good book?' he asked.

'I read a book once, a good book!' quoted Nigel.

'What is it?' John asked.

'*Kabloona.*'

'That *is* good!' Bennett said. 'All about the sex life of the Eskimos.'

'It isn't *all* about the sex life of the Eskimos,' Paul said.

'There's only one chapter about the sex life of the Eskimos.'

'That's the only chapter Bennett read,' Nigel said.

'What is the sex life of the Eskimos?' John asked.

'It only happens in the spring,' Paul said.

'That's no good. What do they do for the rest of the year?'

'Recuperate. You've no idea.'

'May I have that book, Paul?' Nigel asked.

'Sure. Anyone got anything to read? I could do with a real sex book this time.'

'There aren't any real sex books in the camp,' Bennett said. 'The German censors won't allow them – think it's bad for our morals.'

'It's not the censors,' Pomfret said. 'It's the Red Cross. Quite right too. You're all sex-obsessed as it is.'

'I bet the goons think we're homo,' Nigel said. 'Look at the child's hair – nearly down on her shoulders. Why don't you get it cut, John?'

'I want to see how long it will grow.' He saw no reason to explain, yet, that like Peter's beard his long hair was a kind of disguise in reverse. The identity photographs the Germans had taken would bear little resemblance to either of them when Peter shaved off his beard and he cut his hair.

'It says a lot for the British character that we can all be locked up together and nothing at all like that has ever happened,' Bennett said. 'I'm twenty-eight and I've never met a pansy yet.'

'You're not the type, that's why,' Nigel said. 'Not manly enough.'

'Let me tell you – ' Bennett began aggressively.

'Hey, Nig,' Peter interrupted quickly, 'we didn't tell you – Gilbert the Gelding's proposed digging a tunnel under the horse.'

Nigel laughed. 'He really must be as clueless as they say.'

'Oh I don't know,' John said. 'After all, it *is* the idea of the century. Very intelligent of him really.'

'The absent-minded genius,' Nigel said. 'If you're not careful you'll grow up like him – hey, that's an idea. Do you know how they persuaded him to have his head shaved?'

'You leave my hair alone.' John pushed splayed fingers protectively through his tangled mop.

'Chap rushed into their room and said "There's a new order from the S.B.O. We've all got to shave our heads as a demonstration against the Hun." Well, they argued who was to be the first and someone said, "Gilbert's the newest arrival, let's do him first.' So they sat him on a stool and got a razor and soap and shaved his hair off. Just as they'd finished, another type rushed in and said, "You know that order to shave our heads – well, it's been cancelled!" ' '

'Prep-school sense of humour,' John said. 'If anyone touches a hair of my head – ' He drew a forefinger across his throat in menacing pantomime.

The lights flickered twice. 'Five minutes to lights out,' Bennett said unnecessarily. 'You types had better get to bed.'

When the lights went out Peter crossed to the window and opened the blackout shutters. The night air was clean and cool after the smoke-thick overheated atmosphere of the room. The compound was flooded with moonlight. The sand was silver and the posts of the wire fence stood out straight and dark and edged with light. The top of the watch-tower was silver too. Even the yellow searchlights seemed powerless against the silver of the moon.

'The goon's in his box and all's well with the world,' he said.

'Hope the bastard falls out of it,' Paul said.

8

The camp barber was clipping the hair of a newly arrived prisoner. On a bench along one wall sat other clients, looking at German magazines and waiting their turn. In one corner a variety of musical instruments was stacked in an untidy heap. Near the window stood a tall, gangling prisoner with a shaven head and long sensitive face. He had a violin tucked under his chin and was playing a low, sad melody which rose and fell and endlessly repeated the same few notes. He gazed out of the window, seemingly unconscious of the people behind him. Except for the low notes of the violin, the sound of a blue-bottle buzzing against the mirror and the snip-snap of the barber's scissors, the room was silent.

It was nearly tea-time. Outside in the compound a football match was coming to an end. The audience was drifting away. Before long the compound would be deserted while the prisoners had their tea.

The new prisoner was presently astounded to see a naked, brown, tousle-headed, sand- and sweat-stained figure crawl into the room on all fours, dragging along with him a khaki-coloured bag tied at the neck with string. Without saying a word, ignored by the barber and the waiting clients, the strange figure crawled to a point near the window, opened a trap in the floor and disappeared from view, pulling after him the plump khaki bag. Then another, fully-dressed, figure crawled in with another bag, followed by others who formed a human chain, passing the bags from hand to hand down to the naked man under the floor.

The vacant-eyed violinist stopped playing in the middle of a bar. At once the trap was closed on the man under the floor.

The human chain picked up the musical instruments and began to tune them.

One of the ferrets sauntered past the open window. He did not look in. He would have seen only a prisoner having his hair cut, the waiting clients, and a group of musicians practising in one corner of the room.

There was a loud knock on the door. The violinist resumed his melancholy tune. The other musicians laid down their instruments and opened the trap. Twelve empty bags were handed up through the hole in the floor and the naked one emerged. He carefully dusted the moist sand from his body on to the floor near the trap. He was handed his clothes in silence and in silence he put them on. The loose sand was brushed into the hole in the floor and the trap carefully replaced. The empty bags were collected and taken away, one man staying behind to sweep the floor with his handkerchief to remove the last traces of sand.

.   .   .

Soon the space below the floor of the barber's shop was filled. The bags of sand were then carried out of the canteen by the male voice choir which rehearsed in the next room. The full bags were passed up through a trapdoor in the ceiling to Nigel, who spread the sand evenly between the joints in the beaverboard ceiling. They could not put much sand in the roof as the weight threatened to bring down the ceiling; so another trapdoor was made over the kitchen. The bags were again handed up to Nigel, who carried them, one by one, across the rafters to the new trapdoor, where he hid them until the evening.

Next door to the kitchen was the office of the 'kitchen goon' – the German who supervised the issue of the prisoners' rations. After he had left for the night the bags were handed down into the kitchen where David was waiting to receive them. When all the bags had been passed down into the kitchen they were carried through into the kitchen goon's office where they were handed down through another concealed trapdoor, and the sand hidden under the floor.

During the daytime the kitchen goon sat in his office, unaware of the results of the previous evening's work lying directly beneath his feet.

•   •   •

Three days after Odell's scheme went into operation the ferrets pounced again. Peter and John had dug thirty-six bags of sand that morning and Peter had been out in the afternoon to bring in twelve of them. After helping Phil to pass the bags up to Nigel in the roof he had washed himself in the kitchen and was walking back to the hut when he saw the compound gates open and a German army lorry drive at full speed towards the canteen.

He knew what was about to happen and he could do nothing to stop it. The lorry would be outside the canteen doors before the stooges were aware that anything was wrong. The dispersal team was in the roof and under the floor. It was finished. All those months of work would be wasted. And their carefully laid shoring, the brick piles and the cunningly made trap would be exposed, lying on the surface, a pitiful heap of boards and sheets of blistered plywood.

He felt sick and walked blindly on round the circuit, his hands in his pockets, walking hard to fight down the sickness and the choking obstruction in his throat. Someone passed him and said something about 'Bad luck'. He could not reply. They had been digging, inch by inch, for three months and now the tunnel would be discovered. Three months of pinning your faith to a hole in the ground. Three months of waking up in the morning just a little happier because you were doing something to get out of the place. Three months of jealous anxiety that the hole would be discovered. Subterfuge and improvisation, hilarity and panic. Every inch of the narrow hole had been scraped with their bare hands and a bricklayer's trowel. And now it was all going for nothing.

He would recover. In a few hours he would be grinning and saying, 'It was a lousy tunnel anyway'; but for the moment he was very near to tears.

Soon he was joined by John and they walked on in silence.

Peter spoke first. 'Have they caught Phil and the others?' He was deliberately casual.

'No. Lucky we started an hour earlier this afternoon. Phil was just climbing out of the kitchen window as the goons rushed in at the door. He was the last one out.'

'Where did Nig go?'

'He climbed down into the canteen and joined the choir. The goons found them singing *He shall give His angels charge over thee*. The Feldwebel stood under the trap while they sent a ferret up from the kitchen side. All they got out was the ferret.'

'They'll find the sand in the roof,' Peter said.

'I'm afraid they will. They turned the singers out but Nigel stayed behind as long as he could collecting the sheets of music. When he left they were tearing up the floor of the barber's shop.'

'Looks as though we've had it.'

'There's still a chance. They may not connect the horse with it. They may think we were dispersing the sand from somewhere else. Or if they do think of the horse they may think it was part of the stooging system.'

'Were there any bags left in the kitchen?'

'Only under the kitchen goon's floor. They'd all finished except Nig and Phil who were stowing the stuff away under his office floor. When the alarm was given they still had three full bags, so they stuffed the three full ones with the nine empty ones down the hole, covered it up, and Phil went out of the window while Nig went up into the roof and down into the canteen.'

'That was damn' good work.'

John laughed. 'It was Nig and Phil. They'd rather go to the cooler than leave a trap open. If the ferrets don't discover the trap in the office floor all they'll find will be a lot of sand in the roof and under the barber's shop and nothing to tell them where it came from or how it got there.'

'If they do find the bags we're finished,' Peter said. 'They're much too big for the goons to think we carried them under our coats. If they do find them they'll know the tunnel's somewhere in the canteen and when they can't find it they'll either watch the bloody place so closely that we can't work or they'll connect them with the horse. If only we could lay a false trail away from the canteen we might stand a chance.'

'Let's walk round there,' John suggested, 'and see what's going on.'

There was an armed guard posted outside the canteen. From inside came the sounds of hammering and the hoarse commands of the German N.C.O.

'They're enjoying themselves,' John said gloomily. 'They're tearing the bloody place to pieces. And we'll be the ones to get the cooler for wilful destruction of Reich property.'

Peter did not speak.

'This puts paid to Odell's scheme,' John said. 'The ferrets will ransack the camp looking for the tunnel and more dispersal. They're bound to examine all the roofs – especially after finding our sand in the canteen roof.'

'Have you got the rest of the bags?' Peter asked urgently.

'There are the twenty-four full ones in the tunnel and a few odds and sods in my bunk.'

'Let's go and get them,' Peter said, 'and bung them in with Odell's sand. If that's not discovered it will be OK; and if it *is* discovered the bags won't do Odell any harm. But it'll make the goons think our dispersal was part of Odell's tunnel. I don't think trouser-leg bags have been used before and they're bound to put two and two together and think Odell's men got them in some way or other from their hut to the canteen. If we can trick them into thinking that the canteen sand and the bags came from Odell's tunnel we can lie low for about a week and then go on using the canteen for dispersal. They won't search there again for a while once they think they know where the sand came from.'

'Right,' John said. 'You go and fix it with Odell and I'll fetch the bags and meet you in his room.'

•   •   •

The next morning when the prisoners went out on *appell* they took with them enough food to last them the day. They knew the camp would be searched hut by hut and room by room, and during the previous evening they had hidden most of their *verboten* possessions behind the panelling of the walls and in the sand under the huts. Some of them, risking the possibility of a personal search, carried their most cherished possessions with them.

During the day the ceiling of Hut 64 collapsed, burying the searchers in a deluge of sand. The ferrets soon found the tunnel and with it the bags that Peter had hidden.

Apparently satisfied that this was the only tunnel in existence, the Germans called off the search and took the senior officer of Hut 64 to serve his sentence in the cooler.

•   •   •

That evening Stafford, a senior member of the Escape Committee, came in to congratulate them on their luck. He was an old hand at the escaping game and had been the leader of the abortive *dienst* at Schubin which had given Peter and John their first experience of tunnelling.* He brought with him the weekly extra rations.

'Stooges are out,' he said. 'More than usual tonight because of the flap. Ferrets found the trap in the floor of the kitchen goon's office – Winyard was over there getting water just before lock-up time.'

'That means they've found the bags,' Peter said.

'What are you going to do?'

'Nothing,' Peter said. 'Nothing for a week – or perhaps more. We shall take the horse out every day and vault as usual. But no digging. No digging until we're sure they're not suspicious of the horse. We'll get one of the vaulters to knock it over at least once when there's a ferret around. Then we shall start again and carry on as we were before. We're just about under the trip-wire now and it would be silly to rush things. We'll rest for a week and then work all-out until we're through.'

'The horse needs re-upholstering,' John said, 'and we've got to replace those twelve bags. We'll do that during the next week, and get our clothing fixed up.'

* This story is told in *The Tunnel* by Eric Williams (Collins).

'Have you decided on your route yet?'

'We thought we'd go up to Stettin and try to stow away on a Swedish ship.'

'How are you travelling? As Poles?'

'No,' John said. 'Middle class French artisans. Not ex-P.O.W.s but French craftsmen who've been brought over from France. My French is fairly good.'

'What are you wearing?'

'I've got my own brown shoes,' John said, 'and a pair of Australian navy-blue battledress trousers that I swapped for a pair of khaki ones. Jim Strong's let me have his air force mackintosh and I've got a beret that I swapped with a Pole in the last camp. All I need really is a jacket of some sort and a civilian shirt and tie.'

'We can let you have a shirt each,' Stafford said. 'And there's a Fleet Air Arm jacket that ought to fit you. I'm afraid one sleeve's torn and a bit bloodstained – but if you wash it and take the gold braid off it should pass. You can either cover the buttons or replace them.'

'We've got buttons,' Peter said. 'Been collecting them for some time.'

Stafford turned to him. 'How are you fixed?'

'Tettenborne's got a black BOAC trench coat – I'm negotiating for that. I shall wear black shoes, and one of the chaps has made a beret out of a blanket that I can have.'

'What about a suit?'

'The Committee have got a phoney Marine dress uniform.'

'Yes. It's hidden away somewhere – underground I think.'

'Ralph has promised me I can have it but only just before we're ready to go. He swears it'll fit me, so I'm trusting to luck and hoping he's right.'

'I'd better get cracking on your papers,' Stafford said. 'What kind of artisans?'

'Engineer draughtsmen – essential to the goon war effort,' Peter said. 'Not forced labour – volunteers from France.'

'Do either of you have any qualifications?'

'Well, Pete can draw,' John said, 'and I speak some French. So between us . .'

Stafford laughed outright. 'What more could they want! Let me think for a minute. The *Ausweis* and *Arbeitskarte* are easy. So is the police permit to travel. But you'll need a letter from your firm transferring you from one factory to another . . . My God, you two are lucky bastards. I think we've got just the job – a works in Breslau with a subsidiary in Anklam – and that's just north-west of Stettin.'

'The god in the box,' John said.

'Oh – the Committee has its uses. We'll let you have a pocket compass and a torch later on – but the battery's nearly exhausted. You know about all neutral ships being searched? The dock police use tear gas bombs now and specially trained dogs.'

'Yes, we'd heard about that,' Peter said. 'I suppose you've no Swedish seaman's papers? We could drop the French cover when we reached Stettin and it would give us an excuse to hang about the docks. We're taking navy-blue rollneck sweaters which'll help to make us look the part. Switching our identity might make things easier booking in at hotels round the docks too.'

'I don't think we have,' Stafford said, 'but I'll check. I still don't like the idea of staying in hotels. Too many police checks.'

Peter said nothing. Stafford recognized this obstinacy – the singleness of purpose that had taken the tunnel so far – and he turned to John.

'I agree with Pete. No one has tried it yet and very few people have got home – none from this camp. Our papers will be good and I think the bolder we are the less suspicious the Germans will be. Besides, it'll be late October before we're out and it's going to be pretty cold sleeping in the open. If we don't get a ship at once – and it'd be a miracle if we did – we'll have to go somewhere at night and there's less risk in hotels than in hanging around station waiting-rooms and public lavatories. We've talked the whole thing over and that's what we've decided to do.' He said it with finality.

'Perhaps you're right,' Stafford said. 'I know what it's like to be without a base of some sort. It gets on your nerves, having nowhere to go – no place where you can relax and have a bit of a breather . . . I've got an address in Stettin,' he added. 'It's a brothel, but I don't know whether I ought to let you have it.'

'Don't you think we're old enough?' John asked.

'It's not that. I've had the address for some time – ever since I was out myself, but I never got as far as Stettin – and the place may have been bust wide open by now. A Pole told me about it in Schubin – they were Polish girls and they hid Allied prisoners and airmen who were on the loose. But these places can be more of a danger than a help. The Hun might have rumbled it and be using it as a trap.'

'Do Germans go there?' Peter asked.

'No, I believe not. It's a brothel for foreign workers and Germans aren't allowed in. But as I say, it might be a trap. I'll give you the address just before you break. You'll have to commit it to memory. Wouldn't be safe to write it down.'

'We'll remember it,' John said. 'I've never been to a brothel.'

'Well, I wish you luck,' Stafford said. 'I think you might make it. You're breaking before the big North Compound tunnel after all. You could even be home for Christmas.'

'Long before,' John said.

'Have a drink on me in Shepheard's, will you?'

'We'll have a drink on you in every pub in Town,' Peter promised.

9

When they reopened the tunnel at the end of seven days they found that the sand on the roof and walls had dried and considerable falls had occurred. It took them another week to clear the fallen sand and to shore the tunnel in the dangerous places.

It was now early October and the long hot Silesian summer was over. All through September the digging had been controlled by the weather. Once the trap was lifted and the workers were in the tunnel it took them a full fifteen minutes to get back to the shaft, close the trap and prepare to be carried in. They could not afford to be caught out by a shower of rain. If it started to rain the vaulters could not continue without arousing the suspicion of the guards. Nor could they run for the shelter of the canteen leaving the vaulting-horse out in the rain. The obvious thing was to carry the horse in with them, and they could not do this with the trap open and two men in the tunnel. So they studied the weather carefully. If it looked at all like rain they vaulted without digging; and with no one in the horse they took the opportunity to knock it over, to demonstrate the innocence of their activity.

The nearer they got to the wire the more reluctant they were to risk being caught by the rain. But they were keenly aware that Winyard's railway timetable expired at the end of the month, and they knew that if they were held up too often by the weather the tunnel would not break in time. Caution about digging on a doubtful day had to be weighed against the necessity to finish quickly; and they began to get dogmatic and short-tempered in their discussions.

Philip was more upset than the other two by a sudden

change of plan. They would part from him in the evening having arranged to vault immediately after breakfast the following morning. Philip would arrive in their room, dressed for work, only to find that owing to a change in the weather they had decided not to dig. Ten minutes later, if the sky showed signs of clearing, they would decide to dig after all, and the vaulting team would be assembled at a moment's notice.

It was trying for all of them. They were physically tired after more than three months of digging, and now their nerves were becoming frayed by continual anxiety and sudden changes of plan. Peter told again and again the story of the old and the young bull, and fumed inwardly at the delays caused by the more and more frequent spells of bad weather.

•   •   •

The sky was low; a fine grey mist swirled among the tops of the pines. It was no day for digging, and the vaulters had claimed a day of rest. Frustrated, in silence, Peter and John walked the circuit. As they passed the football pitch and the two sand pits which marked the entrance to the empty tunnel they saw a crowd of prisoners jostling under the overhang of the canteen roof. At the front of the crowd the tall figure of the chief ferret, Charlie Pilz, was pinning a new notice to the board.

They went over and joined the crowd. Peter heard a prisoner shout, 'It's about escape!'

'Is it in English?' another asked him. 'If it is, read it out.'

The rest were quiet while the first man read: *To all prisoners of war. To escape from prison camps is no longer a sport . . .*

There were cheers and boos from the assembled kriegies. 'Quiet!' someone shouted. 'Let him finish.'

. . . Germany has always kept to the Hague Convention — more boos and cheers, soon suppressed — *and only punished recaptured prisoners of war with minor disciplinary punishment. Germany will still maintain these principles of International Law —* 'Good show!' 'Jolly decent of 'em!' — *but England has besides fighting at the Front in an honest manner —*

Cries of 'Thanks!' – *instituted an illegal warfare in non-combat zones in the form of gangster commandos, terror bandits and sabotage troops even up to the frontier of Germany* – Cheering broke out, to be suppressed by a shout of 'Let him get to the point, for God's sake!' Peter and John, on the outer edge of the crowd, silently agreed.

– They say in a captured secret and confidential English military pamphlet: Quote: *"The days when we could practise the rules of sportsmanship are over. For the time being, every soldier must be a political gangster and must be prepared to adopt their methods whenever necessary. The sphere of operations should always include the enemy's own country, any Occupied territory, and in certain circumstances such neutral countries as he is using as a source of supply."* Unquote. *England has with these instructions opened up a non-military form of gangster war* – 'What about the Occupied countries?' 'What about Lidice?' 'They're the gangsters!'

– Germany is determined to safeguard her homeland, and especially her industry and provisional centres for the fighting fronts. Therefore it has become necessary to create strictly forbidden zones, called Death Zones, in which all unauthorized trespassers will be immediately shot on sight. Escaped prisoners of war, entering such Death Zones, will certainly lose their lives. They are therefore in constant danger of being mistaken for enemy agents or sabotage groups. Urgent warning is given against making future escapes. In plain English: Stay in the camp where you will be safe. Breaking out of it is now a dangerous act. The chances of preserving your life are small. All police and military guards have been given the most strict orders to shoot on sight all suspected persons. Escaping from prison camps has ceased to be a sport.

The last part of the notice had been read without interruption. The stunned silence which followed was broken by a babel of confused opinions. Charlie was hovering on the fringe, watchful, assessing the reactions of individual prisoners. He smiled mock-ruefully when one man called out to him, 'You'll be out of a job, Charlie – *Ostfront* for you!'

'Nothing to do with us.' Peter spoke more loudly than usual, and drew John away towards the circuit.

'It's going to affect our plans,' John muttered. 'I wonder where the Death Zones are?'

'They'll probably put up a map with them marked in red.' Peter was determined to make a joke of it. 'Pinpointing all the military targets and secret installations.'

'It must be true about the commando handbook,' John said.

'Bloody clots.' Peter laughed. 'What can you expect from the Army!' John did not rise; he was too preoccupied.

'The Luftwaffe would never wear it,' Peter said. 'They've always been more insistent on officer status and correct behaviour than we have.'

'That's just the point.'

'We can't let it make any difference,' Peter said urgently. 'We're nearly out.'

'Perhaps we'd better do what Phil's doing – go all the way on a fast train. Then we won't run into any Death Zones by mistake.'

'The minute we get off the train in Stettin we'll probably be in a Death Zone,' Peter said. 'The Baltic ports are bound to be *verboten* – the whole coast I expect. And every other frontier. You need a special permit to visit the South coast of England, now.' He did not want to change the plan. 'No – ours is the best way for us. Phil speaks fluent German so he's OK on a fast train – especially travelling as a Norwegian on the way home after a business trip. It's slow local trains without corridors for us, once we're well away from Sagan. We'll catch the six-thirty express to Frankfurt and get there before the alarm's given, then take the local one to Küstrin at nine-forty – with different tickets to cover our tracks. In Küstrin we'll buy more tickets for another local stopping train to Stettin. Piece of cake.' When John did not react he added, 'I expect they're bluffing anyway. You know how they do.' But he wondered what effect the notice was having on the organizers of the big tunnel in the North compound. If all two hundred chaps got away as planned the goons might well panic. Thank God, he thought, we're breaking first.

•   •   •

When the tunnel reached the wire John became convinced that it was veering to the left. Peter, in charge of construction, was equally convinced that it was straight and that the home-made compass they had been using had put them where they wanted to be. After days of argument they decided to put it to the test.

Peter crawled to the tunnel face with the rope of the basin tied to his ankle. He took with him a thin iron poker about four feet long. John sat in the shaft holding the other end of the rope, and Nigel sat astride the horse apparently resting after an energetic bout of vaulting. Philip stood gazing out through the wire, hands in pockets, shoulders hunched; in the hopeless, forlorn, typically kriegie stance.

Prisoners were strolling slowly round the circuit. The sentries brooded in their boxes. It was a still, sunny October afternoon and the whole camp had an air of lassitude.

Lying full length at the end of the tunnel Peter scraped a pit in the floor in front of his face. He placed the end of the poker in the pit and forced it slowly upwards through the roof of the tunnel, using a corkscrew motion to avoid bringing down the roof. It was hard work. Steady trickles of sand fell, covering his head and shoulders. Inch by inch he forced the poker upwards until the end was flush with the roof of the tunnel. He scraped the sand away from the bottom end of the poker and pushed it higher. By the sudden lack of resistance he knew that it was through, protruding above the surface of the ground. He gave two tugs on the rope to tell John that the poker was showing. John knocked on the inside of the horse; and Nigel sent a messenger across to join Philip.

Philip, without moving his head, frantically scanned the ground in front of him for the end of the poker. He could not see it.

Minutes passed. Peter became impatient and began to move the poker slowly up and down. Then Philip saw it. He scratched his head. Nigel kicked the side of the horse. John pulled the rope. Peter pulled down the poker.

The end of the tunnel was well under the wire, but fifteen feet to the left of where Peter had expected it to be.

* * *

After the next morning's digging Peter, John and Philip re-laxed by walking round the wire and completing their plans for the break.

'We'll have to mole the last ten feet,' Peter said. 'We're under the wire now and we've twelve days to go to the end of the month. If we're lucky with the weather we shall have done another six feet by then. That puts us about three feet outside the wire. The ditch is about twelve feet beyond the wire – if we can manage to strike that it will give us some cover for the actual break.'

'We'll still be in the light of the arc lamps,' John pointed out.

'I know – but the light from the lamps extends for about thirty feet outside the wire, and we can't possibly push the tunnel on as far as that and get out by the end of the month. And we *must* time the break so that we just have time to leap down to the station and catch a train. If we get out and then have to hang about waiting for a train we stand a good chance of being picked up right away.'

'Pete's right,' Phil said. 'We'll have to get the huts nearest the wire to create a diversion at H hour on D day to attract the sentries' attention.'

'That won't be easy,' John said. 'Who's going to estimate how long it'll take us to mole ten feet?'

'We'll have to over-estimate it,' Peter said. 'Then add half as long again. If we reach the ditch before the time we've said, we'll just have to lie doggo in the end of the tunnel until we hear the diversion start.' He turned to Philip. 'Will you fix it?'

'Yes – I'll get that laid on. What about the outside sentries?'

'They don't come on until an hour after dark. John and I have been sitting up all night watching them. There are two on the side where we're breaking. They each patrol half the wire, meet in the middle, turn back to back and walk to the end. If it's raining they stand under a tree. They walk pretty slowly. When the diversion starts they're bound to stop, and then they and the goons in the boxes will be looking inwards towards the noise. We should get past them and into the woods before they start patrolling again.' He spoke confidently; but thought of tommy-gun bullets and the sharp cry in the night at Schubin when Alan had been shot on the wire. 'Lucky our clothes are navy blue,' he said.

'I've been thinking about that,' Philip said. 'The Red Cross have just sent in some long woollen combinations ready for the winter. If we claim ours now and dye them with tea leaves or coffee grounds we could put them on over our clothes. It will keep us clean while we're down there and be good camouflage when we get out.'

'John and I thought of going down naked.'

'*I'm* not going to get caught and dragged off to the cooler without a stitch of clothing. It's all right for you nudists – my skin's too white and would show up like hell. There's another thing too – I want to go right along that hole tomorrow and have a look at the end. I don't trust you two. I'm not so green – I've noticed how you've been conning me lately to stay in the shaft. I've got to make certain it's big enough to take me and all my kit.'

'What's all this talk of "all my kit"?' John asked.

'Well, I'm going as a commercial traveller, y'know. I have to have samples. And I've got a black Homburg hat I bribed off one of the goons – that's got to go in a cardboard box to save it from getting crushed. Then I'm wearing an RAF greatcoat –'

'He'd better go down tomorrow and see how big the hole is now,' John said.

'He certainly had,' Peter said. 'But look here, Phil, none of your little games. No widening it while you're down there and saying it fell in. It's quite big enough as it is.'

'Let's get this thing straight,' Philip said. 'You can't go down there naked – you'll have to wear shoes at least, in case you have to run. And I wouldn't fancy running through those woods with dogs after me without any clothes on.'

'We must remember to get some pepper for the dogs,' Peter said.

'Yes – but what about the kit?'

'I like the idea of the combinations,' John said. 'We could wear socks over our shoes and black hoods over our heads.'

'We can't go out in all our clothes,' Peter said. 'The hole's not big enough.'

'We'll wear shirts and trousers under the combinations then,' Philip said, 'and pack all the rest of the kit in kitbags dyed black. We can drag them down the tunnel tied to our ankles.'

'Right, that's settled,' Peter said. 'But we haven't solved the most important problem.'

'What's that?'

'How to get four people and our gear out in the horse.'

'Four people?' Philip sounded excited. 'I thought only we three were going!'

'Yes – but somebody's got to close the trap down after us.'

'Do you mean to say that you haven't arranged all that?' Philip was even more excited.

'As a matter of fact I never thought we'd get as far as we have,' Peter admitted. 'When we decided to ask you to come in we never considered how we were all going to get out once the tunnel was finished. We could have got three into the horse at a pinch, but I'm damned if I can see how we can get four.'

'We'll have to draw lots,' John said.

Philip nearly choked. 'D'you mean to say that you've got as far as this and never considered how we were to get out?'

'Did you?' Peter asked.

'I thought you'd got it all worked out.'

'We'll have to put the kit down the day before,' John said.

'We can't do that,' Peter said. 'If we put three kitbags and a cardboard hatbox in the tunnel we shan't be able to get down ourselves. And we'll still need someone to close the trap after us.'

'There's a solution to every problem,' John said airily. 'We can make a chamber near the end of the tunnel large enough to take the bags.'

'That's a couple of days' work in itself,' Peter said. 'I can't see us finishing up much outside the wire as it is. We've got to get past the path where the outside sentries patrol and we've got to do it before the end of the month. After the end of the month God knows how the trains will run.'

'Pray God it doesn't rain during the next few days,' Philip said.

'We'll have to vault in the rain, that's all. The goons think we're mad already. We'll just have to risk it.'

'What train are you two planning to catch?'

'There's a fast train to Frankfurt at six-thirty p.m. German time,' Peter said. 'It'll be dark by five-thirty and the outside sentries usually come on about six-thirty, when they change the guards in the goon-boxes. If we break at six o'clock we stand a chance of getting out before the night patrol comes on. We don't want to be too early because if they find the hole and sound the alarm before the train goes we'll get picked up at the station.'

'That train will do me too,' Philip said.

'You're definitely not coming with us all the way?' It's just as well, Peter thought. Two obvious foreigners are far less conspicuous than three. And old Phil's much better on his own, we'd only argue if we went together. He'll make his own plans and he'll stick to them, which is something we'll never do. Ours is the better way though. Keep it fluid. You need less luck our way . . .

'I'll go on my own,' Philip said. 'Anyway, it would look odd for a Norwegian businessman to be travelling with a couple of French artisans. I'll make for Danzig and get a Swedish ship there.'

'We'll take a fast train only as far as Frankfurt,' Peter said.

'We'll spend the night there and see how things go. We shall most likely make Stettin in two or three short hops – and most likely we'll get off before we get to the main station, and walk into the town. The thing is to take a fast train first, to get as far away as possible as soon as possible, then get off in case they've traced us to Sagan station and found where we booked to. After that we'll take slow, workmen's trains.'

'I'm going straight on up to Danzig,' Philip said. 'I plan to be in Sweden three days after leaving the camp.'

'I think you're doing the right thing,' Peter said. 'The right thing for you. Speaking German and – '

'I've got it!' John said.

'Got what?' Philip asked.

'The solution to every problem. I go down before the after-noon *appell* – say about two o'clock – and take the baggage with me. You can seal me down, Pete, and I'll dig the whole of the afternoon. One of the ghosts can stand in at *appell*. Then you two come down as soon as you can after that. *Appell's* at three-forty-five, so you'll be down about four o'clock or soon after. You bring someone out with you – the smallest man we can find – to seal the trap down after you. We'll still have the best part of two hours in which to get ready to break.'

Peter wanted to say, It had better be me who goes down; but he couldn't take over John's idea. 'It'll be pretty grim, stuck down there for a couple of hours.'

'Oh, I shall be all right. I'll put an air hole up inside the wire where it won't be seen, and mole on quite happily. I should do five or six feet before you come down.'

'Don't go and bloody well overdo it.' He knew John's unsparing energy once he'd set his heart on a thing. He was all nervous energy and guts once he got started. He took more out of himself than he knew. 'Remember we may have to run for it. Don't fag yourself out digging – leave most of it for when we get down there.'

'I'll take it easy,' John said. Peter knew he wouldn't, but could do nothing about it.

'That's everything then, is it?' Philip asked. 'I'll go along and see the Committee and fix up the diversion for six o'clock. We'll have to let them know the actual date later of course. I want to see about my samples too.'

'What are they?' Peter asked.

'Margarine, packed in wooden boxes – '

'Wooden boxes!' Now it was Peter who was excited.

'Got to keep the different brands separate. I'll eat some of it if I get hungry.'

10

For the next twelve days there was an Indian summer, and they were able to take the horse out every morning and afternoon. Working up to a crescendo of effort they dug faster and increased the number of bags to be carried back at a time from twelve to fourteen and finally fifteen. With the extra weight the bearers were beginning to stagger as they carried the horse up the steps into the canteen; and Peter wondered how they would cope when they had three men inside. The smallest and lightest of the regular vaulters was a New Zealander called McKay. When they asked if he would come out and close the trap after them he agreed immediately.

They decided to break on Friday the twenty-ninth of October. The work went so well that they had time to make a final bulge where John would stow the baggage. They dug the bulge on the twenty-eighth; it was as far as they could go. They reckoned that between them they could dig a further ten feet after they had been sealed down the next evening.

On the morning of the twenty-ninth they brought in the second batch of fifteen bags, and recovered their civilian clothing from scattered hiding places round the camp. Ralph, the Committee Clothing Officer, handed over the phoney Marine dress uniform; to his evident satisfaction and Peter's relief, it proved a good fit. When he had removed the tacked-on stripes from the trouser-legs, the patch pockets, and the epaulettes and insignia from the shoulders, it became an almost-too-good civilian suit for a foreign worker to wear in wartime Germany.

With all their gear mustered and checked, they packed it into kitbags and took them to the canteen hidden in bundles of other kriegies' dirty laundry.

At twelve-thirty John had a substantial meal of bully beef and potatoes, Canadian biscuits and cheese. At one o'clock, wearing his civilian shirt and trousers under a long khaki greatcoat, he left for the canteen with the male voice choir. Peter hurried off to see the duty pilot, who told him there were two ferrets in the compound.

'Where are they?'

'One's in the kitchen, and Charlie's hanging around outside the canteen.'

'Hell!' Peter thought for a moment. 'OK – if any more come into the compound send a stooge off to tell Phil. He'll be in the canteen.'

He ran across to the hut where the S.B.O. lived; and knocked on his door.

'Come in.'

He stood in the doorway, panting slightly. 'Sir – we're just putting Clinton down and Charlie's hanging round the canteen. I wonder if you could get him out of the way for a few minutes?'

'Let me see.' The group captain put down his book. 'The cooking stove in Hut 64 isn't working very well. I'll just stroll over and ask him to report it to the Kommandantur. He might like to smoke an English cigarette with me.'

Back at the canteen Peter found the choir lustily singing *Greensleeves*. John, Philip, Nigel and the vaulting team were standing near the door.

'Can't get started,' John said. 'Charlie's outside and he keeps walking past and looking in at the window. I think he likes the singing.'

'Let's change it to *Run, rabbit, run!*' Nigel suggested.

'There's another ferret next-door in the kitchen,' Peter said. 'The S.B.O.'s going to take Charlie away –'

'I'll deal with the one in the kitchen.' It was Winyard, whose Vorlager *dienst* had not yet broken, come to see John off.

'Fine,' Peter said. 'Then we'll get cracking.' He looked out of the window. The S.B.O. was walking across the compound, a golf club in his hand. Suddenly he appeared to see Charlie, and altered course. 'Here comes Groupy.'

The group captain and Charlie exchanged a few words and they both walked away towards Hut 64. They could hear Tony Winyard chatting with the ferret in the kitchen. Hurriedly John doffed his coat and pulled the long black combinations on over his shirt and trousers. He pulled black socks over his shoes and a hood which he had made from an old undervest dyed black over his head. 'It's bloody hot in this clobber,' he whispered.

'You look like the Ku Klux Klan,' Peter said. 'Ready?'

With the choir singing more loudly than ever, they both crawled under the vaulting-horse; Peter holding a blanket, a cardboard box and fifteen empty bags, John sinister in his black outfit. The three kitbags hung between them, suspended on hooks wedged under the top of the horse. They crouched with their backs to the ends of the horse, their feet one each side on the bottom framework. Then the bearing poles were inserted and the horse was lifted. As they lurched down the steps and went creaking across the compound towards the vaulting pits, they held on to the kitbags to prevent them from swaying and falling off the hooks.

With a sigh of relief the bearers placed the horse in position and withdrew the poles. The vaulting began.

John crouched in one end of the horse while Peter piled the kitbags on top of him. Peter then spread the blankets on the ground at the other end and began to uncover the trap. He collected the top layer of grey sand in the cardboard box, and threw the damp subsoil on to the blanket. Feeling round with his fingers he uncovered the bags of sand on top of the trap and removed them. He scraped the remaining sand away from the damp wood. As he lifted the trap he smelled the familiar damp mustiness of the tunnel. He lifted the kitbags off John's crouching figure and balanced them on top of the trap on the pile of sand.

'Down you go.' He crouched astride the hole while John dropped feet first into the shaft. 'My God, those clothes stink!'

"It'll be worse by the time you come down,' John said. 'It's the dye. Must have gone bad or something.'

As John crawled up the tunnel Peter detached the metal basin from the end of the rope and tied one of the kitbags in its place. One by one John pulled the kitbags up to the face and stowed them in the bulge. Peter then re-tied the basin, and John sent back enough sand for him to fill the empty bags.

While Peter was stacking the bags in the body of the horse, John crawled back for his last breath of fresh air. It was the first time he had been in the tunnel wearing clothes and Peter could hear him cursing softly as he struggled to get back. His feet came into view and then his body, clothed and clumsy in the black combinations. Peter crouched inside the horse looking down on him as he emerged. The shouting of the vaulters outside and the reverberating concussion as they landed on the canvas padding above his head seemed louder than usual.

John straightened up, head and shoulders out of the trap. He had left the hood at the end of the tunnel and his face was flushed. He looked strange with short hair; smaller, older. 'It's hot down there with clothes on.'

'Take it easy,' Peter said. 'For Christ's sake don't overdo it. I don't want to have to carry you once we get outside.'

'I'll be all right. You seal me down now and I'll see you after *appell*.'

'OK – don't make the air hole bigger than you have to.'

He watched John's feet disappear down the narrow tunnel and then he closed the trap. He replaced the heavy bags of sand over it and stamped the loose sand firmly on top of them. He didn't like doing it. It's burying a man alive, he thought. He heard an urgent voice from outside.

'How's it going, Pete?'

'Five minutes, Phil.'

He started to hang the fifteen bags full of sand from the top of the horse. He gathered the blanket in his arms and spread the rest of the sand evenly over the ground under the horse. He sprinkled the dry grey sand from the cardboard box over this, and smoothed it carefully. Finally he gave Philip a low hail that he was ready. The bearing poles were inserted and he was carried back towards the canteen. He could hear the voices of the choir: *'He shall give His angels charge over*

thee . . . lest thou dash thy foot against a stone . . ' In the
dark belly of the horse he laughed softly, releasing tension.

With a last creaking lurch they were up the steps and inside. The old horse is falling to pieces, he thought; hope it
lasts out this evening.

One end was lifted. Before crawling out he passed the bags
of sand to Philip. They began to carry the bags into the band
practice room where the choir was going at full blast.

'. . . *the young lion and the dragon . . . there's a ferret passing the window,*' sang David.

'There bloody well would be,' Peter said. 'Keep an eye on
him. Is Nig in the roof?'

David nodded and went on singing, '. . . *because He hath
known my name . . .*'

'Right – we'll just pass these bags up to him and then we're
in the clear.'

Nigel's anxious face was peering down from the trapdoor
in the ceiling. Peter held out his fist, thumb extended upwards,
and grinned. Nigel grinned back, and lowered his hand for
the first of the bags.

'. . . *with long life will I satisfy Him . . .*'

*   *   *

Back in the mess Peter first trimmed, then shaved off his
beard. In the mirror he had made from a smoothed-out Klim
tin and nailed to his bunk, he watched his features emerge,
round and unlined. John had looked years older with cropped
hair. Without his thick wiry black beard he himself looked
younger than his thirty-two years, innocent and inexperienced.
Somehow, discarding the beard was his final commitment to
the escape; and he was impatient to get on with it. This two
hours' wait with John sealed down the tunnel was going to
be the worst time of all. It was touch and go now. At any
moment until they reached the shelter of the trees the scheme
might be blown. At any moment the four-and-a-half months
of back-breaking effort might go for a Burton.

Stretched out on his bunk he stopped worrying while he
wondered about the origins of 'gone for a Burton'. Airmen

used the phrase, or said 'bought it', as euphemisms when fellow airmen were killed. Both must have stemmed from that brewers' advertisement *Where's George? Gone for a Burton.* What would the first beer taste like? He turned his thoughts back to the escape. Once they were outside it wouldn't matter so much; it was the next few hours that mattered. Outside anything might happen, and they would have to rely almost entirely on luck. It was no use making detailed plans like they'd done for the tunnel. They had a rough idea of what they wanted to do – get to Stettin and board a Swedish ship – but that was all. From the moment they broke out of the tunnel they would have to adapt their actions, maybe their policy, to the conditions and even the people they met.

Always reluctant to ponder imponderables, he let his mind run over the list of things he was taking with him: There was the 'dog food', a hard cake made from dried milk, sugar, Bemax and cocoa; it had been packed in small square tins saved from the Red Cross parcels, and he intended to wear a girdle of them under his shirt. Next there were the linen bags containing a dry mixture of oatmeal, raisins, sugar and milk powder; mixed with water it would swell and fill the stomach, preventing that hollow aching sickness that comes from eating ill-balanced, concentrated food. He had sewn one of these bags into each armpit of his trench coat as an emergency ration in case they became separated from the attaché-case which held the bulk of their food.

The attaché-case was already down in the tunnel, at the bottom of his kitbag. Mentally he re-checked its contents: the food, clean socks, shaving gear, rollneck sweater, soap, a few sheets of paper, and pen and ink for minor alterations to their documents. German cigarettes and matches.

He got to his feet and went through his jacket pockets: the wallet which held the papers and the Reichsmarks, the pocket compass and torch supplied by the Committee, two handkerchiefs, cigarettes bought in the town by one of the tame guards, a length of string, a pencil, a pen-knife, his beret and a comb.

It was no use, he couldn't be still. He went out on the circuit and walked round, over the tunnel; thinking of John moling away down there, sweating, not knowing the time, not knowing whether the tunnel had been discovered, out of touch with everyone. John digging away, trying to get as much done as possible before he and Philip joined him.

He went unnecessarily to the abort, checked with Philip on the timing of the diversion for the break, and then walked with Nigel round and round the circuit while they waited for *appell*.

Nigel broke a long silence. 'David and I . . .' he hesitated, diffident. 'We thought we'd have a bash at the tunnel tomorrow – that's if you don't mind. The chaps could take us out after lunch and we'd stay down there until dark.'

'But – what about your leg? We wanted to ask you to come in with us – before we asked Phil. But we thought –'

'I know,' Nigel said. 'John told me. I'm glad you didn't. I'd only have held you up. And Phil deserves it.'

'Are you and David going together?'

'Oh no – I'd hold him up too. I'm going as a discharged soldier – dumb from shellshock as well as wounded. Hitching lifts on my way home to Bavaria from the *Ostfront*. I'll try to get into Switzerland if I get that far. They've got the papers ready. David's jumping goods trains – heading for France.'

'Well, jolly good luck to you both,' Peter said.

'I just wanted to know . . .' he hesitated again, 'to ask whether you could camouflage the hole a bit before you leave.'

Peter could see the complication, the necessity to stay there in the light of the arc-lamps; but Nigel deserved the chance. David too. 'I'm second man out,' he said. 'Phil's the last. It rather depends on how far we can mole. If we come out in the ditch we might manage it.'

'We don't want to jeopardize your effort,' Nigel said. 'We just thought –'

'I'll talk to Phil. You have everything ready in any case. Even if we can't cover the hole there's always the outside chance. The ghosts'll take our places at morning *appell* so if the hole hasn't been seen by then you've got a chance.' If it's not been discovered by then, he thought, we shall be well on our way.

'I don't expect I shall get far,' Nigel said. 'Nowhere near

any of the Death Zones. But I'd like to have a bash . . . I shall miss you after you've gone. It's been good fun, the vaulting.'

'I expect they'll take the horse away when they discover the tunnel,' Peter said. He wanted to thank Nigel for all the help and encouragement he'd given them, but he knew that he could not do it. To thank him in words would put the thing on a formal basis and it was beyond that.

'You will see my wife, Pete?'

'First thing when I get home. Don't take any risks, will you, Nig?'

'You know me,' Nigel replied. 'I'm dumb enough to forget I'm dumb and yell "Goon in the block!" when I see my first policeman.'

      •   •   •

With *appell* safely over, the vaulters assembled in the canteen for the third time that day. Peter's knees felt loose and for a moment he did not want to get into the horse. He felt that three was an unlucky number, that the guards in the watch-towers were bound to be suspicious when they saw the horse being brought out again, after the evening *appell*.

The moment passed and he wanted to get on with it, quickly. As he pulled on the evil-smelling black combinations, he heard Nigel instructing the four men who were to carry the horse. He looked at Philip, unrecognizable in his black hood; and then at the third man, McKay, stripped for lightness and holding the cardboard box ready for the dry surface sand which he would sprinkle over the bags on the trap after he had sealed them down.

Nigel came over and handed him a bottle of cold tea for John. 'Give the child my love,' he said, 'and tell him to write.' He turned abruptly and limped over to the window.

Peter and Philip crawled under the horse, stood crouching one at each end, and held McKay suspended between them. The bearer poles were pushed into position and they braced themselves on these. The four men lifted the horse. It creaked protestingly and seemed to Peter to sag in the middle. One

Showing how three men were eventually carried. Two are wearing
combinations and hoods dyed black to make them less conspicuous
when breaking from the mouth of the tunnel. The third man is to
replace the sand over the tunnel. The hooks are for bringing in the
bags of sand when removed from the tunnel.

of the bearers slipped as they came down the steps; recovered
his balance; and the horse went swaying and jerking across
the football pitch.

Once the horse was in position over the shaft Philip sat on
McKay's back at one end while Peter removed the trap. As he
lifted the wooden boards he listened for sounds of movement
at the end of the tunnel. It was silent. He turned to Philip.

'I'll carry on up the tunnel and see how John's doing. You
fill some bags from the bottom of the shaft for Kiwi to take
back, and then stay down this end. I'll send the stuff John's
dug back in the basin and you leave as much as you can this
end, then spread the rest along the floor of the tunnel as you
come.'

'Right. It's sixteen-oh-five now.' Philip was looking at
the Rolex wristwatch he had borrowed from a member of his
mess. 'We'd better get cracking.'

Peter dropped feet first into the vertical shaft. McKay,
stoically silent in the discomfort of the journey from the canteen, eased out from under Philip and spoke at last.

'My bloody oath!' He was staring in wonder down at the
tunnel entrance. 'Is it as small as that all the way?'

'Smaller.' Peter slid to his knees, edging his legs and feet
into the back burrow. 'Thanks a lot, Kiwi. Don't forget to
smooth the surface sand –'

126

'My bloody oath! Good luck, mate.'

Stooping awkwardly in his tight clothing Peter managed to get his head under the lintel of the opening and slipped head first into the tunnel. He waved his legs in farewell, and squirmed inch by inch along the hundred feet that had taken them so long to dig. Now that it was finished and he was crawling down it for the last time, he was almost sorry.

He switched on the torch. Stafford had been right about the battery. Even so, it was a help. As he inched forward he could see heaps of loose sand dislodged by John's clothing. He noticed all the patches of shoring, built with difficulty in darkness, strangely unfamiliar in the light. Near the end of the tunnel he flashed the torch ahead and called softly to John. He was afraid to call loudly for he was now under the wire and not far from one of the watch-towers.

He came to the bend where they had altered course, and saw the end of the tunnel. Where he had expected to find John there was nothing but a solid wall of sand.

John must have been digging on steadily and, banking up the sand behind him, had completely blocked the tunnel.

Peter began to bore through the wall of loose sand. After about three feet he broke through. A gust of hot fetid air gushed out; and there was John, sweat- and sand-covered, hands and face streaked with black dye. A fringe of hair, wet and caked with sand, plastered his forehead. He looked pale and exhausted in the yellow light of Peter's torch.

'Where the bloody hell have you been?' he asked.

'It's not four-thirty yet.'

'I thought it must have gone six. I seem to have been down here for ever. I thought the roll-call had gone wrong and I'd have to go out alone.'

'Everything's under control,' Peter said. 'Nig sent you some tea, with his love.' He pushed the bottle through. 'I'll just get this sand back to Phil and then I'll join you.'

He pulled the empty basin up the tunnel and sent the first load back to Phil, who filled the empty bags they had brought out and stacked them in the shaft. When all twelve were ready he hung them in the horse, and gave McKay the word to replace the trap and seal them in.

As Peter and John worked on they had a certain amount of fresh air from the air hole under the wire. Philip, back in the vertical shaft with the trap closed above him, had none. When he found himself gasping for breath he crawled up the tunnel and joined in the moling.

They worked feverishly, trying to get as much as possible done before the breaking time. John, in front, stabbed at the face with the trowel and pushed the damp sand under his belly towards Peter, who lay with his head on John's heels collecting the sand and squirmed backwards with it to Philip, who banked it up as a wall behind them. They were now in a narrow stretch of the tunnel about twenty-five feet long and two feet square, ventilated by one small hole three inches in diameter.

They were working for the first time in clothes and for the first time without the fresh air pushed up the tunnel from the open shaft by the movement of the basin. They were working three in the tunnel and they were anxious about the air; Peter and Philip especially, because they knew from flying how lack of oxygen could create a sense of euphoria so that a man got careless and made stupid mistakes. They were working for the first time by the light of a torch, and in the light the tunnel seemed smaller and the earth above more solid. By now the prisoners had been locked in their huts for the night. If the tunnel collapsed the three of them would be helpless.

They worked fast, steadily yet silently. None of them wanted to be the one to break the rhythm of the work.

At five-thirty Peter called a halt. 'Half an hour to go,' he whispered. 'We'd better push up to the top.'

John nodded his agreement, and began to push the tunnel uphill, towards the surface. It proved farther than they had expected and they thought they would never get there. Then John broke through – a hole as large as his fist. Through it he caught his first glimpse of the stars. The stars in the free heavens beyond the wire.

'I'll dig out the whole width of the tunnel,' he whispered, 'just leaving a thin crust over the top. Then we can break that quickly, at six o'clock exactly. There'll be less risk of being seen while we wait.'

Peter gripped his ankle in reply and squirmed back to Philip to warn him to get ready. He retrieved John's kitbag from the third bulge, pushed it ahead of him up the tunnel, and tied it to John's ankle. He returned to the bulge, extracted his own bag, and got Philip to do the same for him. He dragged it behind him towards the mouth of the tunnel where John was resting. Philip followed, pushing his own gear ahead of him, in front of his nose. It was five-fifty, and they were ready.

At six o'clock John broke through to the open air, pulling the dry sandy surface down, choking and blinding himself and making him want to cough. As the sand settled they heard the sound of the diversion coming from the huts nearest the wire. There were men blowing trumpets, men singing *My Brother Sylveste*, men banging the sides of the hut and yelling at the top of their voices.

'They're overdoing it,' John whispered. 'The silly bastards'll get a bullet in there if they're not careful.'

'Go on! Go now!' Peter said. He was scared. It was too light. The hole was some feet short of the ditch, on the edge of the outside sentry's path.

John hoisted his kitbag out of the tunnel and rolled it towards the ditch. He squeezed himself up out of the hole and disappeared from view.

Peter stuck his head out of the tunnel. He looked towards the camp. It was brilliantly floodlit, he had not realized how brilliantly. The high watch-towers were in darkness and he could not see whether the guards were looking into the camp, at the noisy huts, or in his direction. He pulled out his kitbag and pushed it into the ditch, wriggled out of the hole and dragged himself full-length across the open ground and into the ditch. He expected every second to hear the crack of a rifle and feel the tearing impact of its bullet in his flesh. He lay, out of breath, in the shallow ditch and looked back.

The hole was in the full light of the arc-lamps. It would be impossible for Phil to stay and cover it.

The diversion in the huts reached a new crescendo of noise.

He picked up his kitbag and ran blindly across the road, into the pine forest where John was waiting.

Outside

I

Once they reached the shelter of the trees they did not wait for Philip but walked slowly on, away from the wire. Peter could feel his heart thumping high up inside his chest. He wanted to run but he forced himself to walk slowly and carefully, feeling with his feet for the brittle dry branches and pine cones that lay among the needles on the forest floor. His tunnelling clothes were wet with perspiration and the keen night wind cut through them. He was cold, but they must get deeper into the forest before they could dress.

They heard no shots and knew that Philip too must have gained the safety of the trees unseen.

Peter stopped behind a big pine, leaned his kitbag against the trunk and looked back at the camp, floodlit like some gigantic empty stadium.

'Come on, Pete,' John whispered. 'We'll have to move if we're going to catch that train.'

But Peter stood for a moment longer gazing at the compound that he knew so well; the wire that he hated, the huts which held so many of his friends.

'*Come on!*'

As they walked deeper into the forest, John began to laugh under his breath, giggling at first, then shaking with long gusts of low uncontrollable mirth.

'What the hell's the matter?' Peter whispered. 'What the hell are you laughing at?'

'It's you,' John said, gasping, 'you look like some great mother bear mincing along carrying a baby in her arms . . .'

'Bloody funny.' But he too was laughing; laughing with the release of strained nerves and the triumph of escape. Lying at the end of the tunnel, waiting for the diversion, he'd thought they would never make it across the road and into the forest in the full light of the arc-lamps, the full view of the watch-towers. Now they'd done that he began to think that every-thing was possible, that they'd make it all the way. Such confidence was dangerous, he must watch it.

'Let's get out of these combinations,' John said. 'Get cleaned up and dressed like human beings.'

'Not yet. Lay the trail away from the railway station. We'll hide them near the side of the road to Breslau.'

Now they threaded their way between the trees on a route parallel to the camp, using the lights as direction beacons.

'I'm bloody cold.' John was trembling with a mixture of cold and fatigue.

'So am I. Not much farther.' He realized that John must be exhausted after all the moling, and that he still had the task of buying tickets ahead of him. It would have been good to spend the night in the forest and catch an early train; but they could not risk it. They must press on this evening and put miles between themselves and the camp before the alarm was given. With the tunnel exit so near the sentry's path there was no chance it would not be seen.

When he judged they were about a mile from the station Peter called a halt. He looked at his watch. Twelve minutes past six; about right – they would not have too long to wait for the train.

Quickly they stripped off the black combinations and the socks from their shoes. They washed one another's faces with their handkerchiefs and took their civilian jackets, berets and mackintoshes from the kitbags.

At the bottom of the kitbags they had each packed a small travelling bag. Peter opened his, a fibre attaché-case, and took out a tin of pepper. He put the combinations, socks, hoods and kitbags together in a heap and sprinkled them liberally with the pepper, holding his nose to prevent himself sneezing.

Fully dressed in suits, mackintoshes and berets they doubled back towards the railway, making straight for the bridge that led to the station, a high metal footbridge which crossed the line. They gained the road on the far side.

'Let's keep to the right,' Peter said, 'then we shan't be facing oncoming traffic.'

They met several people on the road. A local train had evidently just pulled in. Hope to God they're not waiting at the station, Peter thought; hope the alarm hasn't gone and we don't find a posse of guards waiting for us.

'If we're recognized we'll cut and run,' he said. 'They won't shoot with all these people about. We'll separate. I'll meet you by the water tower in the forest. Then we'll walk. Once they know we're out all the stations for miles around will be alerted.'

'It's OK.' Warmer, cleaner and properly dressed, John was keyed up for the journey. 'If the alarm had gone we'd have heard it. We'll catch the train all right.'

*   *   *

Outside the station everything was in darkness but inside the booking hall the lights were bright. Peter walked over to the timetable on the wall while John, holding his own and Peter's identity cards and police permission to travel, joined the queue at the booking office.

Peter turned to watch him as he moved slowly to the head of the queue. To him the grey-blue RAF mackintosh was glaringly obvious. But the beret and John's lean dark face looked French enough. A young slight figure in a beret and trench coat carrying the travelling bag he had made himself out of a canvas bedroll. He seemed unconcerned as he stood in the queue waiting his turn at the booking-office window; but Peter saw him draw in his underlip and could guess how nervous he was feeling.

Then he was at the window, talking to the girl behind the grille. Peter glanced towards the main entrance; it was crowded with people leaving, people arriving. If things go wrong, he thought, I'll wait until he gets within three feet of me and then we'll both charge together. We'll get through that lot all right.

He turned back to the ticket office. John was leaving, coming over to him with the tickets in his hand. Peter joined him and they waited at the barrier for the passengers to leave the platform before they were allowed through.

Peter stood watching the passengers coming out through the barrier; and saw the *Hauptmann Doktor* commanding the camp hospital. His heart pounded and he wanted to run. The doctor spoke good English and they had talked every day during Peter's week in bed. Then he remembered that he had shaved his beard. As the doctor came by within two feet of him Peter stooped and fumbled with the fastener of his attaché-case. When he straightened up the doctor had passed and John was pushing him through the barrier and on to the platform.

The ticket clerk had told John that the Frankfurt train was running late. They walked to the end of the platform and studied the lie of the land.

'That was a damn' close shave,' Peter said, pleased with his own joke. 'If the alarm goes before the train gets in, we'll jump on to the line and down that embankment. We'll circle the town, and if we get separated we'll meet at the water tower.'

'We'll hear the camp sirens from here,' John said. 'We'll wait until the last minute in case the train arrives before they get here.' He sounded confident, dangerously confident.

'No,' Peter said, not wanting it to be too easy. 'No – we'll go as soon as we hear the sirens, get away before anyone gets suspicious. If they find out we've gone it'll be no use catching the train – they'll telephone Frankfurt and catch us there. It'll be better to get right away from the railway and out into the country.'

'If the train leaves before they get here we can jump off before it reaches Frankfurt.'

'It wouldn't be worth it. If we hear the sirens we'll get out right away and take to the woods.'

'Don't worry,' John said. 'We're OK. We've got the tickets now.'

•   •   •

The train steamed into the station half an hour late, and still the sirens had not sounded. It had no lights and was crowded. They had to stand in the corridor. Peter, wedged near the door, stared out of the window and listened to the rat-a-tat-tat of the wheels and the shriek of the whistle as they hurtled through village stations. Every minute is taking us further away, he thought; we're going to make it. John was squeezed between a burly German soldier and an old woman. He was leaning back against the side of the carriage with his eyes closed.

They stood all the way. The time for the Frankfurt-Küstrin connection came and went, and they knew that they would get no farther than Frankfurt that night. One of those things, Peter thought; let's hope there's an early train tomorrow. Can't spend the night in the station though. We'll be too obvious.

It was ten-thirty p.m. when they pulled into Frankfurt station. They climbed down on to the platform and hurried to the barrier. Passengers were not being asked to show papers; they were merely handing in their tickets. Relieved, Peter pressed on towards the barrier, but John pulled him back and steered him towards another exit further away. They passed through into a spacious booking hall.

'What was all that about?' Peter whispered.

'That one was for soldiers only, you clot. Come on, let's get out of the station and find an hotel.'

They left the booking hall with its dangerous crowds and bright lights and walked out into the darkness of the cobbled streets; foreign streets of which they had no experience, in which nothing was familiar, with signposts and shop signs in Gothic script. It was strange after the close confinement of the prison camp, exciting to be walking along the streets of a town, at night; fugitives surrounded by enemies and unable to speak more than a few words of the language. *Ich bin Aüslander,* Peter thought. He stuck close to John as they made for the centre of the town.

John came to a halt outside a large hotel. 'Let's try this one.'

Peter hesitated.

'We've got to do it sooner or later,' John said. 'Better to do it now, late at night when the porter's tired. We'll see how he reacts.'

'It's not worth it,' Peter said. He did not want to push today's luck too far. 'Let's sleep in the country tonight.'

'Snap out of it, Pete. We decided against the country months ago. The railway was easy and the hotels are going to be easy too.'

It was a large hotel which would, in England, have been of the Victorian period, but it had been modernized. The walls of the entrance hall were covered in green plastic paint and there was a carpet of modern geometric design on the floor. Through the glass doors Peter could see some people sitting in a lounge on the left of the entrance hall.

John went straight up to the hall porter's desk at the far end. He spoke respectfully but with assurance, adopting the role of a member of a defeated nation, but a free worker and not an ex-prisoner of war. '*Haben Sie, bitte, ein Doppelzimmer frei?*'

The porter said something Peter did not understand. John thanked the man and moved towards the door. Peter followed him out on to the street.

'What did he say?'

'He said all the rooms were taken.'

'I don't like it,' Peter said. 'We don't even know if foreign workers are allowed to stay in hotels. Did he seem surprised?'

'I don't think so. I don't see why foreign workers shouldn't stay in hotels.'

'They do some funny things in Germany. They have separate brothels for foreign workers, I don't see why they shouldn't have separate hotels too.'

'We'll try a smaller one next,' John said. 'Let's go back to the station. The cheaper hotels are usually there.'

They tried four more hotels and finally found themselves back outside the railway station.

'What do we do now?' John sounded depressed.

'Let's go out into the country. Let's get right out of the town and sleep under a bridge or something.'

136

'All right. I don't think I could face any more hotel porters.'

*   *   *

They walked for two hours, passing from the industrial city through an area of fine, large houses into the suburbs; through the suburbs and at last out on to a country lane running between flat fields.

'This is as far as I go,' John said.

'We can't sleep out in the open,' Peter said. 'We must find some sort of cover.'

'I've had it. I must sleep. It's been a helluva day.'

'Let's go just a bit further. We're bound to find a barn or something soon.'

They walked on, John stumbling and muttering to himself about sleep. Peter, tired himself, his limbs heavy, his eyes pricking as though he still had sand under his lids, his mouth dry; knew how exhausted John must be after the afternoon's digging, the bad air and the strain of waiting for him and Philip. But this was how escapers got caught, and he determined to push on until they found somewhere to sleep unseen.

They came to a large house standing back from the road, a fine brick house with a high-pitched roof. A typical, solid, German farmhouse. There was a notice fixed to one of the brick gate pillars. John stood close to the gate trying to read the notice which was surmounted by a cross.

'It's a *Kloster*,' he said. 'A convent. I wonder if the nuns would give us sanctuary.'

'Not in Germany. In France or Holland perhaps, but not in Germany. Imagine an escaping German prisoner going to an English convent and asking for sanctuary. No, it's no use asking for help in Germany. Let's get on.' He caught John by the arm. 'Did you ever hear the story of the airman who baled out over France and got into a convent?'

'No.' John did not seem interested.

'It was in 1941. One of our chaps baled out during a sweep

137

over France and after walking for a couple of nights he made contact with a priest who took him to a convent just outside his village. The nuns put him in one of the cells and fed him well enough, but all he had to read was a Bible in French and as he wasn't much of a linguist it rather bored him. He'd been there about a week and one morning as he was looking out of the window of his cell he saw an attractive nun picking flowers in the convent garden. At least, he couldn't see whether she was attractive or not, but she was slim and seemed young. I suppose at some time or other he'd read Boccaccio and some of the ideas had stuck, because he climbed out of the window and ambled across to make contact. This nun was bending over a flower bed, so he stopped behind her and said in his best French, "Mademoiselle, I have been here a week and yours is the first attractive back I have seen. Are you a novice?" He was working out the next sentence when the "nun" turned round and said in a deep, masculine Cockney, "Don't be fuckin' silly, mate – I've been here since Dunkirk!" [2]

But John did not laugh. He was too tired.

They trudged on down the road. Luckily there was no traffic. Shortage of petrol, Peter supposed. Then he saw a concrete drain running through a deep ditch and passing as a tunnel under the road.

'That looks possible, let's try it.'

'I could sleep standing up.'

They slid down the weed- and scrub-covered slope. Before they reached the mouth of the drain they found a secluded spot hidden from the road above. They opened their bags and ate the sandwiches of corned beef which they had brought with them from the camp. They were hungry, but almost too tired to chew.

When they had eaten they settled down to sleep. They slept just as they were, in mackintoshes and shoes and berets, their heads on their bags, side by side on the rough damp ground.

An hour later Peter woke shivering; in spite of his thick woollen underclothes, two shirts, rollneck sweater, marine uniform and a mackintosh. He rose quietly to his feet, afraid of waking John, but John was already awake.

'I wonder if they've found the tunnel yet.'

'Not till the morning,' Peter said. 'We'll get an early train – we'll be on a local before the alarm is given. They won't find it till daylight.'

'Hope you're right. God I'm cold.' John sat up, shivering uncontrollably. 'Think I'll walk a bit, to get warm.'

'Better not. Better stay where we are. Hard to explain if we're stopped, walking about at this time of night – '

'I suppose you're right. Let's put my mackintosh on the ground to lie on, and put yours over us.'

They swung their arms to restore the circulation, lay down and fell asleep again, huddled together for warmth; but they woke later because their backs were cold. So they lay back to back, knees drawn up to chest, and slept fitfully until about an hour before dawn.

*   *   *

Nigel is lying sleepless, looking at the dim shapes of the sleeping ghosts, wishing the shapes were Peter and John. He has made his final preparations. His papers, food and shabby *Wehrmacht* uniform are hidden deep in the sand below the hut. If the tunnel is not discovered he will dig them up just before the routine afternoon vaulting session. If it is discovered, they will remain hidden until the search is over and then be handed back to the Escape Committee.

Just before six p.m. the prisoners in Nigel's room had put out the lights and opened the blackout shutters. They heard the diversion and checked that it was dead on time. A quarter of an hour later they knew that the tunnel must have broken; when seven o'clock came and there had been no shots, no sirens, they relaxed their vigil, hopeful that the escapers had caught their train.

Nigel looks at his watch. Nearly midnight. With any luck they will have left Frankfurt for Küstrin by now. It will be less disastrous for them, now, if the tunnel is discovered; and he is half-hoping that it will be. He tries to visualize that narrow suffocating tube through which he has never crawled. He remembers how Peter and John had looked towards the end, when the tunnel was nearing a hundred feet

– how exhausted they'd been and how, each time, it had taken them a little longer to recover. It must have been the lack of air as much as anything. Now there is an airhole under the coiled wire between the fences. Surely, he thinks, the dogs will smell it out before this afternoon . . .

He thinks of his wife and nine-year-old son, and wonders whether he ought to go. The war cannot last for ever. If he stays where he is he will get home in due course. All the talk of a Second Front the radio boffin had passed on must mean that the end is in sight. Besides, there is his leg. And that *Achtung* notice. The others had dismissed the threat, seemed to have forgotten all about it. Would the fact that the goons had put up the notice be enough excuse to shoot? Wouldn't it be enough excuse to say they'd published that they'd renounced the Convention? After all, the British handbook had been for our own chaps, the Germans were actually warning the enemy.

It would be madness to go.

Suddenly, through the open window, he hears a shout. Then more shouting, and abrupt silence. He gets out of his bunk and hobbles over to the window. Near the spot where the tunnel would have broken torches are flashing. A guard is running, there is more shouting, lorry engines are starting up in the Kommandantur.

He goes back to bed and within seconds is asleep.

2

Before it was light they rose stiffly to their feet and brushed themselves down. They left their hiding place and walked back the way they had come, into the town. It was still dark when they reached the suburbs but everywhere the German people were hurrying to work. As they neared the centre they met the early morning trams; and by the time they reached the railway station it was almost light.

The booking hall was crowded. Peter followed John as he threaded his way towards the notice board; feeling safer as part of this early morning crowd, less vulnerable than when they were walking in the open street.

John studied the board for some minutes, then turned and made for a less crowded part of the hall.

'We're in luck,' he said. 'There's a train for Küstrin in an hour's time. And it's a local stopping train.'

'An hour,' Peter said. 'Let's try to get a cup of coffee, it'll thaw us out.'

'It may be rationed,' John said. 'But after all we're supposed to be foreigners. Can't be expected to know everything.' He made for the Red Cross stall near the barrier.

'No,' Peter said. 'Not there.'

'Why not?'

'They're for troops only.'

'How do you know?'

'Got it from one of the guards in the hospital. Started boasting about our Red Cross and he unbuttoned and told me about theirs.'

'Well, let's try the waiting-room.'

It was warm and busy and smelled strongly of tobacco

smoke. They managed to find a place at one of the tables and sat there awkwardly, without speaking. The people round them were mostly in uniform. They seemed uninterested in the two Frenchmen sitting silently in the middle of the room. Peter took out a packet of German cigarettes and offered it to John. John pulled one out and thanked him in fluent French. Peter grinned in apparent comprehension, shrugging his shoulders in what he hoped was the French manner.

Minutes passed. Peter began to wonder why no one had come for their order, then realized that there were no waiters. It was a 'help-yourself' counter, with a big middle-aged woman presiding over a large urn. John's back was to the counter and he had not noticed this. Peter kicked John's foot under the table, but John merely smiled reassuringly. There was an abandoned newspaper on the empty chair next to Peter. He picked it up, appeared to study it, then took a pencil from his pocket and wrote in the margin NO WAITERS – HELP YOURSELF. He passed the paper to John who tore the margin off, folded the scrap of paper and pocketed it. He yawned elaborately and looked at his watch; said something in French and walked over to the counter.

The coffee was ersatz and not very hot. It was made from acorns – the same type that the Germans had issued to them in the camp. The rations weren't so bad, I suppose, Peter thought. Coming straight from an RAF station they seemed foul enough, but by the goons' own standard I suppose they weren't so bad. None of the soldiers and workmen sitting at the tables round them looked very fit. We're too fit, he thought. Although if I were hunting an escaped prisoner in England – which God forbid – I shouldn't go for a fit-looking chap. Unshaven, yes. He ran his hand over his already bristly chin. Have to shave again soon. But none of these Germans look as though they shaved this morning. It'll do for today. Like to clean my teeth though. Daren't go to a wash-and-brush-up place – even if they have 'em – too intimate. Have to stick it, I suppose. Wonder what John's thinking about? Looks a bit strained. Wish I could do more to help. Bloody useless, not knowing the lingo. I must try to do all the worrying about policy, and let him do the talking. He's good though. Looks

142

more French than the French. Wonder if I look French? More like an Italian with my black hair, brown eyes and five o'clock shadow . . . Glad we didn't try to travel as Germans – too young to be out of uniform. And we're not Nordic types – more Mediterranean, both of us. Non-Aryan.

The Germans in the waiting-room looked down-trodden and thin, almost half-starved. Hitler's master race, he thought. They don't look arrogant, they look as though they expect to be kicked around. And my God they do get kicked around. Everyone in goon uniform seems to kick everyone else around. Or is it just the language? Do they sound as if they're bitching when they're not really. You've got to know a language to know a people. But they're miserable looking bastards. Who wouldn't be miserable on potatoes and sauerkraut. Kartoffel. Immer bloody Kartoffel. He remembered the rotten potatoes he'd had to peel for the mess when he'd been duty cook.

·   ·   ·

Each hut has been surrounded by armed guards. The ferrets are going methodically through every room, looking for vacant bunks. The German-speakers soon learn from their 'tame' goons that the tunnel mouth was discovered at the midnight change of guard. A sentry relieved from the watch-tower nearest the tunnel put his foot into the hole, and raised the alarm. The patrol outside the wire was reinforced and a ferret – human – was put down the hole. When he reported that he could not get through the banked sand to discover where the tunnel started, the Lager Offizier diverted attention to the huts in an attempt to find out the identity of the missing prisoners.

But the prisoners are not co-operating. They get permission to visit the night *abort* at the end of their huts, and return to different rooms. There are not enough guards to control this movement. When the ferrets, frustrated, object that the prisoners are not in their usual beds, the German-speakers point out that there is nothing in camp regulations decreeing this *verboten*. The count becomes more confused as the search goes on.

At last the search is called off. The ferrets stamp out into the compound locking the doors of the huts behind them. There will be no hot water for tea this morning.

* * *

Again Peter stood back from the queue while John bought the tickets. Together they went up some steps and across a footbridge, down the far side and along to the barrier at the end of the platform.

John handed the tickets to the collector. The man handed them back and said something Peter did not understand. John replied in halting German. The collector shouted and pointed first to the tickets and then to the destination board which read KUSTRIN. John inspected the tickets, and blushed. He turned away, pocketing them, and led Peter back the way they had come.

'What's the matter?' Peter whispered.

'They gave me tickets to Berlin instead of Küstrin. I'll have to go and change them.'

'No,' Peter said, 'It'll need too much explanation. Keep them and go to another grille and buy two more. It's worth the extra money.'

John looked relieved. 'OK. I was wondering how to say it.'

At another grille in the booking hall John bought two more tickets; this time he checked that they were for Küstrin before he moved away from the grille. At the barrier the ticket collector was shouting at someone else. John proffered the tickets, and he thrust them back irritably, without pausing in his tirade or taking note of who was using them. They walked through on to the platform.

'Get into a crowded compartment,' Peter said.

Leading the way he climbed into a third-class compartment which was more like a cattle truck than a passenger coach. It was a non-smoking section, separated from the rest of the coach by sliding doors. Through the glass of the sliding doors he could see that there was not even standing room there.

'We'll stay here,' he said. 'Perhaps no one else will get in.'

They sat there until the sliding doors were opened by a German soldier. He shouted angrily and began to push them out of the compartment. If only the bastards wouldn't scream so much I might be able to get the gist of what they're saying, Peter thought as he scrambled after John on to the platform. The man stood in the doorway, shouting after them as they walked on down the platform.

'What the hell's wrong now?' Peter muttered.

John drew a deep breath. 'That carriage was reserved for Russian prisoners of war. I saw the notice on the side as we got off.'

'Definitely not the place for us!'

They climbed into another third-class carriage; this one was full of civilians, and they stood together at the end of the compartment, trying to look inconspicuous.

The train stopped at every small station, and passengers got in and out. It seemed to Peter that the journey would never end. At every stop he expected the *Bahnhof Polizei* to enter the compartment on the lookout for escaped prisoners; there was no chance, now, that the alarm had not been given. He wondered what kind of search had been set in motion, and waited nervously for the train to move again. At one of the stops they managed to get seats and they sat with closed eyes so that no one would talk to them.

 ∗   ∗   ∗

The prisoners have been paraded at one end of the football pitch. They are standing in companies, each company consisting of the occupants of one hut. In the centre of the pitch the Germans have set up a table and three chairs. The table is covered with boxes of indexed files containing photographs, fingerprints and brief descriptions of every prisoner in the camp. The chairs are occupied by the Chief Security Officer, the *Lager Offizier* and Charlie Pilz.

Hut by hut each prisoner is summoned by name to the

table. He is told to recite his P.O.W. number, which is checked against his photograph and description in the file. Once identified he is told to parade at the other end of the football pitch; and his file is transferred to another box on the table.

Progress is slow. Some prisoners seem to have gone deaf and cannot hear their names. Others mistake a name similar to theirs for their own. Two, sometimes three, prisoners reach the table at the same time. Some have grown beards or moustaches since their photograph was taken; others have shaved them off.

Nevertheless progress is made. As the numbers of those checked grows and that of the unchecked diminishes, the Escape Committee stages a diversion. Wings Cameron has come on parade carrying a rugby football. The prisoners from his hut have been passing the ball to one another. Gradually they make their passes longer and longer. Soon what had once been a compact squad of officers on parade has degenerated into a ragged bunch of kriegies throwing a rugby ball. The guards, used to the intransigence of the prisoners, do not try to stop them. Everyone, including the guards, is bored by the length of time the parade is taking. They begin to wonder whether it will be over before the midday meal.

With a wild cry Wings Cameron punts the ball straight at the table where the check is taking place. In the mad scramble to retrieve the ball the prisoners from his hut overturn the table. The files spill from the boxes and are scattered over the ground. Wings dives on the ball and rushes towards the group of prisoners at the wrong end of the pitch, chased by his hut-mates.

Checked and unchecked files, checked and unchecked prisoners are no longer neatly separated. The identity parade ruined, the Germans march the prisoners back to the huts and lock them in.

They wonder what the Germans will do next.

Within half an hour a message from the S.B.O. is delivered to each hut by a prisoner escorted by a Feldwebel. The Kommandant has informed the S.B.O. that he is most displeased at the incorrect behaviour of the RAF officer prisoners – behaviour he considers tantamount to mutiny. There will shortly be a second parade and if similar misconduct unbecoming to officers and gentlemen takes place the Kommandant fears that he will not be able to prevent bloodshed. You will therefore co-operate this time.

The prisoners' mood of elation at the success of the tunnel and their concealment of the escapers' identity sobers to one of tense apprehension. At midday exactly a convoy of army lorries roars up to the gates and brakes in a cloud of dust. Combat troops in full battle order, with steel helmets, automatic weapons at the ready, pour out and are marched smartly into the compound. They are followed by the Kommandant and the senior members of his Staff.

The bugle sounds. The doors of the huts are unlocked and the prisoners file out escorted by the camp guards. Suddenly there is a warning rattle of tommy-gunfire. Laggards come running from the end hut.

The parade is drawn up in ranks of five. Soldiers armed with tommy-guns are stationed in front of and behind each file. This time the identity check is made in good order. By two p.m. the Germans have discovered who the escapers are. The three ghosts are marched off to do their spell in the cooler. The troops are marched out of the compound. The adjutant dismisses the parade.

The excitement is over and the prisoners resume their humdrum routine. A few, seeing the horse carried away by the ferrets to be placed in the Kommandantur 'escape' museum, sense the loss of one more privilege; others are relieved that they will not feel obliged to vault again. All share a sense of satisfaction that they gave the escapers the chance to get as far away as possible before the Germans could circularize their descriptions.

*　　　*　　　*

There was no identity check at the barrier. They left the station and walked out into Küstrin. It was a small town, much smaller than Frankfurt, and Peter did not like the look of it. Its sole reason for existence seemed to be the railway junction. There was no local stopping train to Stettin until the evening and it was not safe to wait all day at the station.

They left the station square and walked down the main street. It was quiet, sleepy. The few people about seemed to have something to do, somewhere to go. It felt strange to be free to walk along a street in day time, to see shop windows and cars and motor buses with their wood-burners attached to the luggage carrier or towed behind on two-wheeled trailers. It was strange to be among people who had a purpose in life, who were not just passing the time until the next roll-call or waiting for the soup to arrive.

They passed a queue of women outside a baker's shop and were sure that all eyes were following them, taking in details of their age, height, colouring, clothes. They quickened their pace until they came to a bridge over a river. It was a hump-backed bridge and they could not see the other side. They had been told in camp that all bridges were guarded; but they did not know. Their only idea of what to expect was culled from kriegie gossip, from rumour and from a smattering of information supplied by prisoners who had been outside.

'It's not worth it,' Peter said. 'Fancy getting caught crossing a bridge. It's too true to form. Let's go back and try a different direction.'

They walked back to the main street and took another road out. It led them to a public park.

'We'll eat here,' John said. 'People always picnic in parks.'

They rationed themselves to a cubic inch of the dog food and ate two of the Canadian biscuits they had saved from the Red Cross parcels. When they had finished John rummaged in his canvas bag and produced a clothes brush. They used this first to brush their hair, then their mackintoshes and lastly their shoes.

'I shall have to shave soon,' Peter said.

'You look all right. Razor blades are scarce in Germany – good as currency,' Tony said. 'Besides, you look more French like that.'

'I'm thirsty. We should have brought some water.'

'We'll go and get a glass of beer.'

'Oh, it's all right – ' hastily – 'I'll carry on. We're all right as we are.'

'We're doing fine,' John said. 'We've been out nearly eighteen hours and we're well on our way.'

'They don't know which way we went, that's one thing.'

'I wonder if they've alerted all the railway stations?'

'Do you think we ought to walk from here?'

'I was just wondering.'

They sat in silence for a while.

'Look here,' John said, 'we're losing our grip. We said the open way was the best way – and here we are skulking down side roads and talking of walking. Let's go into the town and have a beer.' He stood up purposefully.

'Here comes a policeman,' Peter said.

John turned round. A policeman was walking slowly towards them down the path which led back to the street. 'That settles it. Let's go and have that beer!'

Without appearing to hurry Peter rose from the bench and they walked towards the policeman.

'Say something in French just as we pass him,' Peter said. 'Say something intelligent in case he speaks French.'

When they were within a few paces of the policeman John broke into voluble French. Peter tried to look as if he understood; he pushed out his lower lip and shrugged his shoulders non-committally. Then they were past. John stopped talking and they listened, expecting the policeman's footsteps to stop – a shouted hail – the footsteps pursuing them. But the sound of footsteps retreated and they walked on to the park gates.

'What were you talking about?'

'I couldn't think what to say, so I told you all about a letter I'd had from Tante Annette who said that she'd been in bed with bronchitis and that my sister Marie was having another baby.'

'Good show! That effort calls for a beer.'

'They serve a coupon-free meal in some of these places.'

'Yes, I know. It's called a *Stammgericht* or something.'

'Well, let's go and have one. My belly's flapping against my backbone. That dog food isn't exactly filling.'

Just off the main street they found a *wirtshaus*, went in and sat down. It was a large room with heavy dark wooden tables and chairs. The only other customers were four men sitting at a table in the window. They looked like local tradesmen.

Their table was at the other side of the room. It had a redand-white check tablecloth and a menu upright in a wooden holder. A waitress came from the kitchen and stood by their table. *'Was wollen Sie?'*

'Zwei Glas Bier, bitte,' John said.

'Helles oder dunkles?'

John hesitated, made up his mind. *'Dunkles, bitte.'*

'Wir haben nür helles.'

She turned sharply and left them. Peter saw John pull out a handkerchief and appear to sneeze violently; his shoulders were heaving.

'What's the joke?' he whispered.

Muffling his voice with the handkerchief, John said, 'She asked if we wanted dark or light and when I said dark she said they'd only got light.'

'Christ,' Peter said. 'We're nearly home.'

The waitress came back with two glasses of beer on a tin tray. It was light beer in tall glasses, and each glass had a white collar of foam.

'Danke schön.' John handed her a coin. She groped in the pocket of her apron and counted out several smaller coins which he returned to her. *'Danke sehr!'* she said, and smiled.

John lifted his glass and winked at Peter. 'Not bad, eh?' he said when the waitress was out of earshot. *'A votre santé!'*

'. . . *santé!'* Over the rim of his glass Peter was watching the men at the window table. They had stopped talking and were all staring. Wonder what we've done wrong, he thought. Wonder if foreigners are allowed in here. Wish we knew more about it. It's all this working in the dark. It would be dicey enough if we knew what to expect, but working in the dark like this we might barge into anything. Don't even know if there *are* French workers sculling around Germany on the loose. Was it wrong to give her a tip? She didn't seem surprised – pleased but not astounded . . . Wonder if we can smoke in here.

He looked again at the men by the window. One was smoking a pipe. Peter took out his cigarettes and offered them to John, who took one and thanked him in French.

The waitress returned carrying a tray loaded with four big white pottery bowls. They were steaming and the smell made Peter's mouth water. She set one in front of each of the men. He watched closely. Money passed, but no coupon. This was the coupon-free meal. As she turned away from the window Peter caught her eye. He gestured towards the table in front of him. She smiled and vanished into the kitchen.

The *Stammgericht* was a stew made from swedes, potatoes and carrots, but no meat. It was a generous helping, filling and warm. With full stomachs came renewed confidence.

'What do we do now?' John asked.

'Better not stay here. It'll look obvious if we stay here too long. Let's walk round the town.'

But in the streets their confidence quickly evaporated. Everyone else seemed to have something to do. Peter tried to imagine how as a stranger he would kill an afternoon in a small English town; here, as foreigners, they were even more conspicuous. They tried looking into shop windows; but the goods were few and shoddy, and the two strangers attracted the attention of the woman or girl or old man behind the counter inside the shop. All the time the feeling of being noticed grew more acute.

'I hate this place,' John said suddenly. 'Let's get out of it.'

'The Stettin train doesn't leave for hours yet. We've got to wait for it.'

'We've got to do something. Why not go back to the park?'

'No – all the women will be there in the afternoon, with prams and dogs. We'd stick out like – like bulls in a herd of cows.'

John giggled. 'Haven't seen one I'd stick out for yet,' he said. 'Seriously though – this hanging around's beginning to get on my nerves.'

'Let's look at this objectively,' Peter said. 'What would we do in an English town if we had a few hours to waste?'

'Go to the public library or a museum.'

'Or to the cinema. Why not go to the cinema?'

'The cinema!' John said it with scorn. 'We escape from a prison camp and the first afternoon out we go to the pictures.'

'Safer than the streets,' Peter said.

'I bet we're the first escaped kriegies to go to the pictures.'

'That's why we'll get through. Keep it fluid. Do the natural thing. What could be more natural than going to the pictures?'

They walked back to a cinema they'd passed earlier in the day, feeling better now that they were going somewhere, and less conspicuous. There was a short queue; mostly children, with a few women, an old man and some soldiers. They were the only young men in civilian clothes, and they stood in silence at the end of the queue hoping that no one would talk to them.

It was not a comfortable cinema. It smelled fusty and most of the seats were broken. Peter found himself next to a young soldier who sat sleeping, his head fallen forward on his chest. He remembered the cinema in Cambridge. Of how he would go there in the afternoon when he had been flying the night before, and of how empty it would be up there in the balcony with the chattering of the children in the pit below. Of the soft lighting and the organ music before the film began. Of how he himself used to fall asleep as soon as the lights went down and the credits were flashed on the screen. Of how the sound of a shot or the sudden scream of the heroine would jerk him into wakefulness only to fall asleep again and wake finally with a dry mouth before staggering out into the strong afternoon sunshine to have a meal before meeting up with his crew at the Lion for the evening's drinking. Remembering, he fell asleep until John roused him when it was time to go for the train to Stettin.

It was nearly dark when they came out of the cinema. They began to walk quickly towards the railway station at the far end of the town.

'What was the film about?' Peter asked.

'Oh – it was an escapist sort of film. A comedy about a Berlin family on holiday in the Alps. There was nothing about

152

the war in it. I saw you were asleep and was rather frightened you'd wake up suddenly and say something in English.'

'I was too tired for that – slept like a log. I feel much better now.'

'If Nig and David were lucky they'll be just about to break,' John said. 'I was thinking back in the cinema – if the tunnel's not found until after they get out, and the ghosts managed to cover for us, the goons might think that Nig and David are the only ones out and not know about us at all.'

'They haven't a hope of getting out. If we'd reached the ditch and covered the hole, they'd have stood a chance. But we didn't and it's bound to be blown by now. The goons'll know who've gone too. Let's not kid ourselves.'

'Hope they haven't got round to alerting these chaps,' John muttered as they climbed the steps into Küstrin's small booking hall.

Peter watched him square his shoulders as he approached the grille; and cursed himself for having been so positive. John now had to buy the tickets for Stettin, potentially a most dangerous destination to ask for. A Baltic port, a frontier with the outside, neutral world; an unlikely place for the casual traveller to want to visit in wartime. Thinking perhaps it might look more natural if he was there too, he moved to John's side.

'*Papiere!*'

John produced their *Ausweis*, and waited.

'Your permission to travel!' The woman clerk seemed both bored and impatient, not suspicious, Peter thought.

John passed her the *Polizeiliche Erlaubnis* and the *Bestätigung* from their firm. The clerkess glanced at them cursorily, and pushed them back, then handed over the two tickets for Stettin.

John picked up the tickets and the papers. They walked away from the grille; jubilant, not daring even to exchange glances. Again Peter felt the elation he had experienced in the forest. Was it all going to be as easy as that? When they got to Stettin?

His euphoria lasted until the train steamed in and he saw that although not an express it was a corridor train. All the coaches were full and again they had to stand. They were packed so tightly in the darkened corridor that Peter was able to reassure himself that it would be impossible for a search party to move down it. But it was a strain to stand there, surrounded by the enemy, frightened all the time that he and John were about to be discovered, with nothing to do but think and worry about what kind of a hunt the Germans were mounting.

An hour later the train pulled in to a large station. Most of the passengers left, and a number of them went to the buffet where Peter could see them drinking soup. He and John were hungry and thirsty; but they stayed in the darkness of the carriage rather than brave the lights of the buffet.

When the train started again it was less crowded. They were able to sit on their bags in the corridor. Before long they were both asleep.

Shouts wakened them with a sickening jerk. A ticket collector was forcing a passage along the corridor. Behind him were two of the *Bahnhof Polizei*, the railway police.

Hastily John pulled out the tickets. Peter watched the men work their way down the corridor, inspecting tickets as they came. In most cases the ticket collector merely said '*Weiter!*' as he handed a ticket back to one passenger and turned to the next; but occasionally he demanded identity papers and passed them to the police for examination.

This is it, Peter thought. He glanced at John who was white-faced and silent at his side. Next to him an old woman squatted on a small sack which seemed to hold potatoes. As the officials came closer she showed obvious signs of panic. By the time the ticket collector reached her she was almost crying with fear.

'*Ausweis, bitte!*' the ticket collector shouted.

The old woman fumbled in her shabby handbag. The collector stood waiting, tapping his foot. She produced a grimy piece of paper. He thrust it back angrily and shouted again. Speechless she continued to proffer the piece of paper.

'*Polizeiliche!*' the man shouted. '*Polizeiliche!*'

The old woman could not speak. The ticket collector grew red in the face. '*Polizeiliche!*' He was screaming now.

The old woman said nothing but sat hopeless on her sack.

The collector turned and harangued the policemen. One of them pulled her roughly to her feet and began to push her down the corridor. Peter could hear her whimpering as she was jostled towards the guard's van at the rear of the train. The second policeman picked up the sack of potatoes and moved off in the opposite direction.

The collector turned to John, who handed over their tickets and waited for the demand for papers. The collector glanced at the tickets and gave them back without speaking. He moved on to the next coach.

Peter broke out in a cold sweat. They had passed their first train check. Their papers had satisfied the clerks in three booking offices but so far they had not been inspected by the trained eyes of the police. A terrified old woman had saved them this time. The memory of the scene made him feel sick. There was nothing you could do for her you clot, he told himself. You were lucky. She wasn't. He prayed that their luck would hold.

*   *   *

The train began to slow down. Peter was wakened by the changing tempo of the rhythm of the wheels. He looked at his watch; just before eight o'clock. With rising excitement he wakened John who had been sleeping stretched out with his head in the corner of the corridor which they now had to themselves.

'We're running in,' he whispered. 'If the train stops outside the station let's get off. There aren't enough passengers aboard now to make a crowd on the platform. I think it would be safer to jump off outside the station and walk into the town.'

'We'll be OK.' John was still half-asleep.

'We might need a special pass to get as far north as this.'

'You need a special pass to go anywhere,' John said. 'We'll be all right.'

'If the train slows down we ought to jump.' Peter did not like this confidence in John. It had been easy enough in the camp to talk of travelling openly; but now, having got so far, he did not want to take any risks.

John got stiffly to his feet and dusted his trousers. 'OK – as you like. That was a pretty good sleep. I'm hungry. What about a spot to eat?'

'We'll go into the lavatory and make some porridge.'

In the lavatory at the end of the coach Peter opened his attaché-case and took out a linen bag of dry oatmeal and a small tin. He mixed a small quantity of oatmeal with water from the tap over the basin, and handed the tin to John.

'I hope the water's all right,' he said. 'We should have brought some purifying tablets.'

'There's a lot of things we should have brought. We'll get by. It's a cinch now. We're halfway to Sweden.'

'In terms of miles.'

John was looking happy, full of confidence. 'Let's go right in.'

'Not if the train stops. If the train stops we get out.'

But the train did not stop. Before long they steamed into Stettin station.

There were more people travelling than Peter had thought, and they were swept towards the barrier by the hurrying crowd. John pushed on forward to see if there was a paper check. The passengers were handing in their tickets and passing off the platform without showing any papers.

The two of them were at the barrier. A quick tightening of the stomach muscles as they came under the lamp – a moment's panic – and they were through and free to go into the town.

3

When they came out of Stettin station it was raining. A cold wind blew in from the Baltic bringing with it a fine, steady rain that whipped their faces as they stood in the bomb-damaged station square.

'We've got to find shelter of some sort.' John buttoned the collar of his mackintosh. 'Let's try the hotels. We'd better get in somewhere before midnight. There may be a curfew for foreigners in this town.'

'It's Saturday night.' Peter was still doubtful about the hotels. 'We haven't much hope of getting in.'

'We'll have to try – unless we stay in the waiting-room until morning.'

'No fear! Waiting-rooms are the most dangerous places. Police check every two or three hours. Why not sleep out again?'

'It's too wet – and I'm cold enough already. Besides, we must find somewhere to shave. Come on!'

Bent against the driving rain they walked quickly through the dark, strangely quiet streets, past the shells of bombed buildings gaunt and forbidding in the surrounding blackness. There were piles of rubble in the streets and the pavements were broken and uneven where the bombs had fallen.

'Pretty good mess, what?' Peter said. 'I wonder if any hotels are still standing. We could sleep in one of these bombed-out houses.'

'Too risky. They might think we were looting. Get shot for that in Germany. Hope your crowd hasn't chosen Stettin as their target for tonight.'

'Weather's too duff,' Peter said. 'Hope there isn't a curfew here.'

'We'll know as soon as we try the first hotel. Even if there is I can explain that the train was late getting in – though I can't see what reason we can give for stopping off here instead of going straight on to Anklam.'

'You can say that as it's Sunday tomorrow we thought the factory would be closed – and we thought it would be better to stay here for the weekend and go on up to Anklam on Monday morning.'

'I doubt if I could say all that in German.'

They walked on down the wind- and rain-swept street, peering into each doorway as they passed.

'It's this infernal blackout,' John said. 'It's worse than London.'

'I wonder what Phil's doing,' Peter said.

'If he hasn't been caught he'll be in Danzig – he planned to be there by last night. He's either on a Swedish ship or in a police cell by now.'

'He wasn't equipped for sleeping out.'

'No, he won't sleep out. Phil's is an "all or nothing" effort. He's either at sea or back in the cells.'

Peter laughed. 'I bet he's sitting in the hold of some bloody great freighter eating margarine samples and feeling superior. I don't think he gave very much for our chances.'

'That's why he didn't come with us.'

'I'm glad he didn't,' Peter said. 'Three would have been too many. He'd have been binding all the time because it's raining. Remember how he used to bind when we didn't dig because of the rain?'

'We must have been pretty infuriating,' John said.

They stopped outside an imposing stone building with a classical portico and mahogany revolving doors.

'It looks like a club.' Peter was doubtful. 'There's nothing to say it's an hotel.'

'Perhaps they don't, always. We might as well try anyway.'

John shouldered his way through the revolving doors. Peter followed, feeling disreputable and ashamed of his appearance. The carpets were too deep, the air of solid established wealth too strong. He caught John by the arm.

'Let's get out of this!' he whispered.

He moved towards the swing doors. John, infected by the sudden panic in Peter's voice, moved with him. They hurried through the swing doors and out into the concealing darkness of the street.

'What the hell's the matter?' John asked.

'I don't know. I don't like it. Let's try somewhere else.'

'For Christ's sake!' John said. 'What was wrong with it?'

'I don't know – it seemed wrong. It didn't seem the sort of place foreign workers would stay at. Let's try somewhere else.'

'For Christ's sake!' John repeated wearily. 'We can't walk round all night looking for hotels.'

'All right – we'll try the next one. But I've got a hunch about this place.'

'You're always getting hunches. And I'd got my German all ready.'

They walked on through the streets until they came to a smaller building with a dimly illuminated sign which read *HOTEL*.

'What about this one?' John asked.

'That looks all right.'

The lobby had linoleum on the floor and smelled of disinfectant. In one corner was a box for the night porter. The box was empty. In the opposite corner, linoleum-covered stairs rose crookedly to the floor above.

They stood waiting in the middle of the lobby. The place was silent, apparently deserted.

'I'll go upstairs,' John said.

Peter followed him, not wanting to be left alone in the lobby in case someone came in and started talking to him. On the floor above was a landing with several doors. One door was open. They could see beds standing in rows, neat and orderly, as in a barrack room.

'This is no good,' Peter said quietly.

He led John quickly down the stairs and out through the lobby. Then they were in the street again, and it was still raining. John was growing angry.

'What the hell –' he began, but Peter went on down the street and he had to hurry to catch up with him. 'What was wrong that time?'

'That was too cheap,' Peter said. 'It was a sort of a doss-house.'

'What if it was? It's a bed and it's dry.'

'They're likely to ask questions in a place like that. It's too cheap. They're likely to have police checks and God knows what. It's the sort of place they look for deserters in. We want a more expensive place.'

'You said the first place was too expensive. We can't afford to be choosey.' John was shivering; cold, wet and angry.

'We've got to be choosey – that's just what we've got to be. If the place is too cheap it's dangerous because it's liable to police checks – and if it's too luxurious it's dangerous because we're conspicuous. What we want is a quiet, respectable family or commercial hotel.'

'Then we'd better ask a policeman,' John said sarcastically.

'We might do worse than that.'

'Don't be bloody silly!'

They were both angry now. Angry and tired, frightened and wet to the skin. Angry and bewildered because they hadn't imagined it would be like this; angry because they were suddenly without a plan. They'd got out of the camp. They'd got to Stettin. And now they didn't know what to do to achieve their objective.

Presently they were at the bottom of a hill, walking along the main street towards the centre of the town. They had tried several more hotels but all were full.

'It's no good,' John said, at the end of a long exhausted silence. 'It's Saturday night, there's not a hope. Let's walk out of the town and find somewhere to sleep.'

'OK.' Peter said it with relief. 'We really will get a hotel tomorrow,' he added. 'Now we'll find somewhere dry to kip down tonight. Under a bridge or something.'

'Which way shall we go?'

'South, I think. North it's the sea, and east and west we go along the coast. Safer inland.' He took the small compass

160

from his jacket pocket and studied it by the shielded light of his torch. 'We'll go back to the central square and then take the main road going south.'

They found a long straight concrete road which appeared to lead in the right direction. There was a cemetery on one side and large brick buildings on the other.

'If the worst comes to the worst we can sleep in the cemetery,' John said.

'It'll be locked. They always lock cemeteries at night. Frightened of body-snatchers.'

'We can climb over.'

'It's not worth the risk. We might be seen. Anyway it wouldn't be very comfortable.'

'No, but it would be quiet.'

They walked on past the cemetery, past more large buildings, until they came to a suburb of small houses with front gardens.

'This looks like going on for miles,' John said.

'I wish we knew if there was a curfew.'

'Even if there is, I don't expect it's till midnight. What time is it now?'

Peter stopped and looked at his watch. 'Just after eleven-thirty.'

'Well, there's nearly half an hour to go. We'll push on and see what we come to.'

They walked on down the long straight concrete road, with the rain beating at them, running down their faces and inside their collars, soaking their trouser legs, bouncing back off the pavement; steady, continuous, drumming rain.

*   *   *

The policeman was walking on the opposite side of the road, but when he saw them he began to cross the road diagonally towards them. He was tall, paunchy, jack-booted and he was wearing a sword.

'I'll talk French,' John said. 'Be listening to me, but look at him as you go past.'

'Let's run when we get level. He won't catch us up.'

'No – he's got a gun. Just look him in the eye. We'll be all right.' He began talking fast in French.

They went on at the same steady pace. The policeman was now on their pavement, approaching them purposefully. Oh God, he *is* going to stop us, Peter though. What shall we tell him? What excuse can we give for walking out here at this time of night?

'Tell him we're going to visit some German friends,' he whispered. John went on talking in French.

They were abreast of the policeman now and Peter forced himself to stare at him expressionlessly. He was more than middle-aged but looked active enough. He had paused as though to accost them, and John let fly a torrent of excited French, waving his hands at Peter and hunching his shoulders. By God, he's wonderful, Peter thought. What an actor! Good old John. And they were safely past the policeman and he hadn't challenged them. But he had stopped. Peter could not hear retreating footsteps and he imagined the man standing there watching them and wondering whether to follow.

'Turn down here,' he said.

It was a narrow side street. Once in it they were out of the policeman's sight. Peter quickened pace as he heard footsteps behind them.

'I think he's coming,' he said. 'I don't think he liked the look of us.'

Abruptly they reached the end of the street. It was a cul-de-sac and there was no way out.

'Hell,' Peter said.

'We've had it now.'

Peter glanced back over his shoulder. Through the rain he could make out the figure of the policeman turning the corner into the side street after them.

'Quick – through this garden. Look as though we're going to the house.' He unlatched the front gate nearest to them and walked up the path. John followed. For the moment they were hidden from the policeman.

'He's still coming down the road,' John said.

Peter tried a side gate leading to the back garden. It was bolted. 'Give me a hand! '

John stooped and locked his hands. Peter put a foot in them and caught the top of the gate. He hauled himself up and stretched down a hand for John. Within seconds they were over and standing, trembling, on the far side of the gate. There was no sound from the house which was in darkness.

'We can't go back,' John said.

'Let's climb over the fence into the next street.'

'OK, but look out for dogs.'

'They'd have been barking by now – they've all been made into *wurst*.' As always when the moment of danger had arrived and he could take action, Peter was happy.

There was a low wooden fence at the bottom of the garden. They climbed it and found themselves ankle deep in newly turned earth.

'It's a cabbage field,' John said.

'Keep to the edge and cut along behind the houses.'

They found a path and followed it along the outside of the fence. It was slippery with mud and they could not see where they put their feet. There seemed no way out.

'We'd better sleep here,' Peter said.

'What? Among the cabbages?'

'No – in one of these air raid shelters.' He had stopped behind one of the back gardens and pointed to a covered trench near the fence. 'Let's crawl in there and sleep.'

They climbed the fence again and crawled into the air raid shelter. It was a trench, W in plan and about four feet deep; so built that it was difficult to lie down and impossible to stand up. The rain had seeped in and formed a thick slime of mud at the bottom of the trench.

'A typical goon effort,' John said. 'No thanks.'

'It's safe enough.'

'I don't only want safety, I want sleep. Let's try another.'

They tried several and finally found a wooden shed with earth banked up at the sides and the top covered with turf. Inside there was a bale of dry straw. As a hide-out for the night it was just what they needed. They took off their mackintoshes and their shoes and socks.

'My God, I could do with a drink!' Peter said.

'Put out the old tin and collect some rain water.'

'I will. I'll put it out now and then we'll have a drink for tomorrow morning.' He rummaged in his case for the tin. 'What about a spot of porridge?'

'It'll take too long to collect the water. I'll have a piece of dog food.' He yawned. 'What I want most is sleep.'

Peter took out the dog food and cut two pieces about two inches square. The hut looked snug in the dim light of the torch John held shielded in both hands. 'We could sleep here tomorrow night too,' he said. 'If we haven't got a ship by then.'

'No – we've got to have a base in town. This is too far out. Besides – suppose there's an air raid and the owners want to use it?' John laughed, relaxed now; and was serious again. 'We must get somewhere where we can wash and shave – we're beginning to look like tramps. Respectability's the thing. My jacket's soaked. Are you taking yours off or leaving it on?'

'I'm leaving mine on – it'll dry quicker that way. If we burrow down in the straw our clothes'll dry on us.'

'We'd better wake before it's light. D'you think that screw's still looking for us?'

'Not with that bloody sword,' Peter said. 'Don't you worry, we'll wake up all right. I give us about three hours and then we'll be wide awake shivering.'

'Not me,' John said. 'I'm really sleeping tonight.'

He burrowed down into the straw and Peter heaped more on top of him. Within minutes they were both deeply asleep.

4

When Peter woke it was still dark. At the moment of waking he thought he was back in his bunk in the prison camp and he put up his hand to rearrange the rolled-up shirt under his head. Instead he felt the straw, and he was fully awake and remembering where he was. He fumbled in his jacket pocket for the torch. Shielding the light under the jacket he looked at his watch. It was five-forty-five. He flashed the torch over John. He was sleeping curled up like a child, one hand under his head.

Peter rose quietly and opened the door of the hut. It had stopped raining and there was a keen wind. The sky was paling in the east, a few stars showed in the full zenith, and scattered remnants of cumulus cloud chased one another across the horizon. The air smelled good and clean.

Well, this is our second free dawn, he thought. He looked carefully all round him; at the backs of the row of semi-detached houses where not a light showed, and then at the cabbage field behind. In the distance he could hear the faint clanking of a shunting train. Close at hand a cock crowed suddenly. It was Sunday morning, perhaps people wouldn't be getting up so early. Better get moving though.

He stooped to where he had left the tin. It was half full of water. He went back into the hut and mixed some oatmeal with the water in the tin. He shook John gently by the arm.

'On appell, mein Herr,' he said. 'On appell, bitte, mein Herr!'

John grunted and rolled over.

'Come on, wake up, John! It's getting light!'

John opened his eyes.

165

'Come on, John, time to get cracking. I've made some porridge.'

John ran his fingers through his hair and groaned. 'Hell – I've got a mouth like the bottom of a parrot's cage.'

'It's a lovely morning. Eat some porridge and we'll get out of here before anyone's about.'

'God, I'm stiff,' John said. 'I can hardly move. I think I've got rheumatism.'

'Nonsense – you've been sleeping too heavily, that's all. Here's your breakfast. Leave half for me.'

John began to eat, chewing slowly. 'I'm hungry enough but this stuff takes some getting down.'

'It'll swell up nicely once you get it inside you,' Peter assured him.

John ate half, and handed the tin back to Peter. 'Is that all we eat?'

'I've got some biscuits but I thought we'd save them until we can get a drink.'

John put on his collar and tie and then his socks and shoes. He got to his feet and stumbled towards the door. Peter collected his things together, checked that they'd left nothing in the hut and joined him in the garden.

'Do you think it's safe to go back past the house?' John asked.

'No – too risky now it's light. We might be seen climbing over the gate – or in the front garden. There must be a way out of the field on to the road.'

They scrambled over the wooden fence on to the path along the edge of the cabbages, and followed the fence until they came to an alley between two of the houses. This led them out on to the main road they had used the night before.

'If we don't find a hotel today we'll come back here tonight,' Peter said.

'We shan't need anywhere,' John told him. 'We'll get a ship. This is going to be our lucky day.'

The sun was shining as they came into the city centre and the streets were clean and sparkling in the freshness of the morning. Early workers were hurrying to and fro and the first tramcars were grinding their way up the hill on which the town was built. They walked down the cobbled street which led to the river. There was a sea breeze and the air was full of the sea and noisy with flocks of gulls which swooped and soared in the sunshine.

At last they saw the ships. Some were wearing their wartime coat of dull grey paint; others were painted black and red and white, brave and toylike in the sun. Most of them were flying the red German flag with its black swastika centred in a white circle. A few had no flag at all. None was flying a neutral flag.

And the worst of it was that they all lay at anchor out in the stream. Only the fishing fleet was moored alongside the quays.

'This isn't what I expected,' Peter said. 'I expected the cargo vessels to be moored at the quays.' He was beginning to realize that he had not thought about the escape beyond the railway journey. He had always considered the docks as the objective. Getting to the docks had been as good as getting home to him. Now they were here, and the difficulties were just beginning. From now on they would have to make their plans as they went along. 'They've got to come alongside to load and unload,' he reasoned.

'They may be there because it's Sunday,' John said. 'Let's hang around a bit and see what happens.'

'Better not hang around here too long. This is just where they'd expect to find us. No – first we'd better try a few more hotels and get a room. What we need is a headquarters – and a place where we can shave and clean up. Then we can take our time and make plans.'

They turned their backs to the river and walked up into the town, this time through the shopping centre, with the shops shut because it was Sunday and the streets crowded with people. Some, obviously shift workers, were wearing dungarees under old jackets; others were scrupulously clean and neat, the women gloved, the children in long white socks, on their way to church. There were groups of bored soldiers, apparently on leave. To Peter, they seemed potentially the biggest danger.

He and John walked briskly as though they too had somewhere to go.

* * *

Three hours later they again found themselves down by the docks. All this time they had been searching for a place to stay. Everywhere they had been told that the hotel was full.

John's early morning optimism was crumbling. 'This is a dead loss,' he said. 'I feel inclined to stow away on one of these fishing boats and trust to luck.'

'They won't fish anywhere near the Swedish coast.'

'We could hijack it once we were out in the open sea,' John said hopefully.

'Ha, ha! No – we mustn't be in too much of a hurry. It's taken us four and a half months to get as far as this. We don't want to throw it all away in a few minutes and get marched back to the camp after being out for a couple of days . . . This is all new to us and it's worth giving it some thought. Get out a plan of campaign. Here we are in Stettin and we want to get to Sweden. We've some German money, good papers – we've proved that – and fairly good civilian clothes. We speak a little German – at least you do. We've got a bit of food left and we can always get a *Stamm*. That's an idea. It's lunch-time. What about trying the next pub?'

'OK,' John said. 'But look at the other side of the coin. We've nowhere to sleep tonight – no hotel, I mean. Nowhere to wash and shave. And there's most likely a curfew for foreign workers. We've got to have a base by this evening – or a ship.' He leaned against a low parapet and stared gloomily at the ships lying in the river. 'Look at them – all German. Even if they were Swedish I don't see how we could get out to them.'

'We could swim it in the dark and climb the anchor chain. A German airman got out of London that way in the last war. It was winter then too.'

'Not for me,' John said. 'I can barely keep afloat in the saltiest sea – and there's bound to be a strong current here.'

'Then the only way is to meet the crew ashore,' Peter said.

'Contact some of the sailors and arrange with them to get us on the ship.' It seemed simple to him as he said it; merely a matter of speaking a few words to the right man, perhaps the handing over of a little money.

But John was reluctant. 'I don't like it,' he said. 'How'll I know which chap to talk to? Besides it's spreading the risk. At the moment no one knows we're here – better keep it that way.'

'If we're going to get a ship someone's got to know sooner or later. We've worked to a plan so far – we've got as far as we planned – now we must work to a new one.'

'OK – I suppose you're right. But if we have no luck by the afternoon we must organize somewhere to sleep before it gets too late. I think there must be a curfew – that policeman last night seemed to think we ought not to be out.'

'Oh, he was just being officious,' Peter said. 'Doesn't necessarily mean a curfew. Come on, snap out of it. We'll be all right.' He had been holding back because they were without a plan. Now he could see it clearly: to meet some of the seamen ashore, make their arrangements to stow away safely – away from the docks. Not to go dashing into things, but to work slowly towards the objective.

After a beer and a bowl of vegetable stew in what seemed to be a dockers' café, they walked along the quays again, looking at the men now and not the shipping. They saw armed guards herding a gang of prisoners; haggard men, stooping, thin and weary, with their feet bound in rags and the tattered remnants of green uniform hanging from their backs. By their queer spiked cloth helmets and scarecrow appearance Peter knew them to be Russians. They were barely alive, almost too weak to lift the picks and shovels with which they were supposed to be clearing the gutters. They moved slowly, eking out their meagre strength, never smiling or looking up, doomed to slavery until the war was over.

There were Poles too, workers with a large yellow 'P' on a brassard worn on the arm; Ukrainians and Lithuanians with 'OST' stencilled on their shirts; all of them prisoners working under armed guard. There were the seamen of all the Occupied nations, some in civilian clothes, some in the uniform of their companies. Or were they from the Occupied countries? Peter wondered – might not some of them be neutral? How the hell can we tell. At least those are Frenchmen, he thought, seeing a group of men in an odd assortment of uniform whose azure-blue had deteriorated into a dirty pale blue-grey.

So long as he and John kept on the move and were not too obviously loitering, he felt safe enough in this polyglot crowd and free to move slowly among them, trying to learn all he could about the working of the harbour.

'If we're picked up,' John said suddenly, 'we might try to pass as Frenchmen – after all we've got French papers. If they returned us to this sort of thing it wouldn't be so bad. Far better than being in a British camp. Look at the chance these chaps have of getting away.'

'Let's have a word with one of them,' Peter said.

'I told you – I don't want to talk to anyone. They'll know I'm not a Frenchman by my accent, and it's dangerous.'

'We shan't get anywhere unless we take a calculated risk,' Peter said. 'We've got to speak to someone if we're to get a ship.'

'Yes – but not in the docks.'

'The docks are as safe as anywhere else if you get them alone. Let's pick one that's walking on his own and ask him.'

'Ask him what?'

'Just speak to him in French and ask him – oh, ask him if he can tell you where to stay for the night.'

'Supposing he starts to yell?'

'He won't yell. We'll go down some quiet side street leading away from here and stop one there and ask him.'

'All right,' John said. 'But I don't like it.'

'I don't like it either, but we've got to take the risk some time.'

'All right, I'll try. You stand behind him and if he yells sock him behind the ear.'

'I'll sock him behind the ear all right,' Peter said, relieved that John had agreed. 'I'll clock him with the tin of dog food.'

They went down one of the narrow roads leading off the docks and John accosted some of the more obvious Frenchmen who came along. In every case the man stared at them nervously and hurried on without speaking.

'What the hell's the matter with them?' Peter asked.

'They know I'm not a Frenchman. I expect they think I'm a goon – a sort of *agent provocateur*. Let's give it up, Pete, it's hopeless. I don't even know exactly what these fellows are. They're French all right, but they don't seem to be P.O.W.s.'

'Wait a bit – let's try this one.' Peter indicated a short, olive-complexioned man of about thirty years of age who was walking down the street towards them. He wore a beret like themselves, serge trousers and a zipped leather jacket. Round his neck was a brightly coloured handkerchief. 'He looks a bit more extrovert.'

'It's the last one,' John said. 'I'm dog-tired and frightened of some of the others coming back with the Gestapo.'

He stepped into the Frenchman's path, and spoke to him. Peter stayed by the wall, ready to go to his assistance if necessary. There was a rapid exchange of French, and the Frenchman pointed down the road, away from the docks. He appeared to be giving detailed instructions, repeating himself with heavy emphasis and making many extravagant gestures. Finally he shook John's hand, pumping it warmly up and down. John said something, and the Frenchman looked at Peter, smiled and called, '*Salut!*'

Peter grinned, wondering what it was all about. They'd chosen an extrovert all right, this time. The Frenchman again shook hands with John, slapped him on the back, waved to Peter and walked on down the road.

'What did he say?'

'I think he guessed what we are. I didn't tell him, but I think he knew. The best thing is, he gave me an address. The Hotel Schobel. He advised us not to stay there more than three days because after that they have to send your papers to the police.'

'Good show. Where is it?'

'Quite close to the docks. It's not a posh place but he says that they usually have some rooms free.'

'Let's go there right away, before they're taken.'

* * *

They found the Hotel Schobel in a parallel side street leading off the docks. It was a large building, old-fashioned and shabby. The entrance hall had a tiled floor and a lavish display of carved woodwork and unpolished brass.

They were greeted by the proprietor, a stout German of an earlier generation, with a close-cropped bullet head and half-spectacles, smoking a large curved pipe.

John began his carefully rehearsed question. *'Haben Sie, bitte, ein Doppel-Zimmer...?'*

Yes, the proprietor had a double room. He pulled a bunch of blue forms from a drawer in his desk and handed them to John.

Peter leaned forward to see what John was writing. To his surprise the forms were printed in German, French and English. John was writing slowly, taking care to print in the continental manner they had practised in the camp. MICHEL CONDE, he wrote, Born PARIS 2 OCTOBER 1921. Employed by METALLHUTTENWERK DR HOFFMAN, BRESLAU. Normally Resident PARIS. He completed two similar forms, then handed the pen to Peter, who wrote even more slowly: MARCEL LEVASSEUR, Born LILLE 13 JUILLET 1911, Employed by METALLHUTTENWERK DR HOFFMAN, BRESLAU. Normally Resident LILLE.

The proprietor checked the completed forms against their *Ausweis*, and asked for their police permission to be in Stettin. John showed him the *Polizeiliche* giving them permission to travel from Breslau to Anklam and explained that they wanted to stay in Stettin for three nights so as to arrive in Anklam on Wednesday morning. The proprietor asked for his money in advance. John handed over the marks; and then they were free to go upstairs to their room.

It was a large room, the walls covered with a dark floral wallpaper. A wardrobe stood against the wall opposite the door and a heavily ornamented dressing-table filled the space in front of the single window, obscuring the view and keeping out most of the daylight. There was a double bed covered with a thin floral counterpane, and next to it a tiled stove which looked as though it had not been used for some time. In one corner, incongruously, stood a white washbasin with chromium-plated hot and cold taps.

They put their bags on the dressing-table and saw their reflection in the mirror.

'Toss you for the first wash,' John said.

'You go ahead. This is the first chance I've had to study the plan of the town.'

John stripped and crossed to the wash-basin. His ankles and wrists were black from the dye of the combinations he had worn in the tunnel. He turned on the hot water tap. 'It's a snare and a delusion,' he said.

'What is?' Peter was slitting open the lining of his mackintosh and extracting the waterproof envelope from under the armpit.

'This basin. The hot tap doesn't work.'

Peter laughed. 'Don't you know there's a war on?'

'Oh well – it's a luxury to have cold water on tap I suppose.' John filled the basin and began to try to work up a lather on his body with the bar of German issue soap he had brought from the camp. 'I only wish we'd got the luxury of soap from the Red Cross parcels. This stuff stinks.'

'Too big a risk. Better to smell like the goons.' Peter spread the map of Stettin on the counterpane and pored over it; identifying the street where they were, before concentrating on the waterfront. 'We've been barking up the wrong tree,' he said after a time. 'It's the Freihafen we want. That's where the neutral shipping will be – if there is any. If we cross the second bridge after the railway station it'll bring us straight to it.'

'Supposing there isn't a Swedish ship?'

'There's bound to be, it's the nearest port to Sweden.' Peter wished he were as confident as he sounded. 'But if not, we'll go on to Reiherwerder coaling station and see if there's any chance of stowing away on a coaling barge.'

'Where will that get us?' John asked.

'God knows – I hadn't really thought. It was just something Stafford suggested. Anyway, let's take it one stage at a time. It's the Freihafen for us first thing in the morning.' He folded the map carefully and replaced it in its envelope in the arm-pit of his mackintosh. 'Are you going to shave now?'

'If you don't mind waiting a bit longer.'

'No hurry.' Peter took off his shoes and lay down on the bed. The mattress felt lumpy through the thin feather over-lay. 'Why do you think those forms were printed in French and English?'

John was standing on one leg on his towel, furiously scrub-bing at the other balanced on the wash-basin. 'Oh – they had 'em before the war I expect and they're still using them.' He looked very young; thin and young and full of a nervous vitality in the stale and static atmosphere of the room.

'No wonder they've got an inferiority complex. Just imagine if English hotels had registration cards printed in French and German.'

'No need. English is an international language.'

'Our menus are printed in French.'

'Yes, but that's to kid ourselves that the cooking's good.'

'What couldn't I do to a Châteaubriand steak!' Peter put his hands under his head on the pillow and gazed at the ceiling; conjuring up his ideal meal as he had so often done in the prison camp. 'A Châteaubriand steak – garni with spinach and mushrooms and chip potatoes – Dijon mustard . . . Fol-lowed by green figs in syrup, and Stilton cheese.'

'For God's sake shut up!' John said. 'Make us some por-ridge.'

'Or a grilled Dover sole swimming in butter, with a crisp green salad. Or even a good mixed grill.'

'*Shut up!*' John's hand was trembling as he scraped at the soap on his face with his safety razor.

And suddenly Peter realized that John was near to breaking point: that the hours spent in looking for an hotel and talk-ing to unknown Frenchmen had taken the last of his nervous strength. He cursed his own lack of consideration. He had been pushing John harder than he should. 'You don't want any more porridge,' he said. 'When I've had my wash and shave

we'll go out and get a couple of beers and another *Stamm*.'
It's Sunday evening, he thought. We might even run into some
Swedish seamen ashore.

'No we bloody well won't,' John said. 'We're here now,
safe indoors, and no one's likely to disturb us. We'll stay here
and get a good night's sleep. Even being half-starved isn't going to keep me awake.'

'Food's what you need – you've hardly eaten for more than
forty-eight hours. I had a meal while you were moling. I've
got a bar of chocolate – how about that?'

'Yes, please.' John took it gratefully and ate it there and
then, standing on his towel by the wash-basin, with one cheek
shaved and a thin layer of soap congealing on the rest of his
face. Still munching, he asked, 'Was Kleine Oder Strasse
marked on the map?'

'Yes – but that's our very last resort. Remember what
Stafford said. It could easily have been blown by now. I'd hate
to get caught with my trousers down.'

●   ●   ●

From the outside the East compound of Stalag-Luft III looks
much as always: a black area of shuttered silent huts surrounded by a ring of brilliant light. The white beams of the
searchlights stab the blackness, occasionally revealing the ghost-
like form of a prowling dog.

But inside the huts, where normally a single electric bulb in
each crowded room lights a scene of busy domesticity, there is
darkness too. As a reprisal for the escape, all electricity has been
forbidden for a period of three weeks.

In Peter's and John's old room five despondent kriegies sit
round a flickering goon-lamp made from a strip of pyjama cord
floating in a bath of rancid cooking fat. There has been a long
and heated argument between the 'light brigade' who want the
lamp lit with the shutters closed and the 'pure air league' who
prefer the room in darkness with the windows open. The light
brigade has won the day, and the room is filled with acrid
smoke which makes them cough and brings tears to their
eyes. Bennett has spent most of the evening rendering the fat

to remove the water; the result is, if anything, slightly worse, but he is explaining to the room in general how he managed it. Paul is trying not to listen. Nigel is playing chess with David. Pomfret, who cannot read in this dim light, is gazing gloomily into space.

Not only has the electricity been cut, but the end-of-week issue of Red Cross parcels has been stopped. The mess has no reserve of tins, and all five of them are hungry.

Earlier in the day, at the Sunday morning parade, the Germans announce that the three escapers have been caught; that they are now in police custody and will be either tried for espionage or sent to the *Strafelager* in Colditz Castle. The prisoners pretend to disbelieve the announcement, but their quiet triumph has been eroded. There is still the victory over the ferrets – the impregnable camp has been broken, the long months of vaulting and secrecy about its purpose have been worthwhile – but psychologically the guards have recovered some ground. Unless the three escapers are safely out of the country by now, what the prisoners hope is a lie may soon prove true.

Nigel tries to concentrate on the next move.

5

Timing it carefully they crossed the bridge with the morning shift of dockers and came to the Freihafen. It was protected by a twelve-foot square-mesh wire fence with three strands of wire running along the top. There were floodlights positioned above the wire, and armed soldiers at the gates. The place looked exactly like a prison camp.

They walked slowly round three sides of the dock area. The fourth side was open to the river where a tug was steaming up to a hove-to freighter, hooting peremptorily. Ranged along the quays inside the wire were long wooden buildings which they assumed were warehouses. In the gaps between the buildings, sometimes towering above them, they could see the hulls and the funnels of the berthed ships.

John caught Peter by the arm. 'Look – a Swedish ship!'

In the next gap Peter could see the black hull of a freighter with the yellow cross on blue, and SVERIGE in big white letters painted on her side.

'We'll get on board tonight,' John said. 'We'll come back after dark, climb over the wire and get on board.'

'There's bound to be a watchman.'

'Oh – it'll be one of the crew. They wouldn't have a German watchman in a guarded dock.'

'I don't like it,' Peter said. 'I'd much rather try and get hold of one of the crew ashore. It's sticking our necks out to go into a place like this.'

'We wouldn't be here if we hadn't stuck our necks out,' John said vehemently. 'Besides we can't speak Swedish. If we're going to talk to the crew it'll be safer on board than in a pub surrounded by goons . . . Anyway – she might be gone by tomorrow.'

Against his better judgment Peter allowed himself to be persuaded. John was right, they had to take some risks. By doing nothing they might remain free, at least as long as their money lasted; but they would not be getting anywhere. 'OK. Let's make a recce.'

Trying to look casual, they made a close inspection of the fence and found a spot where a railway siding ran within a few feet of the wire, halfway between two of the floodlights. By climbing on to the truck which stood on the siding they would be able to reach the top of the fence and drop down into the dock area where the light was weakest.

'If the truck's still there after dark that'll do to get in by,' Peter said. 'Now we've got to find an escape route. We may want to come back in a hurry.'

They chose a shed standing near the wire. It was directly in the light of one of the lamps but it seemed to be the only means of climbing the wire from the inside, to get out of the docks.

* * *

After their now standard midday meal of a beer and *Stammgericht* in a café at a discreet distance from the docks they returned to the Hotel Schobel and made their preparations for the attempt on the Freihafen. The socks they had rinsed out the previous evening were almost dry and they stuffed these into their pockets with their shaving gear and soap. Reluctantly they decided they must leave their towels and bags behind. They washed and dressed, putting on the rollneck sweaters over their collars and ties; and went out through the lobby with upturned mackintosh collars so that the proprietor would not notice their change of dress.

It was still only early afternoon. They had several hours to kill until it was dark. They went to the cinema rather than wait in their room. The film was *Paracelsus*, a romanticized life of the famous sixteenth-century Swiss physician, philosopher and traveller. To Peter, understanding nothing of the dialogue, constitutionally unable to suspend his disbelief where writer and director could have no first-hand knowledge of the period, it was an incomprehensible jumble of characters cavorting in doublet and hose to the anachronistic tune of Saint-Saëns's *Danse Macabre;* and he sat huddled in his seat, thinking about the evening ahead of them, worrying that they were taking an unnecessary, uncalculated risk in climbing into the unguarded docks. But he could see John's point of view. They could not stay in Stettin much longer and unless they took some initiative they would never get out of Germany. By the time they left the cinema his natural optimism had reasserted itself.

They walked straight down to the Freihafen in the gathering darkness, and found a sentry patrolling the railway siding outside the wire. They walked on down the road past the siding and stood on the corner, apparently in conversation, watching the sentry. He was doing a steady beat up and down the siding, his rifle slung from his right shoulder, his long belted overcoat reaching almost to his ankles. Not much good as running kit, Peter thought; but then he doesn't need to run, with that rifle.

'Next time he turns back we'll slip in behind the empty truck,' John said, 'and climb on top. We'll wait for him to come past again and the next time he turns away we'll jump smartly down into the docks.'

'Not yet.' Peter said. 'We'll go and have a look at the place where we're going to climb out first. If there's another sentry there we'll call the whole thing off – we might want to come out in a hurry.'

They walked on round the outside of the fence until they could see the shed they had selected that morning; but there was no outside sentry here. On this side of the docks there was not a German soldier in sight.

'Well that's OK,' John said. 'He's guarding the railway siding, not the docks.'

Peter felt committed, but he said nothing.

They retraced their steps to the siding and climbed into the empty truck. Crouching, they peered through a chink in its plank sides timing the sentry's beat. Peter worked out that the man had farther to patrol on his way back to the dock gates – or maybe he chatted to the other guards there. The next time he passed going in that direction they rose slowly to their feet. One at a time they spanned the space between the side of the truck and the wire, and climbed the remaining strands to the top of the fence, removing their feet slowly as they climbed, to prevent the wire from twanging. The wire mesh was slack, and when Peter reached the top the fence swayed so that John, already on the ground inside the docks, had to hold it still while Peter jumped down. The noise of the wire shaking ran along the fence and they were frightened that the sentry would hear and turn round.

Although Peter had been dreading this the whole afternoon, once he was over the fence and inside the docks and creeping in the darkness towards the quay where they had seen the Swedish ship, he felt a completeness that he had rarely felt before; an aloneness, an awareness of himself as a vulnerable entity, a feeling that came only when he was hunted.

He had felt the same elation when he had emerged from the tunnel. It was not only the danger of the thing. He had not felt like this when, as a member of a bomber crew, he had been stalked by night fighters. It was more animal than that; and as he crept forward in the darkness towards the black bulking outline of the shipping beyond the warehouses, he felt a thrill of pleasure in the game that he was playing and an added awareness of the clean air blowing in from the sea.

When they reached the quay the Swedish ship had gone.

At first they thought that they must have come to the wrong quay and they cast around looking for her. They took a bearing on a large German vessel they had seen from the road and realized that they were on the right quay. The ship had sailed.

Hoping to find another neutral ship they began to explore the docks. It was a pitch black night and they had to use a torch to read the names on the sterns of the ships. They had written off two of the quays and were about to move on to a third when they saw a light jerking towards them across the open ground between themselves and the gates.

Peter saw it first. 'Look out, we've been seen!' And he ran towards the sea end of the quay; planning to dodge round a warehouse and double back towards the shed which was their escape route.

There was a whistle and shouting. More lights flashed on from ahead of them at the end of the quay. With John following at his heels he turned sharply to the right between two warehouses and out on to the other side of the quay. They saw some barrels, and crouched behind them. Peter was panting now and cursing himself for having agreed to come into the docks. John crouched beside him, panting too. We'll have to wait here until they call off the chase, Peter thought.

John gripped him by the arm and muttered, 'That's the light we saw.' A soldier with a storm lantern was passing them, walking towards the sea end of the quay.

'He'll be back in a minute. We'd better cut away left – the shed's somewhere over there.'

They crept out from behind the barrels and down the side of the warehouse towards the wire. There was a guttural '*Halt!*' behind them. They started running together, running fast, expecting all the time to hear the rifle crack and feel the impact of the bullet in their backs. There was more shouting now; the pursuit seemed to be coming closer.

Running side by side and running hard they made for the open part of the docks, away from the confinement of the quays. They soon came round the corner of a warehouse going fast and crossed some railway lines.

Peter was panting in earnest now. There was a pain in his side and the air felt like ice water as it went down into his lungs.

Then John was in front, running easily. He turned sharply to the left into a dark alley between two more warehouses. They came to a concrete railway platform raised about eighteen inches above the level of the ground. John dived under it and Peter followed, full length on the dry earth under the concrete and panting so hard that he felt his chest would burst. They lay there panting and spent, drawing the cold burning air into their lungs and expelling it quickly to snatch more.

They lay listening to the sound of the German soldiers searching the docks. Twice they heard loud voices at the end of the alley leading to the platform and they tensed themselves for discovery. But the searchers came no nearer and they relaxed again. Gradually the sounds of footsteps and voices grew fainter. Finally the docks were silent.

They lay under the platform for an hour and a half before Peter judged it safe to come out. They were cold now that the sweat had dried on them, and stiff from lying still for so long on the hard ground. They stood listening, reluctant to leave the shelter of the alley.

'We'd better forget about the shed,' Peter said. 'Damned if I know where it is, now. Let's follow the railway down. There's bound to be an opening where it enters the docks.'

They followed the railway lines, walking softly on the sleepers. They slowed down when they came to a branch in the line, uncertain which way to go. There was a lamp over the points, but they didn't see the sentry until they were right on top of him. Then they stopped dead. He was standing in the shadows to one side of the line.

'Walk on,' John whispered.

They started up again and moved down the line, ignoring the sentry.

'*Halt!*'

They stopped and the sentry came towards them, into the light from the lamp by the points. '*Ausweis, bitte.*'

They took out their wallets and handed him the papers. He looked at them; studying them closely as a man will who does not read easily. Peter could smell the German soldier smell compounded of coarse ersatz soap and tobacco, wurst and sauerkraut. After a few moment's deliberation which seemed to last a lifetime, the man folded the papers, creasing them with his thick fingers, and handed them back. Hope to God he doesn't ask for our dock passes, Peter thought. But the sentry, apparently satisfied, adjusted the sling of his rifle and began to move away.

Then he turned and asked a long question in German; and Peter thought he'd remembered the passes. John replied, gesticulating with his hands when he had to grope for words.

'*Ach so?*' said the sentry, and laughed.

'What did he say?' Peter asked, when they were safely out of earshot, walking on down the railway line.

'He was a bit dim. He asked what all the shouting was

about and I told him some drunken sailor had fallen in the sea and they were trying to fish him out. He seemed to think it was funny – perhaps it was my accent. I think we'd better get to hell out of here.'

'It was a damn' sight easier getting into this place than it's going to be getting out,' Peter said. 'I bet they've got guards posted all along the fence by now.'

'I shouldn't think so – they'd have alerted that chap if they'd thought we were escaped prisoners. Probably thought we were just doing a spot of pilfering. If they've scared us off I expect that's all they worry about.'

'I hope you're right.'

There were no more points with lamps to worry about and they picked their way down the dark railway line until they came to the fence. The gap was filled by a gate constructed roughly of lathes of timber and barbed wire. It was not guarded and everything was quiet now; but they were taking no chances. They lay down by the track and waited, listening, for ten minutes. At length Peter spoke.

'The gate's no good – we'll climb the fence. Creep up to it and when I say "Go!" we'll both climb up together. If we're seen, go like hell when you get to the other side and I'll see you back at the hotel.'

On hands and knees now, they inched their way up to the fence.

'Ready?'

'Yes.'

'Go!'

Running bent double they covered the short distance to the fence and began to climb it as quickly and silently as possible. They expected every moment to hear whistles blowing, men shouting, shots fired by the guards inside the wire. But nothing happened. They jumped down safely on the other side and walked fast for two blocks before they felt safe enough to slow down and talk.

'So much for the Freihafen,' Peter said.

'We were just unlucky.'

'Unlucky be damned! We were lucky not to be caught. We were bloody lucky to get out of there without being shot.'

6

Peter awoke to see John standing fully dressed by the wash-
basin. He was wearing Peter's navy blue mackintosh, with his
beret pulled down low over his forehead.

'Where the hell are you going?'

'I'm not. I've been.'

'Where?' Peter pulled himself up on an elbow and stared
at him.

'Down to the docks.'

'What on earth for?'

'I thought I'd go and have a look round.'

'Then you're a bloody fool. Supposing you'd got caught. I
shouldn't have known where you were.'

'I left a note for you,' John said mildly.

'But why didn't you wake me up and tell me you were going?'

'I woke up and couldn't get to sleep agin. You were sleeping pretty soundly and I didn't want to wake you. I lay there
thinking for a bit and decided that the best time to contact
the French was early in the morning, just as they were going
to work, before it got really light.'

'Why didn't you wake me? I'd have come with you.'

'Well – as a matter of fact –' John looked embarrassed. 'I
thought perhaps I'd have more chance if I went alone. I'd been
wondering why they all seemed so scared when I talked to
them on Sunday. And I came to the conclusion that, firstly,
the RAF mackintosh I've got looks too much like the German
feldgrau and, secondly, the fact that you were hanging around
in the background made them jittery. So I thought I'd go out

on my own in your mackintosh and put it to the test.'

'Yes,' Peter said slowly. 'I see what you mean. Did you have any luck?'

'I'll just get back into bed and I'll tell you all about it.' John undressed quickly and stretched out on his side of the wide bed. 'It's bloody cold out. I'm not getting up again until the day warms up.'

'What happened?'

'Well, it was just as I thought. I got down to that French camp near the docks as they were all streaming out to go to work. I tagged on to a chap who was alone and walked down the road with him. I didn't explain that I was English, just said, "*Bon jour, m'sieur*" and fell into step beside him. I asked him where the Swedish ships berthed and he confirmed that it *is* the Freihafen. Then I asked him where the Swedish sailors go in the evening and he said either the brothel in Kleine Oder Strasse – it must be still working by the way – or the cafés down Grosse Lastadie Strasse. He didn't think there were any Swedish ships in at the moment – told me one sailed yesterday midday, that was ours I suppose. Oh – and you need a dock pass to get into the Freihafen. He showed me his – it's a kind of pink card.'

'Does he work in the docks?'

'They all work in the docks in that camp. They unload the ships.'

'What did he say about a curfew?'

'There's no curfew for foreigners in this town. But all the French workers have to be back in their camps by ten o'clock.'

'Did he make any suggestions?'

'No, he wasn't very forthcoming really. Didn't trust me I suppose. He answered all the questions I put to him but that's all. When I couldn't think of what to ask him next there were awkward silences. These chaps don't speak my sort of French, I think most of them come from the Midi. I had to repeat each question about four times and then I'm not sure I always understood the answer.' John lay quiet for a few moments before he said, 'He must have guessed I was English because he told me there's a chap in their camp who speaks English. He called him Jo-Jo le Corse, or something like that.

185

He said if we went along there tonight this chap would talk to us.'

'Now we're getting somewhere! What time?'

'He said any time after eight o'clock. He showed me where the hut is. We're to climb in over the back fence.' He turned and looked at Peter and laughed.

'D'you mean we're to climb into the camp?'

'Yes.'

'Christ! We nearly get shot after climbing into the Freihafen last night – now tonight you want to go climbing into a bloody prison camp.'

'It's the safest place to talk,' John said. 'Safer than talking in a café.'

'You said that about the docks.'

They both lay silent for a while, warm and comfortable in the large bed, secure behind the locked door, listening to the noise of traffic in the street below, thinking about the day ahead of them.

'Is it very closely guarded?'

John smiled. 'It's not guarded at all. There's an old civilian gatekeeper who books them in and out, but apart from that they come and go as they please.'

'All right – we'll go along there tonight and meet this chap. Let's get up now and have a look at that coaling station at Reiherwerder. They might load colliers for Sweden there. It might not be fenced or guarded like the Freihafen.'

     •   •   •

Reiherwerder coaling station lay about four kilometres up-river from the docks and according to Peter's map it could be reached by tramcar. They decided to follow the tram track out on foot. There were minor docks and coaling stations all along the route, approached by narrow lanes running off the main road. At the entrance to each lane was a swing gate guarded by a watchman's hut.

It was a grey damp morning and they walked briskly to keep warm. There was little traffic apart from a few coal lorries and the occasional tramcar. All the workers they met on the road seemed to be foreign; men with the yellow letter 'P' on a diamond-shaped patch sewn on their jackets, girls with the word 'OST' printed in yellow letters on their blue overalls. They were heavy peasant girls and unlike the solemn-faced men they were laughing as they clattered over the cobbles in their wooden clogs. If only we had a common language, Peter thought, we might get help from them.

As they neared the Reiherwerder they were stopped by a level crossing. A long train of empty coal trucks was steaming slowly into one of the side docks.

'That's the way to get in!' John said. 'Come up here after dark and jump one of these trains. It'll take us right up into the coaling station – probably stop right by the barges. No need to get any more involved with the French.'

Peter waited for the train to clank past before replying. He was afraid of John's impetuosity. He could see no future in the plan. To jump a coal train – stow away on a barge going God knows where. To abandon the safe guise of a French worker and become an escaping prisoner. To go in with no way out. To make the final move that might lose the whole game.

Truck after truck clanked slowly past, unchecked, into the dock.

It would be too easy. Stretch out a hand, a quick jump, and you were in. And then what?

'Let's do it, Pete! Tonight.'

'Look here, John, let's not rush our fences. We need to find out a lot more about it first. We might stow away on a barge and wake up in Berlin – they're more likely to be going inland than out into the Baltic.'

'You said yourself colliers might load at Reiherwerder for Sweden.'

'Yes – *might*. We don't *know* if they do. We've got to be sure.'

'The best way to find out is to go in and see.'

'No it isn't. The best way to find out is to ask the French. Come on – we might meet some Frenchmen who work in the Reiherwerder station. They could tell us.'

'And they could tell half Stettin what we're doing! That's

a risk, if you like. I think it's damn' risky talking to any-one.'

'Not as risky as climbing into places haphazardly. Just suppose we were French workers, as we pretend to be. Even then we'd be breaking the law by going into the coaling station. By not breaking any laws we can stay here as long as our money lasts.'

'Yes, but where's it getting us?'

'Oh, we're not doing so badly. We've only been here a couple of days and we're getting to know the score. There's this Frenchman tonight. After all, time's no object, we don't have to rush things.'

'Then what the hell have we come to Reiherwerder for, anyway?'

'Now you're just being silly.'

'I'm not being silly. We get chased out of the Freihafen, so we come out here. We find a good way of getting in, and you want to cry off.'

'I don't want to cry off. I just want to be certain of the next step.'

'How can you be certain of it – how can you be certain about anything here?'

'We can be more certain after asking this Frenchman about it tonight. After all they've been here longer than we have. We wouldn't have got a hotel if it hadn't been for a French-man.'

'That's true. We were lucky that time. He might just as easily have given us away.'

'That's true too.'

'Then what are we arguing about?'

'I don't know. Let's push on to Reiherwerder.' Peter suddenly realized that they had been arguing heatedly in English, their voices rising as their tempers rose. His last words had been spoken as the clanking of the train died away round a corner, and the clear English tones rang across the street. 'Come on, John,' he muttered. 'Sorry if I lost my temper.'

There was a bridge at the entrance to Reiherwerder. On the far side was a barrier guarded by a German soldier. They stood for some minutes watching pedestrians crossing the bridge.

'It's all baloney about crossing bridges on the right-hand side,' Peter said. 'They cross on both sides.'

'Yes – what's more, if you go across in a tram you get over without having to show your papers.'

'You might have to show them to the conductor when you buy your ticket,' Peter said. 'You probably need a special pass too – like the one you were shown for the Freihafen. No – it's not worth going any further until we know more about it.'

They turned their backs on the bridge and started to re-trace their steps towards Stettin.

'Look, John – there's a Frenchman over there. Go and have a natter to him.'

'You're always wanting me to natter to Frenchmen,' John said good-humouredly. 'What do you want me to ask this one?'

'Oh – whether the Swedish ships load coal here, if you need a special dock pass – that sort of thing.' Peter felt the helplessness of his position. 'I'd do it myself if I could – I'll do all the talking tonight, to save you.'

They crossed the road and John spoke to the Frenchman. Peter listened; he could understand more or less what John was saying, but not a word of the Frenchman's reply. A tram came along and the Frenchman broke off the conversation and ran to board it. Peter made to follow but John held him back.

'What did he say?'

'He gabbled a sort of argot I couldn't understand. It was quite useless really. I didn't want to get on the same tram in case he wanted to carry on talking in front of the Germans.'

'Never mind. We'll take the next tram back to town and get some lunch. Then let's go to some of these cafés in the Grosse Lastadie Strasse – another Swedish ship may have arrived.'

After a short wait at the next tram stop they boarded a car which took them to the centre of the town. They went back to their hotel room and ate some porridge; had a beer and *Stamm-gericht* in the nearest café; and began exploring the Grosse

Lastadie Strasse. Frightened to stay too long in one place they went from café to café, having a beer in one, a cup of acorn coffee in another. Everywhere they felt conspicuous, felt all the time that people were watching them, that their clothing was not right, that their very silence made them stand out from the other customers. They saw no Swedish seamen.

As it grew dark it became more difficult. Because of the blackout they could not see inside the café before they entered. After stumbling into one full of German soldiers they decided that it was time to wash and brush up before going to the French camp.

•　　•　　•

It had been easy getting into the camp. John had no difficulty in finding the hut; and now they were standing in a room full of Frenchmen and smelling again the odour of captivity.

There was a silence when they came into the room, a sudden silence then a resuming of the conversation in a lower key. There was a closer drawing-together of the men seated round the table, and some laughter and loud remarks from men on the bunks against the wall.

John's contact of the morning was there. When he saw them he rose to his feet, mumbled a few words and went out through a door at the back of the room.

'Where's he gone?' Peter asked.

'I didn't get it – fetch the chap who speaks English, I suppose.'

While they waited Peter looked round him at the familiar scene. The room was very like the one they had lived in. Here perhaps the smell was stronger than he had known it; that unmistakable, unforgettable prison smell compounded of male bodies, clothing that had been worn too long, tobacco smoke, stale food, goon-lamps – and the night *abort*. This room was dirtier and showed less ingenuity and improvisation, but these men had to work for their living. Stuck to one wall was the German poster *KEIN ARBEIT – KEIN ESSEN*. Basically however it was the same room, the same bunks, the same wooden clogs under the bunks.

It was the men who were different. Peter felt the resentment all around him. He did not feel among friends. The French-men were eating, spooning up some kind of stew from large enamel plates; and as they ate they watched the strangers standing awkwardly by the stove waiting for John's contact to return.

'I wish that chap would hurry up,' Peter said.

'Not a very promising bunch, are they?'

Reluctant to say more in case some of them understood English, Peter stood beside John, simulating indifference, until the contact returned with a short dark-moustached man whom he introduced as Jo-Jo le Corse. His part finished, he re-seated himself at the table and resumed his meal.

The Corsican took them along to his room, farther down the corridor. Here the occupants were more polite. They stood when the two Englishmen entered and offered them coffee and black German bread. In return Peter produced a packet of cigarettes.

The Corsican had been halfway through his meal. He ex-cused himself in broken English, explaining that he was the camp barber and had to follow his trade after the day shift returned from the docks. He was a thin, sharp-featured man of about thirty-five. He looked cleaner than his room-mates and wore a collar and tie.

His English was not as good as they had hoped. When Peter began to ask him about Swedish ships and how they could contact the crews ashore, he did not understand and John had to take over and ask the questions in French. While they were trying to communicate in English the other Frenchmen were silent; but when John spoke in French they all replied to-gether at such a speed that Peter found it very difficult to follow.

'*Je vous prie, messieurs,*' John said, smiling, '*lentement, lentement!*'

The barber silenced the others and answered John's ques-tions. He regretted that he personally had no opportunity to contact the Swedish seamen on their behalf as he did not work in the docks. But he had friends in another hut who actually boarded the ships to stow the cargoes and he would ask their advice. He sounded confident, but he also made it sound too simple. Was there anything else he could do to help?

Perhaps he could tell them whether seagoing ships loaded coal at Reiherwerder?

'*Pas du tout!*' one of the other men cut in. 'Reiherwerder is for the barges only. It is only of interest because some go right through to the River Rhine and one can reach France that way.'

John was running out of questions. He seemed satisfied, and rose to his feet, thanking their hosts. To Peter it seemed less than promising; it was a feeler, nothing more. Before leaving they traded cigarettes for black German bread. The Corsican accompanied them to the main door of the hut. They asked him to tell all his customers that there were two British escaped prisoners looking for a neutral ship out of Stettin. He said he would tell a few that he trusted, by no means everyone. They offered a reward to anyone who helped them. He pooh-poohed the idea. He wished them a good night's sleep and was turning back towards his room when Peter stopped him.

'How will you let us know if you have news? We have to change our hotel tomorrow.'

'Please?'

John translated.

'Ah – how stupid!' He slapped his forehead. 'Go for your *Stammgericht* about eight o'clock in the evening to the Café Schiff opposite the main entrance to the Freihafen. It is run by a good man, a Communist. Do not contact him – he says that the less he knows the less he can tell the Gestapo when they interrogate him. If I have news I will send someone to you there.'

They got safely out of the camp and walked back towards the hotel.

'Good chap that Corsican.' John was in a buoyant mood. 'He'll be able to help if anyone can. Quite a satisfactory evening.'

'It was all right as far as it went,' Peter said. 'But we can't sit back and wait for one chap who might or might not do something. We've got to hedge our bets.'

'What on earth do you mean?'

'Talk to some more Frenchmen ourselves. This Jo-Jo type's not actually working in the docks. We want to find a Frenchman who can tell us immediately a Swedish ship berths and where – someone who can introduce us to the crew ashore.'

'Good God!' John said. 'We've got a reliable intelligent chap working for us now. Do you want every Tom, Dick and Harry to know we're here?'

'No – *chaque Alphonse, François et Henri.*' Peter came out with it proudly.

John was convulsed. When he could speak again he said, 'I'm banking on Jo-Jo – he'll fix us up all right. We don't have to worry any more.'

7

Peter was shaving in front of the mirror over the wash-basin.
He finished shaving and began to wash himself down with a
face-cloth he had cut from the tail of his shirt.

'What's the programme for today?' John was still in bed.

'We'd better go and have another look round the Freihafen
this morning.'

'I thought you decided against climbing into the docks.'

'I don't mean climb in – I mean see if another Swedish ship
has berthed yet and mark down a few cafés for this evening.
Do a recce on this Café Schiff place. You can't see what you're
doing in the dark.'

'Oh God, are we going to start all that café-stalking again?'

'It's the only thing to do, John. We made one contact last
night but it's not enough. We've got to get every Frenchman
in the town working for us.'

'I don't like it,' John said. 'The Corsican didn't seem too
trusting – and you want to trust the lot.'

'We'll pick 'em carefully. No one's given us away yet.'

'There's always a first time. And it'll be our last.'

'We won't tell 'em where we live. We'll just make a rendezvous like you did with the last chap. We're bound to strike
oil sooner or later.'

'Better make it sooner then. The money won't last for ever.
We've got to move out of this hotel today.'

'Shall we sleep in that hut again tonight?'

'Good God no!' John pulled the eiderdown up round his
ears. 'We'll find another hotel. The trouble is to find one that
isn't full.'

'Our papers seem all right,' Peter said.

'The papers are all right for the moment – but what about the date on them? We were supposed to be on our way to Anklam five days ago. I know there's been a weekend but it's Wednesday now and sooner or later one of these hotel chaps is going to get suspicious.'

'Ah well, we've only enough money for another three days anyway,' Peter said cheerfully. 'Three days should be enough if we work at it.'

There was a brief silence; and John changed the subject. 'What do we have for breakfast?'

'We've enough porridge for one more meal, And there's the bread we got from the French last night.'

'Let's go down and have breakfast in the dining-room. I'll get washed.' John threw off the eiderdown, rose to his feet and stretched.

'Too risky. No sense in running into trouble.'

'Come on, Pete. A hot drink'll do us good.'

'It's too risky. What the hell. It's not worth risking everything for a cup of coffee.'

'We go into cafés and drink coffee – I don't see the difference. Come on – we'll take down some of the bread and eat it with the coffee. Start the day with something warm inside us.'

'All right – we'll go and see what it's like. But if there are any goons in uniform there it won't be worth risking.'

'We'll take our bags with us,' John said.

The dining-room was on the ground floor. It was only half-full and they sat at a corner table with a banquette seat, with their backs against the wall. A waitress came over to them and John ordered coffee. She brought two cups and a pot of coffee, but no sugar. John poured the coffee and they knew at once by the smell that it was made from acorns. John took the bread from the side pocket of his mackintosh. It was wrapped in a copy of the *Völkischer Beobachter*. Peter looked round the dining-room to see if anyone was watching them. There was an old lady at the next table, staring into space, and on the far side of the room an elderly couple were each reading half of the morning paper. At a centre table a middle-aged man who looked like a commercial traveller was writing in an exercise book. Except for the heavy smell of German tobacco smoke and an occasional 'Heil Hitler!' from the foyer they might have been in some English provincial hotel.

They sat there eating the bread and drinking the acorn coffee. Relaxed, Peter sat back on the seat; they were fooling them all along the line. He glanced casually through the glass-paned door, and stiffened suddenly. Two German officers were crossing the foyer.

There was no other door out of the dining-room. What he had always feared was to be trapped in a room with only one door and the Germans coming towards him. He had dreamed of it in the camp.

The German officers gave a perfunctory 'Heil Hitler!' as they came into the room and the door swung to behind them. They made straight for the table where Peter and John were sitting. Peter felt his stomach contract, and the piece of bread he was eating stuck in his throat. Always he had that sudden contraction of the stomach and the desire to run when danger threatened. The exhilaration came later. First there was the blind unreasoning panic to get away, to get the hell out of it. Only after that came the exhilaration and the trembling at the knees.

But the two officers were talking to each other, not looking at Peter and John. They were an Oberst and a Major and both were carrying black briefcases. The major was wearing breeches and jackboots and had a white scar from the left eye to the corner of his mouth. He wore an ornamental dagger slung from chains on his waist-belt, and on his collar the red flash of the artillery. The Oberst was less flamboyantly dressed. He was in slacks and shoes and carried no dagger, but from the top button of his uniform jacket hung the insignia of the Knight's Cross of the Iron Cross.

What are we supposed to do? Peter thought. Do we stand up when they get here? Do we speak to them? Do we 'Heil Hitler!'? I suppose this is their usual table. Is it done for foreign workers to eat at the same table as German officers?

He went on eating his bread and sipping his coffee. There was nothing they could do. They could not walk out leaving their coffee and bread on the table. They just had to sit there and take it as it came and trust that their luck would hold.

The officers seated themselves on the opposite side of their table. They both had thick colourless indoor skin, and closely-cropped hair. The Oberst wore pale-blue rimless spectacles and his mouth was small and tight. He ordered coffee from the waitress who had followed them to the table; and turned and asked the Major some questions.

Peter glanced at John out of the corner of his eye. He doesn't look worried, he thought. We're OK, we'll be OK. We'll just finish the bread and coffee and then we'll get up and walk out.

The Major opened his briefcase and took out a bundle of papers. He put on a pair of colourless rimless spectacles and began to explain the papers to the Oberst. For God's sake listen, John, Peter thought, this may be important. He grinned in-wardly. Don't be a clot. Colonels don't discuss military secrets in front of foreign workers over a hotel breakfast-table.

They drained the last of their coffee. John looked at Peter and raised his eyebrows. They rose without speaking, picked up their bags and mackintoshes and walked out through the foyer into the street.

'What were they talking about?' Peter said. 'Could you get any of it?'

'I couldn't follow it very well. It was some educational scheme I think. There was a lot about the *Hitler Jugend* and the *Hitler Mädchen.*'

'Preparing for the next war, I expect,' Peter said.

They set off at a steady pace and walked round the three sides of the Freihafen. They located the Café Schiff – closed at that early hour – but could see no Swedish shipping in the docks. Peter had imagined that there would be at least one Swedish freighter a day. Stettin was the nearest German port to Sweden, and the German war effort relied on that country for ball-bearings and Bofors guns. Perhaps at this stage of the war the goons were producing their own. He began to wonder whether Danzig mightn't be a busier international port, whether Philip had had more sense in going there. But Philip might have been caught by now. There was no future in such idle speculation. The important thing was not to miss the next

Swedish ship which docked; and to be sure of that they must have enough contacts among the French who worked in the Freihafen.

They did the round of the dockside cafés, drawing a blank. Late in the morning they decided to try the Café Schiff. They entered it through swing doors at the bottom of three steps leading directly off the street; and found a low-ceilinged smoky room full of seamen and dock workers sitting at round metal tables, drinking dark beer out of tall glasses. On the walls there were no pictures of the Fuehrer, nor did the customers give the Nazi salute on entering and leaving.

They chose a table in the corner nearest the entrance doors. Here they could talk without being overheard. In the quieter cafés they could not talk in English and had to sit in silence, slowly sipping their beer. If they wanted to talk they had to go to the lavatory, and they usually found other customers there. But here they could talk comfortably against a background of argument and chaff.

Peter had noticed two young Frenchmen at a table on the opposite side of the room. Their dark hair and fresh healthy complexions looked warm and vital compared to the Germans around them. They sat with their heads close together, arguing. They look just like us, Peter thought. We must look exactly like that when we're whispering together. I wonder what they're talking about. The longer he watched the more suspicious the French boys seemed. The one facing the room darted nervous glances from side to side as he spoke. On the spare chair at their table were two bundles tied up in coloured cloth.

'Just look at those two,' Peter said. 'Move over there so that you can see them without turning your head.'

John moved over next to him. 'They do look a bit furtive. I think I'll saunter over and find out what they're up to.'

'Good show,' Peter said. 'I think they're the only Frenchmen here.'

'Oh – I didn't mean ask their help, just have a friendly chat.'

He crossed the room, looking as young as the French boys, and as French. He stopped by their table and greeted them.

The two Frenchmen had stopped talking abruptly and seemed scared. He sat down at the table and Peter saw them grow less scared as John pulled something from his pocket and showed it to them. His kriegie disc, Peter thought; I hope no one else can see it. I won't join them, I'll stay here and watch and if they get too suspicious-looking I'll go and warn them.

But John pocketed his *Kriegsgefangener* identity disc almost immediately, leaned back in his chair and took out a packet of cigarettes. He signalled a waiter, ordered more beer and chatted easily. When he had finished his, he bade the Frenchmen *au revoir* and rejoined Peter.

'I scared them out of their wits,' he said. 'They were planning to stow away on one of the coal barges bound for Strasbourg – that's where they come from – and I went up and leered and asked them if they were staying long in Germany. They thought I was a member of the Gestapo and was just playing with them before I ran them in. They were scared as hell.'

'I bet they were.'

'They're only kids,' John said. 'They were rounded up and brought here in cattle trucks at the Releve – they'd never left home before. They're housed in a camp about ten miles outside Stettin and they come in as often as they can with all their luggage wrapped in a bundle, ready to stow away.'

'Did you get any gen?'

'Not much – they don't know any more about it than we do, rather less if anything. Money is their difficulty. They said a pal of theirs saved up forty marks which was the price an Alsatian skipper of a coal barge wanted for taking him on as an extra hand, and the fellow took it and handed their friend over to the Germans.'

'What a bastard.'

'They know who he is and they say the next time he comes to Stettin he'll get a knife in his back. That's if he ever comes here again. He won't if he's got any sense.'

'Where do they try to stow away – Reiherwerder?'

'Yes. They know a chap who works there – alternate day and night shifts and when he's on nights he lets them have his pass during the day. That way one of them goes in and looks around for a barge bound for the Rhine. If and when he finds one they reckon to go back at night and stow away on it.'

'Climbing in,' Peter said. 'Better to have two passes even if they're forged. If we haven't got a Swedish ship by the time we run out of money, that just might be a way out. We ought to be able to contact one of the escape lines in France.'

'That occurred to me,' John said, smiling. 'I asked for the loan of the pass – I thought you could make a couple of copies, it doesn't look very complicated.'

'I should be able to.' Peter was pleased to take some of the weight off John's shoulders. 'I brought some Indian ink and a sheet of carbon paper. And some thin card which ought to do. I should be able to fake 'em all right. When do we get the original?'

'They're using it this afternoon but they said they'd borrow it again tomorrow, use it in the morning, and let us have it for the afternoon if we meet them here at the same time.'

'Unless they're already on their way by then,' Peter said.

'I rather doubt it,' John said. 'They were dead serious, but not *sérieux*. If you see what I mean . . . You were quite right about the barges though,' he added. 'They do go slap through the middle of Berlin.'

'Then they'll be our very last resort,' Peter said. 'But I'll forge the passes just in case.'

They decided they had been long enough, for that morning, in the Café Schiff and moved to another café for their midday *Stammgericht*. Then they were out in the street again, at a loss what to do next. John wanted to postpone looking for a hotel until later in the day, arguing that then he could tell the proprietor that they were on their way back from Anklam and would be catching an early morning train to Breslau. Peter saw the sense in this, and proposed that they should spend the afternoon tackling some more Frenchmen on their way between the docks and the camps; but John dug his heels in. In addition to the nervous strain of doing all the talking to strangers in a foreign language and the constant fear that any one of them might give the alarm or that he might choose a German in mistake for a Frenchman, he felt the cold more keenly than Peter did. He was not only cold but he was hungry; the vegetable stew they'd had for lunch, though temporarily filling, was not nourishing, and their supply of oatmeal and dog food was nearly exhausted.

Peter gave way and suggested the cinema. So for the third afternoon in their five days of freedom they took refuge in a cinema and although they both knew that it was getting them nowhere, its warm anonymity gave them time to rest and forget their hunger. That afternoon they both slept through the main film, and when they emerged into the fading daylight they discovered that neither of them had any idea of what it had been about.

Refreshed, they tackled the problem of a room for the night. Perhaps because it was not the weekend they found one at the first hotel they tried. The large blonde middle-aged woman wedged behind the desk could not have been less interested in their documents. She took their Reichsmarks, handed them a key, and returned to her needlework.

The room was small, clean and impersonal, with pale beige walls and a grey-white bedcover. It reminded Peter of the cell in which he had spent his solitary confinement in Dalag-Luft after capture, and made him restless to get going again. It was too early for the evening call at the Café Schiff. He did not like to propose so soon another assault on the French and asked John what he would like to do to fill the time.

'Let's go and have a look at that brothel.'

'It wouldn't be open yet, would it?'

'I don't know. What time do brothels usually open?'

'God knows.'

There was a short silence.

'Where did Stafford say it was?' John asked.

'Seventeen Kleine Oder Strasse.'

'We could go and have a look at it.'

After checking the direction on Peter's map they left the hotel and cut down a cobbled street which led them out on the Bollwerk. There was a mist-ringed moon rising above the river and the streets shone wetly where they were lit by the shaded street lamps. They followed the river for a hundred yards and then turned left. Kleine Oder Strasse lay on their right hand, a narrow winding alley cutting darkly between the old houses. They followed the alley until they came to number seventeen, a tall house whose blackout was complete. On the righthand side cf the door was a white-painted sign on a black wooden board: NUR FUR AUSLANDER.

'Doesn't look very glamorous,' Peter said. 'Not even a red light.'

'If they're all Polish girls as Stafford said, they probably hate the goons. They'd make a good contact with the Swedish sailors.'

'You most likely have to show your papers as you go in. Doesn't that notice say "Foreigners Only"?'

'Yes.'

'It's too dangerous. We were told not to go there except in dire need. And you could hardly call this dire need.'

'Depends what you're going in for,' John said.

'Do you want to go in?'

'I wouldn't mind. Don't you?'

'It's too dangerous. It's nearly a year since Stafford was given the address and the Gestapo are bound to have got on to it by now. They've probably got one of their own girls in the place as a spy.'

They stood looking at the face of the tall dark house with the abrupt and unequivocal sign.

'Why don't we go in and have a look round?' John asked. 'Not tell 'em we're British – act like real French workers.'

Peter laughed. 'No – let's wait till we get to Sweden. That's the object of the operation.'

* * *

By eight o'clock that night they were sitting in the Café Schiff, eating a *Stammgericht*. It was no better and no worse than the coupon-free meal they had had in all the other cafés; a stew of potatoes, swedes, carrots and turnips without a trace of meat or herbs to give it flavour. Peter tried not to keep looking at his watch to keep track of the time; but they both knew when eight o'clock came and went without a message from the Corsican.

'I'll try one more Frenchman tonight,' John said, pushing his bowl away and wiping his lips. 'Provided you choose him.

Then I've had it.'

'That fellow looks all right.' Peter indicated a man he had been watching, a thickset wild-eyed man who was leaning across his table haranguing his companions. His eyes were alight with enthusiasm and he seemed to be urging them to do something against their will.

'Wait till he leaves the others to go to the lavatory,' John said. 'We'll follow him in and while I talk to him you stand behind him in case he yells. He's the last one though. If he's no good I'm finished for the night.'

'OK. I'll fix him if he tries to yell.'

But the man did not go to the lavatory. He looked at his watch, excused himself and walked quickly out of the café.

'After him!' Peter said, and they left their unfinished beers on the table and followed him out on to the street.

They caught him just as he was turning the first corner. '*Pardon, m'sieur*,' John began; and the man stopped and looked at them. '*Nous sommes prisonniers de guerre anglais –*' The Frenchman took him by the arm before he could say any more and hurried him back into the Café Schiff.

Peter followed. They sat down at the table where they had been sitting before. The Frenchman seemed tense and excited and still gripped John by the arm. His former companions had observed his return and were watching the three of them. The Frenchman spoke to John in a fast whisper.

Why must he look so bloody furtive? Peter thought. Why does he have to make the whole thing look like a conspiracy? And he cursed himself for picking him.

'He wants to see our kriegie discs,' John said.

Peter took the grey metal identity disc from his pocket and passed it to John who handed it with his to the Frenchman. The Frenchman took them and rubbed his hands together, the discs between his palms. '*Mon Dieu, il fait froid ce soir!*' he exclaimed, shivering theatrically, cupping his hands and blowing into them, peering at the discs. Apparently satisfied, he handed them back to John under the table, ostentatiously looking round the room while John grabbed them. By this time most of the customers were eyeing them curiously. The Frenchman began talking to John in a low voice, his mouth hidden behind his hand.

'He's going to take us to another café,' John said. 'He says it's the one the Swedish sailors always use.'

'He'll put us all in jail if he's not careful. What the hell's he want to act like that for?'

'He says he's a member of the French Resistance. He says that the café he wants to take us to is *sympathique*.'

'OK,' Peter said. 'Let's get out of here.'

Sympathique, he thought, they're all sympathetic. Why can't they talk without looking furtive all the time. Those two boys this morning looked furtive enough but this chap looks like a stage conspirator. Perhaps they always behave like that. Perhaps it's me, perhaps I'm getting nervy. Perhaps the Germans are used to French workers behaving like that and they don't notice it any more. But it certainly terrifies me.

They walked through a maze of side streets to the Frenchman's café. He led the way in, and Peter and John followed. This was brighter than the Café Schiff, and there were women. The Frenchman chose a corner seat and ordered three beers. John tried to pay for it when it came, but the Frenchman pushed the money away. '*Gardez les sous*,' he said, and launched into a long speech.

The French was too fast for Peter and he looked round the room. It was a cheerful place, brightly lit, and a pale-faced youth in a stained dinner jacket was thumping out dance music on a piano. There were a few German soldiers among the customers and they each had a girl. The people looked happier than those in the other cafés. There was a smell of food in the air, good meat food, and the tables had cloths on them.

The door opened and four military policemen came in. They looked enormous as they came in the door and Peter realized how difficult it would be to get out of the place. It was a single door and if only one soldier was standing there it would be impossible to get past him. He looked round for the lavatory and saw a door in the corner marked HERREN. As the military policemen began to check the soldiers' leave passes, he rose to his feet, crossed the café floor and went into the lavatory. It was the usual affair with a small high window opening on to a lane at the rear of the building. He made certain that the window would open and went back to the table. Two of the policemen were leaving, taking a disgruntled soldier with them. The other two sat down beside the girl he had left, easing their belts and calling for beer.

Peter interrupted the flow of French. 'There's a window in the bog,' he said. 'If anything happens we can get out that way.'

'Good show.' John turned again to the Frenchman.

A woman sitting alone at the next table caught Peter's eye and smiled at him in invitation. She had dyed red hair and was heavily made up. He looked away quickly, alarmed, hoping that she would not talk to him. He leaned towards the other two, assuming an interest in their conversation.

The Frenchman was about to leave. As they stood to shake hands the waitress passed their table. The Frenchman stopped her.

'My friends are Swedes,' he said loudly, in German. 'They are lonely in this town. If any Swedish sailors come in this evening please show them to this table.' He turned to John, said 'A demain, mon ami!' and left the café.

'The bog!' John said urgently; but it was too late. The red-haired woman was already at their table, talking earnestly to Peter in a language that was neither French nor German. Peter sat transfixed, wondering desperately how to shake her off. There was only one way.

'Ich bin Ausländer,' he said with dignity, playing his trump card. 'Nicht verstehen.' He lifted his beer glass unsteadily to his lips, deliberately spilling some, and downed the rest of it in one.

The woman turned to John and addressed him in the same language.

'I do not speak Swedish,' John said in German.

'But your French friend said that you are Swedes.'

'My friend here is Swedish. I am French.'

'His accent does not sound Swedish.'

'He is very drunk.'

The woman began to apologize for speaking to them without an introduction. She seemed deeply distressed, about to cry. The two military policemen were staring at the scene from the other side of the café. Peter realized that they had to get out, and soon. He rose clumsily to his feet and weaved between the tables to the door marked HERREN. He heard John say, 'Excuse me, *gnädige Frau!*' and knew he was following.

Safe inside the lavatory, with the door locked behind them, Peter asked, 'How was my German?'

'Terrible.'

'What was she going on about?'

'She's looking for a Swedish sailor. I think he's done her wrong – probably left without paying. She heard that furtive clot say we were Swedes and asked if we knew her boyfriend.'

'We'd better get cracking before those MPs want a leak.'

Peter stood on the lavatory seat and opened the window. He thrust his head and shoulders through the narrow opening, but soon wriggled back, grunting. 'We'll have to go feet first,' he said. 'It's a helluva drop.' By swinging on the water pipe he managed to get his legs up on to the sill and out of the window. He turned on to his side, wriggled through and landed with a thud in the street below.

John managed it more easily, with room to spare. He picked himself up off the pavement, giggling. 'I wonder what they'll do when they find the door locked.'

'Break it down, I expect. We won't go back to that place.'

'You can say that again – not for all the Swedes in Stettin.'

8

They slept late the following morning. This was the sixth day of their freedom and they were running short of money and food. They had eaten the last of their oatmeal and were determined to save two tins of dog food to eat on the ship – when they got one. Although they wore warm clothing they were always cold. The cold came from inside and was a coldness that only food could cure. The constant strain of living in the heart of an enemy city, heightened by the incident of the previous evening, was beginning to tell on nerves that had been sorely tried during the long anxious weeks before the tunnel broke. The longer they were at large in Stettin the greater the danger of their being picked up by chance, or betrayed; the quicker they met someone who would help them find a ship the less the danger. It was this Morton's fork which at one moment made John reckless – wanting to get out of Stettin by any means, in any direction – and Peter urge caution; and at the next made John reluctant to trust more strangers and Peter argue that, without taking the initiative, they would never get on board a ship bound for Sweden.

But after the near-disastrous meeting with the Swedish-speaking German woman even Peter was beginning to feel that they could make one too many chance acquaintance. After a long lie-in, and a good wash and shave, they did the round of some of the more promising dockside cafés without trying to make any new contacts. At midday they kept the rendezvous with the two boys in the Café Schiff and borrowed the Reiherwerder pass; bought them a *Stammgericht*, and then went to the Hotel Sack where the boys had heard that French workers often stayed. They got the last free room but were told by the proprietor that it could be for one night only; all the hotels in the town, he said, were fully booked for the weekend.

The Hotel Sack was modern and steam-heated. There were two beds with no space between; each made up with its sheet-enveloped eiderdown cover.

'*Wunderbar!*' John threw off his outer clothing, kicked off his shoes and sank down into the mattress. Within minutes he was fast asleep.

Peter opened his attaché-case and extracted from it a flat tin box. Inside the box were bottles of red, blue-black and Indian ink, a camel-hair brush, a razor blade, two mapping pens, a small metal ruler and an india-rubber. He laid everything out neatly on the dressing-table top and studied the pass carefully. It was a piece of thin pale pink cardboard about the size of a playing card. In the top left-hand corner was a photograph of the holder – roughly the same size as the photographs on their *Ausweis*. Thank God Stafford had supplied duplicates. To the right of the photograph was the superscription. Below these in black German-gothic lettering was the usual bureaucratic questionnaire: Name, age, sex, nationality, height, eyes, hair. Under this the signature of the Chief of Police. In the bottom left-hand corner was the well-known imprint of the eagle with spread wings surmounting a wreath-encircled swastika.

Peter noted with satisfaction that all the particulars had been filled in with pen and ink – he did not feel capable of reproducing typescript accurately. It was not the shaping of the letters so much as the intensity of the ink that was difficult to reproduce. The only way was to trace it through the carbon paper, and this was slow work, easily spoiled.

The sheet of thin card the Escape Committee had provided was almost as thick as that on which the pass was printed. He cut two pieces of the right size; cutting them carefully with the razor blade and metal ruler on the glass top of the dressing-table. He was totally absorbed in what he was doing, forgetting even the ultimate aim of the work. He would be absorbed for the rest of the afternoon and would finish the job with aching eyes and stiff shoulders; but rested and in some way renewed by the intensity of his concentration. It had been the same in the prison camp when he had been painting scenery for the theatre, or a water colour; he would realize suddenly that an afternoon had passed with him absorbed and unaware that it had gone.

He gave the two pieces of card a wash of clear water and left them to soak. He mixed a thin solution of red ink and water in one of the tooth glasses and washed this on carefully. He gave them three washes before he was satisfied that they were near enough to the colour of the pass. He left them to dry, flat on the glass above the radiator.

While the pieces of card were drying he took some tracing paper and carefully traced out the spacing of the lettering on the pass. He did not trace the actual lettering; it was too small for that. He was experienced enough to reproduce the German print freehand and with enough accuracy for it to pass for the real thing at a quick glance. Then he traced the outline of the stamp which he would later duplicate through carbon paper on to the forged passes. It was getting dark, and he switched on the electric light.

'How's it going, Pete?' John yawned and turned over to watch him.

'It'll be OK. Need a bit longer though.'

'What's the time?'

'Oh – getting on for five-thirty.'

'Then I'd better go and meet the F.F. while you finish.'

'The F.F.?'

'Furtive Frog. You remember, we said we'd meet him at the Schiff around six this evening.'

'Oh. Yes. For God's sake don't let him talk to any more goons – male or female.'

'Not bloody likely. I'll start off by telling him how damn' silly that was.'

'OK. You come and collect me as soon as you've finished with him and we'll go back there for the evening *Stamm*.'

When the two pieces of card were bone-dry he pricked out the tracing through the tracing paper and started on the lettering. He wrote slowly, taking only sufficient ink on the pen nib to draw one stroke, writing with the paper resting on the sheet of glass so that there would be no indentation made by the nib and the ink would stand up proudly It was careful, finicking work and he paused only occasionally to refill his pipe. When at last he stood back, stretched and looked at his watch it was nearly eight o'clock.

That's OK, he thought, John's obviously staying on at the Schiff in case the Corsican sends a message at eight. He inspected his handiwork. The forgeries were not perfect, not nearly up to the standard of their other papers; but they would do. He stuck the spare photographs on to the two passes with a paste he made by mixing a little dog food with water, traced the stamp through the carbon and carefully forged the signature from the original.

When the ink was dry he placed the two copies at the bottom of his attaché-case, packing the rest of the card and the two reserve tins of dog food on top to keep them flat. The genuine pass he put in his mackintosh pocket; wondering whether the two boys were also waiting at the Schiff and whether he ought to go there himself and not wait for John here. No, he decided. Better stick to our arrangement, we could miss each other en route.

Then he lay on his bed and fell asleep.

●   ●   ●

He was dreaming he had been caught in the tunnel. A fall of sand had pinned him to the floor and he was struggling to get free. It was dark and hot and the sand was smothering him. There was sand in his eyes, in his ears and in his nose, and he was swallowing sand with every breath. The more he struggled the more sand kept pouring down from the roof. Someone was digging down to save him. It was John, he knew it was John, and he kept calling to tell him where he was. He could hear the thumping of the spade as John dug furiously away to save him from being suffocated. If only he could keep the sand away from his mouth he would be all right. He pushed his hands open-palmed away from his face, clearing the sand away, pushing hard against the force of the onrushing sand . . .

Then he was wide awake in the hotel bedroom. The sand

was the pillow smothering his face and the weight of the sand was the weight of the heavy German quilt he had pulled over his chest. The sound of John digging was a heavy thumping on the door. He looked at his watch. It was ten past nine.

A male voice started shouting impatiently in German. Peter was instantly on his feet, searching his memory desperately for the right words to say 'What is it?' Ah –

'*Was ist los?*'

The man outside the door replied with a long speech from which he got only the words *Menschen* and *Kommen Sie nach unten*. Men – come downstairs. He glanced quickly round the room. Everything incriminating was in his attaché-case. Except for the pass in his raincoat pocket and the map of Stettin sewn into the armpit. Should he leave them there or take them down with him . . . ?

There was a final shout of '*Kommen Sie Schnell nach unten!*' and the sound of heavy footsteps retreating down the staircase. What the hell, he thought. If this is it it doesn't matter whether the stuff is up here or on me. For a wild moment he debated whether to destroy the passes he had forged. He told himself not to be a bloody fool, pulled on his raincoat and beret, and went down to the lobby.

Waiting there were the two French boys.

Relief flooded through him and he greeted them happily. They gabbled at him in excited French. He looked round hastily for the hall porter; he was listening to the news on a small radio, taking no interest. Peter thrust his hands in his mackintosh pocket, found the pass they had come for, put an arm round each of the boys in a fatherly embrace and urged them towards the door. With his back shielding the operation from the night porter he handed over the pass.

'*Merci beaucoup,*' he said. '*Au revoir, au revoir, à demain!*' He opened the door, practically pushed them down the steps and slammed the door behind them.

'*Danke schön, mein Herr,*' he said as he passed the reception desk. It was a mistake. The night porter promptly switched off the radio and began another long speech in German.

'*Nicht verstehen! Gute Nacht!*' Peter said, almost panicking. He hurried up the stairs and into the room, locked the door and sat exhausted on the bed. Where the hell was John? he wondered. Surely if he'd been at the Schiff he wouldn't have let those kids come here without him? He found himself sweating and realized he was still in outdoor clothes. As he was hanging up his mackintosh there was more knocking on the door; but softly this time. He unlocked it, and John walked in.

'What the hell did you lock the door for?' John asked. 'Afraid of the goons?'

'I'm not exactly afraid of them,' Peter said. 'I'm scared out of my wits. I've been having visitors.'

John looked alarmed. 'Not – '

'The French boys. Came for the pass. Didn't you send them?'

'No – I couldn't meet them. I haven't been at the Schiff – at least not for the last couple of hours. Had you finished the copies?'

'Yes. They're not bad, but let's say I'd rather not use them.'

'We won't have to.'

Peter realized then that John was jubilant, working up to good news. 'Come on – out with it. Has our barber chum got us a ship?'

'As near as dammit,' John said. 'Wait a minute though. I've got something for you. He delved into his mackintosh pocket and pulled out a large, thick, rather dirty sandwich. 'Sorry I couldn't get any paper to wrap it in.'

'Where'd you get this?' Peter asked through a mouthful of black bread and liver-sausage.

'The F.F. gave it to me. Gave us some money too. Apparently he's a Communist saboteur or something and that accounts for all the cloak-and-dagger stuff.'

'It's damn' good. Here – have half.'

'I had one – that's all for you.'

'Well come on. Tell me all about it.'

'I'd better start at the beginning.' John kicked off his shoes and lay down with his feet on the rail at the foot of his bed. Peter resigned himself to waiting. 'It was bloody cold and wet when I left here – d'you know it even began to snow? I began to think it wouldn't be so bad to get caught. None of the kriegies we met who'd been out seemed desperately disappointed, did they? I mean, the huts were warm enough and we had food of a sort and there were the chaps. And you knew what was going on.'

'I suppose you'll come to the point eventually.'

'It was a bit early so I went round the Freihafen fence to see if there was a Swedish ship. There wasn't of course, but the Russki prisoners were queueing for their soup. God, they're thin and ragged – they looked a damn' sight colder than I felt. Some of them don't even have boots or shoes, just strips of rag bound round their feet . . . But d'you know, I saw one big skinny chap pour half his soup into his mate's cup. It's funny how appalling conditions don't necessarily make men brutish.'

'The warm stench of comradeship,' Peter said. 'It's just because their conditions *are* so bad. You got the same sort of thing more at Oflag XXIB than at Sagan. Once you've got something to lose you begin to compromise. Now, what about the F.F.? And the Corsican?'

'Well, I got to the Café Schiff right on time and the F.F. was there waiting. He signalled me to a table some distance from his and then ostentatiously turned his back on me. Here we go again, I thought. He lit a cigarette and he managed to do even that furtively. So I ordered a beer and just ignored him – wrote him off as a dead loss. I thought I'd wait there for the boys, bring 'em back here to get the Reiherwerder pass, and then you and I would go back to the Schiff for the eight o'clock *Stamm*.

'Then this chap suddenly leaped to his feet and rushed out, passing my table and hissing at me to follow. He led me down the Bollwerk, up Kleine Oder Strasse past the brothel, along another side street, up a short hill and down to the river again. He plunged down some steps and through a doorway. Quite intriguing really. Frankly I thought it might be another brothel and I'd get some action at last. Actually it turned out to be a cross between a café and a night club – called the Café d'Accordion – a real dive. Singing, dancing, all that sort of thing.

'He was meeting two chums there – just as furtive as he was. When we'd settled down over a beer he began to level. Told me they were members of a French Communist Resistance group, come to Stettin to sabotage the German war effort; that they couldn't do anything to help us get out but could offer us money. I told him that was fine and we'd be very glad of it but that we needed food even more because we hadn't got ration books. He promptly disappeared into the kitchen and came back with one of those sandwiches, then when I pocketed half for you he went back and got another.'

'Not a bad chap really,' Peter said. 'Did you get the money?'

'Yes. A hundred marks.'

'Good show. That'll keep us for a few days.'

'He said it would be far safer to make an arrangement to sleep in one of the French camps than different hotels especially with our phoney papers.' John laughed. 'Not his camp, mark you. When we finished our beers he and his chums left, telling me not to follow for at least ten minutes. Didn't want me to see the direction, I suppose.' He sat up suddenly, swinging his feet to the floor. 'Then it happened,' he said with dramatic emphasis.

Peter waited in silence.

'I felt a kind of prickling at the back of my neck – you know how one does – turned round and there was Jo-Jo the Corsican sitting with one other chap at a table full of empty glasses, staring at me. He beckoned me over and tore me off the hell of a strip for not keeping the eight o'clock date at the Schiff, said he'd sent a colleague there with a message. When I explained and apologized he warned me to be careful of the F.F. who he said was enthusiastic but inexperienced. Then he introduced the man with him as Pierre and handed over to him.

'Pierre said that another Frenchman – *un homme très sérieux* – is going to Sweden the day after tomorrow. He said if this chap agrees we can go along too.' John crossed to the mirror and began to hum *'Auprès de ma blonde'*.

'How?' Peter asked bluntly. 'I thought there weren't any Swedish ships in the Freihafen. If one docks tomorrow it won't be ready to sail the day after.'

'I don't know – I've told you all Pierre told me. We've just got to convince this chap we're socially OK and he'll tell us all the details.'

'Where do we meet him?' Peter wanted to do it now; get it settled.

'Pierre will pick us up at the Café d'Accordion tomorrow evening soon after six o'clock – when he finishes work in the docks. He'll take us to his camp to meet this chap, who's called André by the way. If André agrees we can go with him Pierre says we can sleep in his hut tomorrow night.' John began to take off his collar and tie. 'D'you realize Pete, we might be in Sweden the day after?'

'I hope this chap speaks English,' Peter said.

9

'You're quite sure he said Sweden? Not France? He's not another of these coal-barge addicts?'

'He said Sweden.' John's voice was drowsy, muffled by his bedclothes.

'I can't understand why a Frenchman should want to go to Sweden,' Peter insisted.

'Oh for God's sake!' John sat up with a jerk. 'Perhaps he's got a girl there – perhaps he's wanted for murder in France – perhaps he needs a holiday – perhaps he wants to join de Gaulle in London. I thought we were going to have a good long sleep this morning until it's time to give up the room.'

'Sorry,' Peter said. He was already washed, shaved and dressed. 'I feel a bit restless. I think I'll go for a walk round Freihafen and see what's going on.'

'Don't *talk* to anyone.' John lay down again and settled deeper into the mattress.

'You know me. I can be silent in seven languages.'

'What the hell's happened to you lately? Quoting Hemingway last night and now a goon preacher of all things. I thought you were practically illiterate.'

'Oh – you don't have to go to Oxford to study philosophy . . . Well, I'm off. I can't stick around here any longer doing nothing.'

A fine drizzle of rain was falling and he buttoned his mackintosh tightly round his neck. The cloth beret gave no protection to his face and he cursed the inventor of such idiotic headgear.

It was the first time he had been out in the streets without John. He felt vulnerable, acutely aware and almost lightheaded; an intensification of the mood which had haunted him ever since they had crawled from the narrow tunnel and escaped into the lesser darkness of the forest, a feeling of incredulity, of too-good-to-be-true.

It was raining steadily by the time he got to the Freihafen and he began to regret leaving the warm hotel room. But for him waiting inactive was the worst part. Not knowing the score he could not even plan ahead. This André must have a plan, he thought. If he is going to Sweden it must be by ship. Unless he's stealing an aircraft. He dismissed the idea as absurd.

He walked round the perimeter fence of the docks, hands in pockets, collar turned up round his ears, head bent to the driving rain, and peered sideways studying the shipping. Through the gaps between the warehouses he could see only German freighters; but perhaps there was a smaller Swedish ship hidden by one of the large Customs sheds. In spite of the rain there was the usual dockside activitity. Tall cranes swinging crates against the grey overcast, freight trains shunting, dockers hanging about or circulating in slow motion over the wet cobbles, armed guards and uniformed officials sheltering under the overhanging roofs, tugs hooting. He found it hard to believe that, tomorrow, he might be on the other side of the barrier and hiding in the hold of a ship bound for Sweden.

It was nearly eleven o'clock – about time John got up. He walked quickly back to the Hotel Sack.

John woke to see Peter hanging his wet mackintosh on the radiator. 'Is it still raining?'

'Cats and dogs. Come on – *raus, raus!*' He wrung out his beret over the wash-basin.

'Oh hell. It's warm and dry in bed.'

'They'd never believe us back in the camp,' Peter said. 'We get away and all we do from then on is lie on our bunks. Too typically kriegie . . . Let's try your Accordion place for a *Stamm*, they make bloody good sandwiches.'

*   *   *

When they got there they found the Café d'Accordion closed. It had an abandoned air as though it would never open again.

'D'you think it's been shut down?' John looked worried. 'It was a pretty blatant sort of joint.'

'Oh I expect they only open in the evenings. If it's still closed at six o'clock I expect the Corsican will get a message to the Schiff . . . Let's try the city centre for a *Stamm* – the standard might be higher.'

The café they chose was crowded but they managed to find a table for two. When John had ordered the beers and *Stammgericht* he went to the lavatory, leaving Peter to keep his place. He sat there day-dreaming. At first he did not realize that he was being addressed. Then he looked up and saw the angry German face glaring down at him. *Ich bin Ausländer, nicht verstehen.* He was about to say it when he realized that the German was asking if the other chair was occupied. Nothing could have been more plain; the man was standing one hand resting on the back of the chair, eyebrows raised in inter-rogation.

Oh hell, Peter thought, the blighter will sit down if I don't say something. Inspiration came. *'Das ist besetzt!'* he said, pointing to John's chair, *'aber das ist frei!'* pointing wildly across the café.

The man thanked him and left. John came back.

'Some goon wanted your chair.'

'How did you manage to stave him off?'

'Oh, I explained that the chair was occupied and suggested that he sat somewhere else. He seemed a decent chap. Had quite a conversation with him as a matter of fact.'

After lunch they emerged into the street to find that it had stopped raining. They decided to walk round the docks again. Down the Bollwerk where the River Oder flowed dark and sluggish and the gulls wheeled and swooped in the sky, jeer-ing and shrieking at them because they were earthbound, star-ing at them with beady yellow eyes, diving and soaring in the perfect freedom of flight. Past the flotillas of motor torpedo boats and E-boats, and the ships' pinnaces waiting to dash out to the destroyers moored in the roads off the outer port of Swinemünde. Past the Café d'Accordion, still dark and closed. Over the bridge and out opposite the gates of the Freihafen. There was no Swedish ship in sight.

They went into the Café Schiff for a beer. It was half-empty and they sat in silence, each with his own thoughts about what the evening's encounter would bring.

Peter was thinking about the French. If this thing falls through, he thought, perhaps we'd better make for Danzig. Write off the French completely, not risk the barges which might take weeks to cross Germany to France. Jump a goods train because we won't have the right papers, and gamble everything on getting a ship in Danzig before our money runs out . . .

He found that he was looking at a man seated at the next table. He had seen the face before – noticed it several times, but almost subconsciously. All at once it seemed that the man had been in every café they had visited. The face had cropped up time and again but he had not consciously recognized it as familiar before.

His heart lurched. It had caught up with them at last. He wondered which of the French had given them away. He had always known that it was too good to be true – too easy. Now that they were confronted by it he was almost relieved. He leaned over to John. 'See that fellow at the next table?'

'Which one?'

'By the radiator. The florid type with glasses. He came in soon after us.'

'What about him?'

he *is* following us.'

'Nonsense.'

'He is, I tell you. He's been in nearly every café we've been to the last couple of days.'

'Why the hell should he follow us? If they wanted to pick us up they'd do it without following us.'

'Might want to see what we're up to,' Peter said. 'Anyway, he *is* following us.'

'You're getting the jitters.'

'All right, we'll prove it. Drink up and we'll go to another café.'

They finished their beer and without looking in the man's direction they got up and left. They walked quickly down the street to the next café. They ordered more beer and sat watching the door. The man did not come in.

'Imagination,' John said. 'Let's go back to the Schiff.'

'No. Have a beer here.'

'We'll go back afterwards then. No good being uncertain about it.'

When they got outside it was nearly dark. They turned to the right out of the door and started back down the street towards the Schiff.

'He's behind us,' Peter said quietly. 'He must have been waiting outside.'

John glanced over his shoulder. 'Yes – that does look like the same chap. What the hell are we going to do?'

'We can't keep that date at the Accordion – can't talk to anyone while he's with us. We'll have to drop him somehow.'

'Let's go to the place where we climbed out of the window.'

'No – they'd be on to us as soon as we walked in. Don't suppose they've repaired the lock yet anyway. We'd better separate.'

'OK,' John said. 'Where shall we meet?'

'Can't be any of the cafés he's seen us in. I know – the cinema. The one who gets there first can wait for the other in the queue.'

'Right. When we get to the next crossroads I'll go right and you go left. He may hesitate and then we stand a chance of losing him straight away. If not it's up to the one he follows.'

They walked on at the same pace until they reached the crossroads. Then they separated and began to walk fast. Peter turned left again, then right and out on to the Bollwerk. There were a number of people about, mainly dock-workers. He pressed on, threading his way between them and not looking back. Mustn't let him think I know I'm being followed – if it's me he's following. If he knows that they'll arrest us right away. He slowed down and began to fill his pipe, tamping the tobacco down carefully. He patted his pockets as though looking for matches; pretending not to find any he turned and walked back the way he had come. As he turned he saw the figure of a man slip sideways into a dark doorway.

He walked past the doorway without looking into it, back to

a café where he knew there was a permanent light burning on the counter for customers to light their cigarettes. He lit his pipe at the flame and came out on to the street again. He came out fast and turned in the direction he had been going in the first place, hoping to catch a glimpse of the man who was following him. He did not see him, but both logic and instinct told him that the man was still on his tail.

He walked on down the Bollwerk, crossed the bridge by the railway station and came out on to the road leading to Reiher-werder. There was a tram at the next stop, just about to start. He ran the last fifty yards and jumped on to the platform as the tram gathered speed. The conductor grabbed his arm and shouted at him furiously. Wedged on the boarding platform he looked back down the street; but he did not see his pur-suer.

At the next two stops there was a car close behind and he thought it might have been commandeered to continue the chase. At the third stop there was no car; so he climbed down off the tram and crossed the road. He caught the next tram going back into town. No one else boarded it. He did not get off at the Bollwerk but went right on into the town and made for the cinema. John detached himself from the queue.

'He followed you,' John said. 'I stopped to light a cigarette and saw him chasing you down the street. Did you drop him all right?'

'Yes – jumped a tram and gave him the slip.'

'What do we do now?'

'Let's get out of this. The quicker we get out of here the better. Let's jump a train up to Danzig.'

'Seems a pity to waste all the contacts we've made – just as we were getting somewhere at last. If we go up to Danzig we'll have to start all over again.'

'All right – we'll go to the Café d'Accordion first. We've got to warn your chum Pierre anyway. Don't suppose he'll want to compromise André's plans by taking us to his camp – but you never know. If he doesn't, we'll go straight to the goods yard and get to hell out of Stettin.'

They heard the hum of voices and the sound of music as they turned the corner into the street. Peter followed John through the wooden swing doors, stumbled after him down three steps and found himself in a long low room dim with tobacco smoke and crowded with people enjoying themselves. Some of them were singing to the music played by a wizened elderly pianist and a hunchback gypsy with an accordion. As Peter and John paused at the foot of the steps, peering round for a free table, the musicians switched abruptly to *J'Attendrai*. Oh God, Peter thought, Pat! Jean Sablon's record of that had been her favourite. For a moment he was back in the camping punt on the Thames that long hot summer before the war, with Pat lifting and dropping the pole in the green shade of the willows, the water cascading off the pole in a shower of diamonds, and himself lying on cushions in the stern lazily working the portable gramophone. Then the moment of grief and nostalgia had passed and he was standing in a noisy café in the heart of an enemy port; his senses alert, his mind observing. Most of the conversation seemed to be in French, although occasionally he could pick out the singsong tones of Scandinavia. What damn' bad luck, he thought, to get on to this place just as we're forced to change our plans.

They stood by the bar, drinking beer and waiting for a table. Next to Peter, leaning with both arms on the zinc top, was a big middle-aged man with a long scar from below his left eye to his jawbone. He looked like a seaman. He was drunk, rolling drunk, and he was gabbling a mixture of German, French and English. He was trying to sell the barman a boiler suit.

'How much?' Peter said in English, with his back to the bar so that the barman should not hear.

The big man turned round and stared at him solemnly. 'How much? What money you give me? I spik English, I spik German, I spik Dutch. I spik French, I spik all languages . . .' His head lolled loosely on to his arms, then he jerked upright. 'I pinch 'em from a lighter.' He flung an arm affectionately round Peter's shoulders. 'I pinch 'em from a lighter tied alongside my ship. Now I sell 'em, see? I spik English, I spik

American, I spik –'

'What's your ship?' Peter asked quietly. 'Where is she?' He suddenly felt reckless, wanting to seize an opportunity, to gamble everything.

The man did not want to talk quietly. 'I spik Swedish, I spik German . . .' His voice trailed away and he went out like a light, flat on his face on the floor, knocking John's beer from his hand. He lay sprawled among the feet of the people at the bar, the spilled beer soaking the back of his jacket and his hair.

Peter's mood of recklessness evaporated as quickly as it had come, and he found himself sweating. He saw a free table by the wall and led John away to it.

'Did you think he was Swedish?' John asked.

'I did at first – but not now. More likely a Dane or Norwegian.'

'I thought you'd gone mad, talking to him in English.'

'I think I did too. A case of any port in a storm I suppose . . . D'you think this chap Pierre gave us up before we got here?'

'I don't know. I suppose he might have. What's the time?'

'Past seven.'

They sat in silence, sipping beer; worrying how long they should wait before giving it up and trying for Danzig. Peter watched a waitress edge her way between the close-packed tables, balancing a tray full of glasses of beer. A young Frenchman at one of the tables she passed put his arm round her waist and began to croon at her in burlesque German.

'*Ach, mein Liebe,*' he said. '*Ach, mein Liebling, mein Liebchen!*'

With her free hand she thrust his arm away contemptuously. He made an obscene gesture and laughed. He was about twenty-five, tall and powerful-looking, with a dark face and angry brown eyes, a wide full mouth, straight nose and unruly hair. He wore a scarf round his neck and his jacket was too short in the sleeves. He was sitting slouched back in his chair, a cigarette dangling from the corner of his mouth; just drunk enough to do as he pleased. He looked as though he usually did as he pleased, Peter thought. He looked like a man to help you if he wanted to help you – not a man to be frightened to help you.

'Why not ask that chap over there if he knows where we can find Pierre?' Peter said, pointing him out to John. 'He looks a good type.'

'It's bloody unlikely. There must be hundreds of Pierres in Stettin.'

'We can't wait here much longer. That chap may have followed you here last night.'

'Oh – all right. I suppose anything's better than you accosting drunks in English.'

John rose, crossed to the Frenchman's table and greeted him, pointing to where Peter sat, inviting him to join them. There was a rapid exchange; and when John returned, followed by the Frenchman, both were smiling.

'Some of your hunches aren't bad. This is René and he's going to take us to Pierre – he's in the same camp. Knows Jo-Jo too – in fact Jo-Jo asked him to look out for a ship for us.'

'Have you told him we're being followed?'

'Yes – he wants to leave right away. Reckons the sooner we're off the streets the safer for everyone.'

'I'm ready.'

As Peter pushed back his chair he glanced round the café; the quick furtive glance that he had scoffed at in the French but had unconsciously acquired himself. And in that quick glance he saw the man who had been following them.

He was standing with his back against the bar, staring at them through his glasses, sipping a beer.

Peter felt a sudden anger against the fate that had lured them on with every promise of success only to let them down at the very last minute. An idea flashed through his mind: to lead the man down to the waterfront and murder him, throttle him and throw his body into the river. And then commonsense came to his rescue and a fatalism that had grown in him since he had been taken prisoner. They'd had a good run. The only thing was to submit now and go back quietly. There was no use struggling against it. There was a time to struggle and a time to submit. They'd had a good try and now if they were lucky they would go back to the prison camp – to try again. But he had a desperate desire to have the last week over again; to turn back the clock and not make the fatal mistake that had brought the Gestapo on their track. He'd have to work out what it was. He turned to John and tapped him on the knee.

'That chap who followed us is by the bar.'

John was saying something to René and René was smiling. Then John told him what Peter had said. René looked at the man by the bar and his smile grew broader.

My God, the man's cool, Peter thought. He watched as René got up, crossed the café floor and exchanged a few words with the man at the bar. The man left the café. René turned to them, laughing.

'That is Jo-Jo's brother. He has been following you for the last two days to see that you do not talk to the wrong people. *Allons, mes vieux* – all your problems are resolved.'

*   *   *

They had some miles to walk before they got to the camp but they walked them cheerfully. This was no longer aimless walking. It was not walking because they dared not stay in one place, because they felt hunted and if they walked they felt less hunted. It was not walking round the docks, round the town, in search of Swedish seamen whom they hardly expected to meet; frightened all the time that they would be stopped and their papers demanded. It was not walking because they were hungry and cold, and if they walked they felt less hungry and less cold. It was walking to get somewhere.

When they reached the camp they went in openly through a main gate. This camp was larger than the Corsican's, built as a Hitler Youth labour camp in the thirties, and not as a wartime prison. There was a three-strand barbed wire fence which was a gesture rather than a defence. The huts were clean and dry. There were ten beds in René's room, ten lockers, and a table and some stools.

René introduced them to his room-mates, sat them down at

the table and placed in front of them half a loaf of black bread, a lump of lard-like margarine and a few slices of hard sausage which he declared was made from horse-flesh. Then he went to find Pierre.

They ate slowly, not talking, exhausted by the crises and triumphs of the day. René returned and told them that Pierre was expecting André, but later that night. He suggested it was better to get some sleep while they could. They shared René's bed and he shared with another man. It was almost good to be back on the hard prison bed; back in the live darkness of the crowded room, the friendly sound of sleeping men, and the sudden-glowing cigarette of the man who could not sleep.

10

René was shaking his shoulder. There was another man with him but in the dark Peter could not see his face. He and John scrambled off the bunk. René said something urgently.

'What is it?' Peter asked.

'Pierre's come for us,' John said. 'André is here and wants to see us now. He's sailing today – what the hell's the time? – and it's entirely up to him whether we can go along too.'

'Hell's bells!' Peter had thought it was already fixed.

As they followed Pierre's torchlight down the corridor, John muttered, 'René told me that this chap André's a big noise and not too easy to get on with.'

'Then you'd better do all the talking,' Peter said. 'Use your boyish charm.'

The tall thin figure ahead of them paused outside a door and said something over his shoulder.

'André wants to interview us one at a time,' John said uneasily. 'Me first because I speak French. You're to wait outside.'

Christ. Schoolboy stuff. 'OK – in you go.'

He sat cross-legged, leaning back against the wall in the darkness of the corridor; thinking they might bloody well have supplied a stool. There was a low murmur of voices from the room, but he could distinguish no words. In spite of the discomfort he nodded off to sleep.

•   •   •

'Your turn now.' John sounded cheerful.

'Everything fixed?'

He giggled. 'I'm not supposed to talk to you.'

What a charade, Peter thought. He rose stiffly to his feet and walked into the room.

It was a smaller room than René's. It had only two bunks but there were three men seated on chairs behind the table. One of them was Pierre. VIVE DE GAULLE and the Cross of Lorraine were daubed roughly in bright blue paint on the wall facing the door. A single stool stood in front of the table.

The men did not get up or offer to shake hands. The one in the centre indicated the stool.

'Please sit, *m'sieur*. My name is André. I believe that you understand a little French but do not speak it.'

'Very little,' Peter said. 'I regret – '

'We will commence,' the man interrupted brusquely. 'What is your name?'

'Peter Howard.'

'Rank?'

'Flight lieutenant, Royal Air Force.'

'Your friend's name?'

'John Clinton.'

'Rank?'

'Captain, Royal Artillery.' Why hadn't they asked John, he wondered. Or were they playing games? He noticed that the third man was making notes.

'How old is he?'

'Twenty-three.'

'And you?'

'Thirty-two.'

'So old? You are an old man to be a flier.' André laughed shortly.

Peter looked at him, not commenting. He saw a sturdy man in his middle twenties, with a smooth round face and greenish-brown eyes. His hair was brown, cut *en brosse*. A tough man, Peter decided, but conceited. He resolved not to lose his temper.

'When were you captured?'

'December 17th 1942.'

The man taking notes said something sharply in French.

'*Si?*' André said, and turned back to Peter. 'You and your friend were in the same bomber crew?'

'No. I told you – he is an Army captain.'

'He was flying with you?'

'No. He was captured in the desert behind the German lines.'

'On what date?'

'December 17th 1942.' He grinned as he said it.

'An extraordinary coincidence . . . Were you wounded when you were shot down?'

'Only slightly.'

'Show me.'

More theatrics. Oh well. He stood and began to remove his jacket.

'No – do not derange yourself. You look tired. Two years is a long time to be a prisoner of war.'

'I was in the bag only ten months.' He spoke patiently.

'Ah yes. *Bien entendu.* One must congratulate you on your successful escape.'

'We're not out of Germany yet.'

'That is true.' André got to his feet and walked round the table to where Peter sat on the low stool. He pulled a packet of cigarettes from his pocket and offered him one.

'No thank you.' He did not like the taste of tobacco before breakfast.

'So? You do not smoke?'

'A pipe. During the daytime.'

Suddenly the man leaned forward and struck him lightly in the face. Peter's reaction was immediate and instinctive. He lunged to his feet, kicked the stool clear, grabbed his opponent's coat lapels in his left fist and swung back his right arm. André ducked his head sideways, dodging the blow. Peter heaved him upright and swung again.

'*Non!*' André said, gasping, trying to push him away. '*Attends! Ecoutes!*'

Peter hesitated, feeling foolish, and slackened his grip. André moved quickly out of range, behind the table. The two men sitting there were laughing.

'What the hell did you do that for?'

'It was a – *une preuve*,' André said, adjusting his rumpled jacket. 'I expected you to react with words in your own language. Then if you had been a Boche stool pigeon I would have known.'

'And now you don't,' Peter said.

'Oh – it worked *assez bien*. You did not shout *Donner und Blitzen* or *Heil Hitler!*, or pull out a pistol or blow a whistle. I am now prepared to believe that you are indeed *un sal anglais.*'

One of the other Frenchmen said something and André smiled ruefully. 'Your friend,' he said, seating himself again at the table, 'reacted in a more civilized fashion. He merely called me *salaud* – and in French.'

'What about this ship to Sweden?' Peter wanted to get on with it.

'*Mais oui*. The ship.' He had reassumed command. 'It is a Danish ship and you may voyage in it as far as Copenhagen. There you will be put in touch with a man who helps Jews across the Oresund to Sweden.'

'But this man –' Peter indicated Pierre, ' – told my friend that you were going to Sweden in the ship.'

There was a moment's silence. André frowned at Pierre and said something in quick curt French. Pierre nodded, embarrassed. André turned back to Peter.

'Yes. I go direct. But I have discussed your case with the man responsible and he agrees that it might jeopardize the escape route of our organization here if you come with me all the way.'

'How d'you think we'd jeopardize it?'

'There are many Nazi spies in Sweden. *Evidemment* you would talk to people when you are there. One has told me that even here in Stettin, in *Germany*, you have talked to people without discrimination.'

'Only to Frenchmen.'

'And to one drunken Dane,' André said. 'The bosun of the Danish ship on which we shall sail.'

Peter digested this, and said: 'Is he your responsible contact?'

'No – it is one of the ship's officers. Be content, he will

interest himself in your crossing to Sweden.'

'I would like to meet him.'

'He speaks no English.'

'All ship's officers speak some English.'

'*Mon ami* – you have the luck that I agree to your coming with me as far as Copenhagen. If you do not wish to come, you have only to say.' With an expressive Gallic shrug, he leaned back in his chair.'

The unspoken threat hung between them while Peter considered. Copenhagen was better than Danzig. And once on board ship, out of Germany . . . 'Thank you,' he said grudgingly. 'I will discuss it with my friend and if he agrees we will be glad to go with you as far as Copenhagen.'

André smiled. 'There is no need to discuss it with Jean – he is enthusiastic.'

Force majeure, Peter thought. That settles it then. 'When do we embark?'

'Jo-Jo le Corse will come here for you later in the morning and take you to a rendezvous with one of the crew. This man will bring seamen's cards and dock passes and accompany you to the ship.'

•   •   •

It was nearly midday when the barber arrived. Peter wanted to cross-question him about the Danish ship and about André's own plans; but Jo-Jo was so pleased that he had found them a way out of Germany, so confident that they would both be equally pleased, that he remained silent. Pointless anyway; they were committed now.

Outside the sun was shining and a fresh westerly wind was tearing the last few leaves off the roadside trees. Jo-Jo chatted happily to John in French as the three of them walked briskly into the town and down towards the Freihafen. Realizing that he was tramping these streets for the last time, that he would soon be out of Germany, Peter's mood changed again to one of euphoria. Careful, he told himself. We're not home and dry yet. Somehow we've got to fix it that we go all the way.

They rounded the corner to the Café Schiff and a man

who had been standing outside began to walk towards them. He was fair-haired, fresh-complexioned, and looked young enough to be a student. He wore a neat short blue overcoat and carried a small-brimmed brushed trilby hat. He held out his free hand to Jo-Jo and smiled at Peter and John.

'The two Englishmen,' Jo-Jo told him.

'Yes, I think so. I am very pleased.' He gave an oddly formal bow, holding his hat in both hands against his chest. 'I take you to my ship.'

'First we drink a beer together?' Jo-Jo seemed reluctant to lose his protégés.

'Thank you.' The boy considered. 'I have brought papers for one. I take one Englishman now and I will come back to the Schiff for the other.'

'You go first, Pete,' John said. 'Jo-Jo and I'll have a beer while we wait.'

'*Bon voyage, mon camarade!*' Jo-Jo wrung Peter's hand, clapped him on the shoulder, turned abruptly and led John off to the café.

Peter realized then that he had not thanked the Corsican, and felt churlish. He wanted to run after him and tell him how grateful he was for all that he had done. He hesitated. Jo-Jo and John went down the steps into the Café Schiff. It was too late.

'We go now,' the Dane said. 'If you are ready?'

He's too young to be one of the ship's officers, Peter thought. He can't be the 'responsible man'. But he might know something.

'What happens when we get to Copenhagen?'

'I do not know.'

'How shall we get to Sweden?'

'I do not know – but it will be arranged.' The boy was looking worried. 'Please. We must go to my ship. I give you the passes now, where no one can see. Then we go through the gates separately, into the Freihafen. Please turn to the right inside. Walk slowly so that I can overtake you. Then follow me, but do not come too close. If I stop to talk to anyone, walk past us and slow down. When we reach the ship follow me very quickly up the gangplank.'

At the gates the soldier on guard was talking to a police-man. They both looked at the passes without interest and waved Peter through. He walked after the Dane across the railway tracks and down to the quayside; openly and in daylight where he and John had crept furtively and in the dark. He rounded the corner of a warehouse and saw the Danish ship. A small black freighter called the *S.I. Norensen*, with *Koben-havn* lettered below the name. There was a rough gang-plank leading steeply amidships. Close by the gangplank Russian prisoners were loading the forward hold under the supervision of a German guard.

The Dane walked up the plank, edged along the side-deck under the high bulwarks and vanished down a companionway in the bows of the ship. Peter followed and found himself in the forecastle. The Dane motioned him to a seat without speaking and went back up the companionway.

Light came dimly through salt-encrusted portholes. Gradu-ally Peter's eyes adjusted and he looked round him. The cabin was triangular, lined on two sides with two-tier bunks. The apex of the triangle was the bows of the ship and at the base of the triangle, next to the steep companionway, was a cast-iron stove with a cream-enamelled kettle boiling on the hot-plate. He was sitting on one of the benches which ran each side of a long deal table which occupied all the floor-space be-tween the bunks. In the shadows of an upper bunk a figure rolled over on its side.

'Ah – *c'est toi, mon vieux*. Where is the good Jean?'

He recognized André's voice and was relieved to find it friendly. 'The Dane's gone back for him.'

'That must be Sigmund. *C'est un brave gars*.'

'When do we sail?'

'This afternoon. Are you a good sailor?'

'I think so.'

'Soon you will be sure. One tells me there is wind. To sleep is the best preventive.' He turned over, his face to the ship's side, and was soon asleep again.

Peter knelt on an empty bunk and looked out of a port-hole. John was following Sigmund along the quay. They both looked unconcerned, normal. It's going to be OK, Peter thought, we're going to make it. But he wanted to see the hawsers being pulled in, to feel the ship move, the roll and lurch of it, to hear the water rushing past the hull and know that they were on their way.

Then John and Sigmund were in the forecastle, warming their hands at the stove. They were in high spirits. 'We got past the guards at the gate with no trouble,' Sigmund said; and Peter realized how dangerous it had been, what a risk he had taken, to fetch them on board. He felt another surge of confidence and knew that they would get from Copenhagen to Sweden.

A heavy body thumped down the companionway, half-fell and righted itself. A big man filled the space between the table and the stove; middle-aged, fleshy, with a long scar white against the stubble of grey beard. His eyes were pale blue, red-rimmed and bloodshot, and he smelled strongly of schnapps.

'This is the bosun,' Sigmund said quietly.

'Yes,' Peter said. 'We met him ashore.'

'You boys all right now. I'm Larensen, see?' The big man grinned down at them. 'Call me Olaf. I'm de head man round here. I send Sigmund for you, see. I fix everything. You don't have to worry now.'

'Excuse me.' Sigmund rose to his feet. 'I leave you now. I am on watch.' He stripped off his shore-going clothes and pulled a thick white-and-black patterned seaman's jersey over his head. He looked solemnly at Peter. 'You will be home for Christmas maybe,' he said, and swung up the companionway.

Larensen was talking to John. 'You an aviator?'

'No,' John said. 'I'm a soldier.'

'A soldier eh?' He pulled a full bottle of schnapps from his coat pocket. 'You boys like a drink?' He took out the cork and wiped the top of the bottle with his hand before offering it to John. 'What you do before the war?'

John took a drink from the bottle and set it down on the table. 'I was at the university.'

'A professor, eh?' He turned to Peter. 'He too young to be a professor.'

'He was a student,' Peter explained.

'He was a professor,' Larensen said.

'All right,' Peter said, 'he was a professor.'

The other foredeck hands came in one by one. Three young men and a boy. In their shore-going rig of smart suits and over-coats the men looked little older than Sigmund had; but when they had changed into sweaters and overalls they too became at once men and more dependable. They clustered round the stove and each took a pull from Larensen's bottle of schnapps. They did not seem surprised to find strangers in the forecastle and no explanations were given.

The boy began to fry eggs and bacon in a deep black pan on the top of the stove. Peter sat on the bench, his back against a lower bunk, drinking schnapps from the bottle as it was passed round, smelling the frying bacon. One of the crew offered him a cigarette but he could not smoke. His stomach was turning over and he was nearly sick from the smell of the frying bacon and the sound of sizzling and spluttering in the pan. He could not understand how André slept on.

It's true, he thought, your mouth does water. He sat there trying to talk to Larensen until the boy placed a plate covered with eggs and bacon in front of him. With an effort he passed it to John. He watched Larensen clumsily cutting thick slices of white bread from the loaf on the table. Then another plate came up and was pushed in front of him. They set to and ate, quickly and thoroughly, wiping their plates with bread when they had finished.

'You boys were hungry, eh?'

'Yes,' John said. 'That was the best meal I've had for a year.'

Larensen opened a cupboard and brought back a large piece of cake on a plate. 'Made from eggs,' he said proudly. 'Our last cargo was eggs – eggs for Germany!' He made a short explosive sound with his pursed lips. 'You boys eat good, then you sleep until the ship ready for sea.'

With a feeling of security and the knowledge that for the moment there was nothing else they could do, they slept deeply. A couple of hours later Larensen woke them with mugs of hot sweet coffee and thick jam sandwiches. He sat opposite them while they drank and ate, his two mahogany-coloured, dirt-grained and calloused hands resting on the edge of the table. Peter noticed that one of the fingers of his right hand was missing.

'Soon I gotta hide you boys,' he said. 'Ship ready for sea now an' German soldiers come search all over – bring dogs and tear gas.' He laughed at their expressions of alarm. 'André! Wake up! You tell 'em I spik truth. That fockin' frowgaiter always sleeping,' he told Peter in a loud aside. 'Thinks the old *Norensen* a fockin' cruise liner. You finished, professor? Now I gotta hide you.'

He edged sideways along the bench towards the bows of the ship and lifted out a panel in the apex of the triangle, revealing a cubby-hole about six feet deep. 'André – you show 'em!'

'*Merde!*'

André slid down from the upper bunk and dragging his blanket with him climbed into the forepeak. Peter and John followed. Larensen stood shining a torch on them while they tried to make themselves comfortable on coils of old rope. There were a few rusting tins of paint, and a strong smell of paint, turpentine and tar. The walls were the sides of the ship, cold steel with water condensing and dripping down them.

Larensen passed a bottle of water, an empty bottle and a funnel into the forepeak after them. 'I leave you dis torch,' he said. 'Don' shine it if you hear voices and don' spik. Germans come down to fo'c'sle, but they won' use tear gas in fo'c'sle. I give 'em schnapps, see? So you keep quiet. You make noise – ' he drew his hand across his throat in cutting gesture. 'Don' smoke or you cough. I fix 'em, see? I fix 'em good. If they bring dog in fo'c'sle I fix 'im too. I got meat and pepper ready, I fix 'im good.'

He replaced the panel, leaving them in darkness. John shone the torch and they settled themselves down to wait. Wrapped in his blanket, André slept. But Peter and John did not feel like sleeping now. They sat crossed-legged on the rope, unable to talk, aware of every step on the deck above their heads. The atmosphere was cold and damp, and in spite of their mackintoshes, sweaters and woollen underwear they shivered. Once they heard the sound of military boots and the whining of a dog and then German voices shouting from the quay. After that there was silence. They were tempted to tap on the panel separating them from the fo'c'sle; thinking it must be over, that they would be able to breathe fresh air and stretch their cramped limbs. They had long since filled the empty bottle and Peter wished that he had not drunk so much coffee. The cold was almost unbearable, waves of cold from the wet steel hull, cold which numbed their limbs and deadened their minds. Escape is all coldness, Peter thought. Coldness and waiting. It's heat sometimes in digging and in running away. But mostly it's coldness and hunger and hanging about waiting. And by God it teaches you patience.

Then they heard the Germans come below into the cabin. They heard the loud voice of Larensen talking German, laughter and the sound of a glass against a bottle; and the heavy dragging movements as the soldiers eased themselves on to the benches that ran along underneath the bunks.

Peter sat there riding it out. He had forgotten the cold now and the fact that his bladder was full. He was listening for an excited tone in the German voices and the sniffing of the dogs. He thought he heard the scratching of a dog's paw but he could not be certain. Through the darkness he could feel John's tenseness as he crouched beside him, straining to hear the voices in the cabin on the other side of the wooden panel.

Then he heard them leaving, heard the triumphant note in Larensen's voice as he followed them up the companionway out of the forecastle. He heard their boots tramping across the deck and heard Larensen clatter back down the companionway and squeeze past the table to remove the panel. After the pitch blackness of their hiding place the dim light of the forecastle was almost blinding.

'I gottem,' Larensen said triumphantly. 'I fix 'em. You come out now. We have somep'n to eat, then I hide you again, in de bilges.'

When they had clambered out into the forecastle and were stretching themselves, he grabbed Peter's arm. 'German guard, look, look, here! You see 'im?' He pointed through a porthole and Peter saw a German soldier in a long greatcoat, rifle slung over his shoulder, standing guard at the bottom of the gangplank. 'He come wit' us to Swinemünde. Make damn' sure we don't take passengers, see?' He laughed and Peter warmed to him. 'We drop 'im off to Swinemünde, then you come back to fo'c'sle. But now you eat and then I take you down to de bilges, eh?'

He cut huge open sandwiches of dry bread and cold fat bacon, with chopped gherkins and bright yellow mustard. When they had eaten he lit a paraffin storm lantern and led them down through a hatch at the foot of the forecastle companionway on to the deck below, down through another hatch into the hold, forward, and through a third hatch, forward again and down into the bilges where the anchor chain was stowed. He placed the lantern carefully on a shelf.

'My watch now,' he said. 'André, you tell 'em keep away from dat chain when we get to Swinemünde.' He grinned at Peter and John. 'When de anchor goes down at Swinemünde you know soon out of Germany.' He climbed back up the ladder and they could hear the hatches clanging as he dropped them shut behind him.

The air in the anchor locker was just as foul and it seemed even colder than it had been in the forepeak, but at least there was more room. Peter wondered why Larensen had hidden them in the cramped cubby-hole during the search; then realized it must have been because the Germans would have searched down here when they searched the cargo space. He turned to André.

'How long before Swinemünde?'

'*Ca dépend.* Four hours at least.' He yawned. 'The only thing to do is to sleep.'

There was a heap of old canvas in a corner. They shared it out and each made himself a bed. They settled down to sleep, André and John heavily, Peter fitfully. He was awake when he heard the slowing-down of the engine, and knew that they had reached Swinemünde. He roused the other two, and they all crouched against the cold hull as far away as they could get from the chain. When the anchor went down the chain ran out, plunging and kicking like a wild animal, thrashing from side to side in the confined space of the locker. All at once it stopped and they heard the lap, lap of the waves against the hull. They relaxed, appreciating the silence and stillness in the locker after the clatter and banging of the chain.

Peter lay on the oily canvas, listening to the slap of the water on the hull. This was the last check. If they passed this now they would be out of Germany. He heard a series of noises which he thought might be the pilot boat coming alongside and pushing off, and he imagined the pilot and the guard leaving the ship and the captain taking over.

Then the anchor came up, the chain dropping heavily into the locker, splashing them with rust and mud. The engine thumped faster and the ship began to move.

II

Peter reached for the torch in the pocket of his mackintosh and flashed it at his wrist. His watch had stopped. He sent the thin beam of light cutting across the nightmare blackness of the chain locker. John lay sleeping with his head on his arm; he looked dirty, unshaven and drawn. André, wrapped in his blanket, face turned to the bulkhead, was a shapeless mound that rose and fell as he snored.

His mouth tasted foul and his lips were dry and cracked. They had all been sick during the night. They had been sick until they had fallen asleep from sheer exhaustion. He himself had felt airsick many times, almost every time he flew; but he had never been seasick before. Not even when crossing the North Atlantic to and from Canada. The *Q.M.* had had stabilizers of course. And he had not had to make the voyage in the bilges.

The *S.I. Norensen* had run into a storm as she left the shelter of Swinemünde. Her plates creaking, propeller racing, the old freighter had pitched and tossed with violent shuddering jerks, and the water in the bilges had swished and rolled, filling the locker with the nauseating stink of fetid salt water, engine oil and the refuse of the years. It had not been so bad while they had the storm lantern. But when the paraffin ran out and they were left in the dark, unable to see but hearing each other's groans and retchings and cascades of sickness, then the locker had become a black, cold, damp, tossing, stinking hell.

He shifted his weight uncomfortably on the hard canvas. Wearily, scarcely caring, he knew that the storm had abated. The motion of the ship had eased to a slow roll and thud. He heard the hollow sound of footsteps on steel, coming nearer.

Incredibly the man was singing *South of the Border* and in English. Then the hatch opened and Sigmund's face was looking down into the locker, pale and ghost-like in the light of the lantern he held.

'Sorry,' he said cheerfully. 'We had to leave you too long. The German coast patrol followed us from Swinemünde. Goes home now, and you come up.' He swung the lantern to take in the scene below him and his smile changed to a frown of concern. 'Were you sick?'

'Just a little,' Peter said. 'Where are we?'

'I think I take you on deck for fresh air. I show you where we are. You come, André?'

'I go immediately to my bed,' André said. 'I prefer not to regard your execrable *Baltique*.'

•　　•　　•

They climbed up and up through the ship and when they emerged through the last hatch on to the deck above the forecastle the clean night air was like a drink of spring water. They stood filling their lungs and looking up at the stars. On the horizon, fine on the starboard bow, were clusters of lights brighter than the stars. As the ship rolled in the swell the lights and the stars swung in a big arc, diamonds juggled by a giant hand.

'You see Sweden?' Sigmund broke the silence. 'We turn North after we pass the Falsterborev lightship, and then we are soon in the Oresund. You can stay on deck with me until I go off watch if you like. I am lookout for shipping, and wrecks.' He rummaged in a large white-painted wooden box which was also a seat, and pulled out two sets of heavy black oilskins. 'These keep you warm, I think.'

'What time do we reach Copenhagen?' Peter asked.

'About eleven o'clock this morning.'

Then, he thought, we start all over again. Just like arriving in Stettin, not knowing the score – but worse, because we have no Danish money and no papers. He was going to ask Sigmund when they would meet the ship's officer who was going to help them when the boy spoke first.

'The officer of my watch is the First Officer. He is the one who says Yes or No to taking stowaway passengers – like you and André. On the way to Swinemünde we talk much because I do not understand why we take André to Sweden and must leave you in Copenhagen.' He broke off and peered into the darkness at the sea ahead.

Peter wanted to say, We don't understand either; but waited to hear Sigmund out.

'No, there is nothing I think . . . I ask how you go to Sweden. We discuss the possibilities for one, two hours, and at last Mr Olesen says I can tell you that you have two choices.' He was speaking slowly, choosing his words.

'What are they?' Despite himself Peter was becoming impatient.

'One choice is very quick but dangerous. The other is very slow but sure.'

'Let's take the quick way, Pete!' John said, at the same moment as Peter said, 'Better be slow and sure.'

Sigmund seemed to be amused by some secret joke. 'You do not wait until I tell you! The quick way – we go within a mile of the Swedish coast when we turn North towards the Oresund, the ship heaves to, we put a rope ladder over the side – and you swim ashore.'

'OK, Pete, you win. We'll walk down.' John turned back to Sigmund. 'What's the alternative?'

'You go with us.'

For several seconds they could not believe that he had said it. It's like climbing a mountain, hauling yourself up the vertical rock-face with pitons and rope, Peter thought, reaching the summit – and seeing a ramblers' path down the other side. He had to make sure.

'What made him change his mind?'

'I explain. I made him a speech. I tell him it is better if we help you than the French saboteurs, because you are trained officers. I tell him John will fight to liberate Europe when Mr Churchill starts the Second Front and Peter will bomb all the German factories. I tell him we must take you because of this. When I stop speaking he says, 'OK, but it is not possible for stowaways to stay on the ship while we load cargo in Copenhagen," and he says what I know already, that there is an arrangement for the Frenchman to go to a safe house but it is not possible to send you there too. I say, that is not a problem, that I will take you ashore and look after you in Copenhagen. And he says, "OK, fine, fine."

'So when I go to the fo'c'sle for my supper we have a big meeting there. I tell my shipmates what we will do and I ask them to agree not to get drunk ashore or bring strangers on board for a goodbye party before we sail again. Larensen was very angry with me – not because of what I say about the drinking but because he says he's the crew boss, he will take you to his house. But he stops being angry when I tell him that my stepbrother's flat is empty while he is fishing in the North Sea and that no one will know, but if he takes you to his house his wife and family will be in bad danger' He drew a deep breath and smiled at Peter. 'You are happy now? Home for Christmas, maybe?'

'Maybe,' Peter said, and grinned. 'So long as we don't have to go all the way in the bilges.'

'No, of course. We stay in Copenhagen two days and then sail for Oslo. With food for the Occupying Army,' he added bitterly. 'The Germans do not worry too much in Denmark because they think we go direct from one conquered country to another. But always we go inside the three-mile limit of Swedish waters, and always, from Göteborg or Strömstad, the Swedish pilot comes out to ask if we have passengers who would like to leave the ship. That way you land in Sweden without getting wet.' The ship's bell rang on the bridge. 'Fine – now I am off watch. We go below and you wash while I cook our breakfast. What do you like to eat?'

'Whatever there is, I'm ravenous,' John said.

'There are two choices,' Sigmund began solemnly; and for the first time since they had left the camp their laughter was carefree and wholehearted. 'One is bacon and eggs,' he continued, 'and the other is eggs and bacon.'

Limbo

I

'Let me out! Unlock this bloody door!' Shouting, he banged with clenched fists on the door of the cell.

He paused, waiting for footsteps in the corridor outside. There was no sound. The guard must be asleep. He looked round for something to help him make more noise. Enough light from a street lamp came through the high barred window to reveal the bucket that he refused to use, a small table, a narrow blanket-covered bed and a four-legged stool. He picked up the stool and swung it against the door. 'Unlock the door, will you!'

At last there were hurrying footsteps. A key turned in the lock and the door opened inwards. The policeman on the threshold was well into middle age, with thin grey hair. He looked tired and vulnerable now that he had shed his helmet and pistol holster.

Peter was ashamed. 'I'm sorry – I didn't mean . . . It was being locked in. And I want to go to the toilet.'

'Please come.' The man beckoned and led the way.

As Peter passed the duty desk on his way back to the cell, the policeman rose, picking up his keys.

'No,' Peter said. 'Leave the door open. Please. Why did you lock it?'

'It is the order of my chief. He gave his promise to the British Legation to keep you here tonight.'

'I know – but there was no need to lock the door.'

'Perhaps you go to café and we lose you and you miss the train. Then my chief has trouble with the Government in Stockholm.'

'The cafés are closed now,' Peter said. 'Leave the door unlocked. I've had enough of being a prisoner.'

'It is true that you and your friend are British officers? That you escape from German camp?'

'We told you.'

'I do it. But you must not tell the chief.'

'Of course not,' Peter said. 'Thank you.'

The policeman held out his hand and Peter shook it. Suddenly he wanted to laugh, and he wanted John to laugh with.

'Please unlock my friend's door too, so that we can talk.'

The man crossed to the door of John's cell and peered through the judas. Slowly he shook his head. 'He sleeps like my son,' he said. 'Let him sleep. We drink coffee and you talk with me.'

'No, thank you. It is very kind of you – but perhaps I will sleep again.'

He knew that he would not, but he did not want to talk to this friendly man who would naturally ask questions that he must not answer. He returned to his cell and lay on the bed with the door open. He looked at his watch. Six o'clock. At almost exactly this time yesterday Sigmund, in dripping oilskins and sea-boots, had clumped down the companionway into the forecastle; wakened him, John and André, and hustled them up on to the dark windswept deck. The *Norensen* was hove-to and a small motor vessel was lying about a hundred yards off amidships, bobbing in the white-breaking waves. In his mind's eye he could again see Sigmund lashing the top of a long rope ladder to cleats inside the bulwarks and hanging it outboard down the ship's side. He remembered his awkward descent of the swinging ladder as the motor boat came closer, engines revving, men shouting; the constantly widening and narrowing gap between its surging floodlit deck and the bottom rungs, with himself the weight on the pendulum; the conviction that he'd never make it; launching his body sideways at a moment when the boat below him crested a wave and rolled nearer; landing in a heap in the heaving deck and strong hands grabbing him as he scrambled unsteadily to his feet, pulling him out of danger and out of the way, to make room for John and André to follow. The white blur of Sigmund's face under his black sou'wester high above them, his voice windborne, calling, Home for Christmas! and their answering yells in unison of Maybe! The genial talkative English-speaking pilot and the taciturn sergeant of police whom he had brought out to take charge of them. Marching along the quiet quay, through the empty streets, to the police station; and the questions they were unable to answer except with their names, ranks and nationalities. The police chief making telephone calls to Stockholm and his impatience when they took hours to come through. A silent André being whisked away in a car by another equally silent Frenchman. He and John, escorted by a policeman, walking through the now busy streets to the municipal baths – and being vigorously scrubbed by a brawny blonde woman. The measures of schnapps, bottles of ice-cold beer, and platter of open sandwiches covered with a snow-white napkin, served in the police station by a waiter from a nearby restaurant. Being ushered into the cells for the night. The deep sleep of complete relaxation. Waking, wanting to urinate – but not in the bucket – and finding the cell door had been locked while he slept.

Perhaps John was awake by now; he would go and see. Together they could relish the irony of escaping from a German prison camp into a Swedish prison cell.

*   *   *

They were served another good meal in the charge-room and then escorted by the same policeman on the long electric train ride to Stockholm. He had changed into civilian clothes and explained carefully that he did not want to cause them embarrassment on the journey. He slept all the way. Peter and John talked desultorily and stared through the windows at red timber farmhouses and matching barns, neat fenced fields, sprawling dark forests and clean cheerful towns. They did not yet feel free. They would not be free until they could go where they wanted and without an escort.

*   *   *

Sigmund leans on the bulwarks and watches the stern light of

246

the pilot boat merge into the lights of the town of Strömstad. He is a little lonely, but also relieved. When the pilot boat did not appear off Göteborg, Strömstad was the last chance. It would have been too risky by far to keep the stowaways on board during the unloading at Oslo in order to land them in Sweden on the return trip. In Oslo a German from the Gestapo, speaking some Danish and keen to learn more, often hangs around in the forecastle; and the final search before the ship sails for neutral Göteborg is always the most thorough.

The sky is paler over Sweden in the east. Soon they are crossing the invisible line into Norwegian waters. He scans the horizon seaward and sees the bow waves of two dark grey warships heading straight for the ship. He races to the bridge and reports the sighting. First Officer Olesen shrugs non-committally and tells the helmsman to hold his course.

Within minutes the German warships are encircling them at speed. The larger slows down and from the bridge an Aldis lamp flashes a signal: YOU ARE UNDER ARREST. PRO-CEED TO HORTEN AND ANCHOR AS I COMMAND. Olesen gives the helmsman the new heading. The ship turns a few degrees to port. Sigmund goes off watch and warns his mates in the forecastle.

As the anchor rattles down in the outer basin of the naval port of Horten a landing craft comes alongside and a party of heavily armed Wehrmacht officers and men board the ship. The Germans go straight to the forecastle. The officer in charge orders the opening of the cubby-hole in the forepeak. He seems chagrined to find nothing there but coils of rope and tins of paint.

The ship's company is herded on deck. While the ship is systematically searched from stem to stern the Hauptmann questions the paraded men one by one; starting with the cabin boy and finishing with the captain. None has ever seen two Englishmen and a Frenchman on board.

The search and questioning having drawn blanks, the captain is ordered to carry on to Oslo and discharge his cargo. One of the warships shadows the *Norensen* up the fjord and does not peel off until the pilot boat and tug meet her at the harbour entrance.

When the gangplank goes down the Gestapo come on board and arrest Larensen, Sigmund, the other three foredeckhands and the cabin boy.

●　　　●　　　●

'Well that's about all for the moment I think. Now you'd better go and get kitted out.' The impeccably tailored military attaché looked from one to the other and shuddered. 'Can't have you showing the flag round Stockholm dressed like that, y'know.' He pressed a button on his uncluttered desk and lifted the telephone receiver. 'Fenning, our office manager, will take you along to the Nordiska Kompaniet.'

Peter glanced at John, then turned to the attaché. 'We'll manage,' he said. 'We'd rather go alone.'

'Oh no you don't. Fenning has to book it. In fact I rather think you're going to have two chaps with you.' He moved the receiver rest up and down. 'Get the Excelsior will you please? Extension 123. Hello? Millington-Butt here. Could you do me a favour and get down to the Legation right away? Good show.'

There was a knock on the door and an elderly man came in.

'Ah, Fenning. These two officers need some clothes. Could you take them along to the NK? In about ten minutes say?'

'Yes sir, of course.' The office manager sounded flustered. 'The same – ?'

'Yes, yes. Complete outfits.'

'I'll collect them in ten minutes then.' The door closed behind him.

The colonel leaned back and said cheerfully, 'The other chap'll be along at any moment. Help yourselves to a cigarette while you wait.' He waved a well-manicured hand in the direction of an engraved silver box on the coffee-table.

'What the hell do we need two for?' Peter was irritated at being treated like an army subaltern. The air attaché was away visiting a small-arms factory in the north of the country.

'Soon see, Howard. Tell Fenning to make sure you're back here by six-thirty to meet the Minister.' Another knock on the door. 'Come!'

The door opened and Philip walked in. He burst out laughing when he saw them. John shot upright in his chair.

'Phil,' he said incredulously, 'where on earth did you get that suit?'

∎　　∎　　∎

After two days' solitary confinement in a cell deep in the Victoria Terrasse Gestapo Headquarters Sigmund is reunited with his shipmates and they are all transferred to the concentration camp at Grini. The Gestapo chief has given instructions to the Kommandant that they be held separately, but the camp has no empty cells and they are housed together in a barrack block. That evening they confer and agree on 'fairy tales' invented by Sigmund with the object of confusing their captors.

The next morning they are marched out and lined up against a wall. The temperature is $-15°$ centigrade. They have only the trousers and sweaters they were wearing in the overheated forecastle at the time of their arrest. They are kept standing against the wall, without food or water, for eight hours, while a relay of Gestapo officers interrogates them.

Larensen is the only one who admits that he has seen stowaways on board the *Norensen*. He is detained, the other five are released. They rejoin the ship in time to sail for Göteborg and Copenhagen.

Sigmund is uneasy that under further interrogation Larensen might tell the Gestapo everything. He worries at the problem of how the Germans knew not only that the *Norensen* carried three stowaways but that they were English and French, and where they'd been hidden during the pre-sailing searches in Stettin and Copenhagen. He knows that both the ship's cook and engineer are pro-German; but he is convinced that even in his cups Larensen would not give the game away to them. He remembers how drunk Larensen was in Copenhagen, in spite of their compact. How he took pity on an ordinary seaman who had broken his leg and was out of work. How – again in spite of the compact – Larensen brought him on board and gave him a bunk in the forecastle. Sigmund wonders whether this man had a loose tongue ashore.

He is surprised that the Gestapo are not on the quayside to meet the *Norensen* when she docks in Copenhagen at the end of her run. She stays in her home port for ten days and the crew are given leave in rotation. His turn is last. By now he is no longer worried. He believes that Larensen, a good man when sober, has taken all the responsibility and that the Germans are satisfied. He enjoys his holiday and sees a lot of his girl-friend Kamma.

As he walks up the gangplank to rejoin the ship the day she sails for Stettin, ten men in Gestapo uniform follow him on board. Once more the entire ship's company is lined up on deck. Larensen's protégé hobbles up, his leg still in plaster. Sigmund tells him, You'd better disappear or they'll think you're one of us and suspect you too. The man seems not to hear. Sigmund repeats the warning.

This time the man answers. His voice is sullen and he does not meet Sigmund's eyes. He says that he works for the Gestapo.

The German officer asks the informer which member of the crew brought the stowaways on board before the ship sailed for Oslo.

The informer points to Sigmund.

2

The clock in the church tower across the road struck five and an early tram ground its way down Birgerjarlsgatan. In the deep-carpeted long-curtained hotel bedroom a thickset figure in burgundy silk pyjamas tossed and turned, cursing, on the softly sprung mattress. The slighter mop-headed figure in the other bed sat up. His pyjamas were sky blue.

'Pete – are you awake?'

'Yes. Damned if I can sleep.'

'They're too soft,' John said. 'You sink in too far.'

'It's not only the bed, it's the lobster I had for dinner. I feel damned ill.'

'I wonder if prison diet did us any permanent harm.'

'Shouldn't think so. They say sailors always react badly to fresh food after a long voyage, but get used to it.' He poured himself a glass of mineral water from the bottle on the bedside table and drank it down. 'How did your dinner party go?'

'Oh – the usual thing. We skolled one another and all that gubbins. As usual I was the only one not in evening kit.'

'The social lion, the guest of honour, the man who escaped from Germany.'

'Yes, I know, it was a bit like that. Where've you been?'

'I took Kristin to the cinema. Or perhaps she took me. Saw a film called *Spitfire*. Pretty sad-making it was too.'

'Did she cry.'

'No, but I did.'

'I saw a film called *Slümper Skorda* or something – *Random Harvest* in English – and I wept like a child.'

'We'll soon get blasé again.'

'Not Phil,' John said. 'He had three baths yesterday, a hair-cut, face massage and a manicure. Then he went and bought some silk stockings and kirbigrips for his wife and ski-suits for the twins.'

'I'm glad he made it. More glad about him than about us in a way.'

'I've often wondered why you were so keen to escape, Pete – having lost your wife, I mean.'

'It was living in a fool's paradise.'

'What was?'

'Oh – living in the camp. When you're in a crowd you don't have to face up to things. Like being in a monastery. So long as you kept your head firmly inside the camp life was quite pleasant – too easy.'

'Chaps could get on with what they wanted to do,' John said. 'Look at Pomfret – he was happy as a king reading books by women novelists. He hated all women – even his wife.'

'That's what I mean,' Peter said. 'It was too easy, being a prisoner. Life'll be complicated when we get home. I don't suppose they'll post me back to the squadron.'

'Why not?'

'Oh – Bomber Command won't let you operate in the same theatre once you've been a prisoner. In case you get caught again.'

'Hell. I hope they'll let me rejoin my regiment.'

'I'd like to learn to fly,' Peter said. 'Not just navigate. They said I was too old at the beginning of the war but I think things've changed.'

'I want some action.' John kicked off the bedclothes and bounced up and down on the mattress. 'I could do with a woman.'

'Doesn't Rita – ?'

'Not a chance. She's a jolly nice girl – good company and all that. But she's set her heart on marrying an Englishman and she's heard they only marry virgins.'

'Bad luck.'

'I'll see Millington-Butt this morning and get him to lay

on a popsie,' John said with decision. 'After all, he's a soldier too.'

'Was, you mean. He's more likely to signal the War Office for instructions.'

'Time they sent us home. I wonder what the hell they're playing at. I thought we'd fly back at once.'

'So did I.'

John turned restlessly. 'Hell – I'm putting the mattress on the floor.' He dragged the mattress off the bed, wrapped himself in the old cocoon-like manner and settled down with his arms behind his head. 'I came past the docks tonight. There was a ship there bound for Germany. I nearly stowed away and went back.'

'Not me,' Peter said. 'God, I was sicker then than I am now.'

'Wonder where André went?'

'And whether Sigmund's still on board. He was getting a bit chokka with Larensen.'

'Remember how angry he was to find Larensen shouting drunk outside that pub in Copenhagen docks?'

'It scared the pants off me. That's why I was so bloody rude to Larensen. I go cold now when I think of it. There he was, helping to get us to Sweden, and I threatened to knock his block off if he didn't stop shouting in English.'

John yawned. 'Nothing to what you threatened to do to that BOAC pilot at Bromma last week.'

'Don't remind me. But he's the one who always seems so damned delighted to have an excuse for not taking us.'

'Four-and-a-half weeks here is quite long enough,' John said. 'Why don't we vamoose – cross into Norway and join the Resistance?'

'I've had joining.' He knew then that the warm stench of comradeship that had sustained him through the months of captivity had been swept away by the cold wind of individual freedom. He lay thinking, then said slowly, 'The best part of escaping was when we were in charge of things. Building the horse, digging, planning – the break itself, and travelling across Germany. The feeling that every minute was vital, that everything one did could sway the balance between success and failure . . . The part I didn't enjoy was when we were in other people's hands – not knowing the score and having no say. First it was the French and then the Danes. Now it's the British. Although we're technically free we can't do a damned thing for ourselves, can't make a single decision. We can't even decide what to wear, because we've only one outfit. Here we are, stuck in Stockholm, having to telephone the Legation every day to see whether they've fixed our flight out – which they never have. I want to go home, get the war over and start running my own life.'

There was no response; John was asleep.

Peter went into the bathroom and had a cold shower. He felt better afterwards but even less like sleeping. He had never suffered from insomnia before. He knew that the root cause was dissatisfaction. Killing time. Maybe they had needed a holiday when they first reached Stockholm but now they had been idle too long. He thought back over the previous day. The lazy lie-in after breakfast in bed. Squash and smörgasbrod lunch with John. The cinema, and back to Kristin's flat for tea. The slim brown-haired girl boiling the kettle, asking him how the English make 'proper' tea, and wheeling the laden trolley in front of the cushioned divan. The gusto with which she tucked in to the cream cakes she had bought especially for the occasion. Then, to please him, switching on the BBC news.

It had taken him straight back to the other flat, in Copenhagen. He saw Sigmund turning the key in the lock, his puzzled frown at the hum of a vacuum cleaner. A young woman with tousled fair hair, cheeks flushed from bending, switching off the machine. Her pleasure as she exclaimed, Sigmund! and the change of expression as she looked over his shoulder at himself and John standing awkwardly on the landing. Her face paling, eyes darkening with fear. She spoke in rapid Danish, asking questions. Sigmund replied in a reassuring tone but he looked worried. The girl put on a fur hat and brown leather coat; glanced at the wall clock; hesitated; then wound the handle of an old-fashioned gramophone – playing *Lilli Marlene*, very loud. Nervously beckoning to Peter and John he crossed the room and knelt in front of the radiogram. She turned a knob and switched it on, but softly, so that they too had to kneel with their ears close to the loud-speakers. They heard the V signal *di-di-di-dah*, *di-di-di-dah*, beaten on an African drum, followed by a BBC accent reading the midday news. They thanked her, touched by the gesture. She smiled wanly, picked up gloves and handbag, kissed Sigmund on the cheek and left the flat.

Sigmund told them that she was his stepbrother's wife. When her husband was away on his trawler she always stayed with her parents but today, feeling energetic, she had come to clean out the flat. He said that he blamed himself for not telephoning first to make sure she was not there; the last thing he wanted to do was involve her.

Soon Sigmund returned to the ship and he and John were alone, with nothing to do for the next forty-eight hours but sleep and listen to the BBC. And play the gramophone loudly, to drown the English voice on the radio.

•   •   •

The clock in the church tower had finished striking eight when he heard whispering and giggling in the hotel corridor, a woman's voice softly cajoling. There was a tentative tap on the door before it was pushed open to reveal four children, girls in long white dresses, golden hair gleaming in the flickering flames of a crown of candles on the head of the tallest. She frowned gravely as she concentrated on walking slowly and steadily into the room, holding a long silver tray. In silence she offered him and John cups of coffee and saffron cakes while her hand-maidens, grouped behind her in the middle of the carpet began to sing *Santa Lucia*.

The last '. . . *Lucia*' dissolved in more giggles and the woman's voice came from the doorway. 'It is the Swedish Festival of Light today. It is our hope for sun and the end of the long northern winter.'

As the door closed behind the small procession he found himself in tears for the second time in twenty-four hours. In spite of his lack of belief he wanted to pray to Santa Lucia that

255

these children of light would never know the dark fear of the girl in whose flat he had been sheltered in Copenhagen.

*   *   *

It is the shortest day of the year and Sigmund has been in Copenhagen's West Prison for thirty days. He thinks maybe he should celebrate. He is alive, the cell is centrally heated, his friends send in food. He has not – so far – been badly treated, merely shown the torture chamber as a threat. It seems that the Gestapo do not know what to do with him.

He thinks back to his second arrest. This time the Gestapo ignore the other three deckhands; Larensen is still in the Norwegian concentration camp at Grini. Only he and the cabin boy are marched down the gangplank and into the waiting car. Real psychologists the Huns, always taking the youngest as the most likely to talk. But the policy doesn't always pay off – it hasn't with young Povl.

Outside Dagmarhus headquarters the Gestapo leave the two of them alone in the car for a few minutes. He and the boy make a dash for it, but they are caught immediately. Instead of taking them into the Dagmarhus their captors bundle them back into the car and drive them to the West Prison.

Regularly every week the two prisoners are interrogated by their jailers. Sometimes one or the other says, 'Oh yes I remember . . .' and a German comes from the Gestapo headquarters to hear one of Sigmund's 'fairy tales'. The Gestapo man always offers them cigarettes, to encourage them to talk, and leaves the packet behind when he goes.

Thirty days is quite long enough, Sigmund thinks. How am I going to escape? Perhaps if I sham illness and get taken to an ordinary hospital . . . He is working on the idea when the door of the cell is flung open by a warder. A well-dressed civilian walks in. He is a Dane and introduces himself as a lawyer. He is friendly and tells Sigmund that he will be free within the hour. Sigmund decides that now the Gestapo is playing jokes on him and telling him 'fairy tales'. The visitor is amused at his incredulity and says he is lucky to have a nice girl-friend and a charming stepmother with influence. His head whirling,

Sigmund begs the lawyer to explain. What he hears does indeed sounds like a fairy tale.

When his stepmother learns from Kamma that he is held in West Prison she goes to intercede for him, to tell the Gestapo what a good boy he is. Before the First World War she spent two years as a children's nurse in Germany. She speaks German fluently and takes with her to Dagmarhus her souvenir of those carefree days, a poesy book with many German entries. She shows the book to the Gestapo officer who interviews her. Idly he turns the pages. He stops and stares first at a handwritten entry, then at the middle-aged Danish woman before him. We have both changed a little, he says, and shows her his own handwriting.

After that, the lawyer tells him, it was only a question of time and the proper channels before the order for your and your friend's release. But do not bank on being left alone for long. Take care.

An hour later Sigmund collects a radiant Kamma and goes home to thank his stepmother. They celebrate his freedom and she tells him that Danes in the Resistance have executed the informer.

3

The month of December moved slowly but inexorably towards Christmas and they were still in Stockholm. Time and again, when they made their daily report by telephone to the Legation, they were told to go to the airport ready to fly that night. Time and again they cancelled their dates for the evening, said their farewells and made the journey out to Bromma; only to learn that the weather was too duff, or the aircraft needed servicing, or it hadn't arrived, or passengers with priority had the only seats.

After months of intensive effort and the nervous strain of the escape they felt increasingly frustrated. They spent the mornings sleeping late, the afternoons playing squash and taking sauna baths, and the nights – once they knew for sure that they were not flying – in carousing. They were fed up with limbo, with being treated as 'the boys' and with being put on show for their achievement. They knew that they were rotting, wasting their time. They wanted to get on with the war.

Christmas Day came and went, with a midday family party at the Residence. The Minister's wife was kind and sympathetic. The Minister himself promised to do all he could to get them home.

On Boxing Day Philip left; even he had been depressed at missing another Christmas with the twins.

When Peter rang the Air Attaché's office at four p.m. two days later he was told that they were to go to Bromma right away because an aircraft was leaving for Leuchars that night. They were at the airport by five. The pilot of the waiting Mosquito said they might as well go back to town. There was no hope of a seat as he had to take two civilian VIPs who had been over on a swan.

Peter and John had been kicking their heels in neutral Sweden one day short of seven weeks.

*   *   *

The door suddenly gave way under their combined assault and they fell forward into the room. On all fours Peter crawled to the bedside table and reached for the telephone. His wavering grab was inaccurate. The bell stopped ringing as the instrument crashed to the floor. With elaborate care, kneeling upright he replaced the telephone on the table. Immediately the ringing began again.

'Better answer it ol' boy.' John had flung himself fully dressed on his eiderdown.

'*Ich bin Hauptmann Zimm!*' Peter bellowed into the receiver.

'At long last.' The voice, a husky contralto, belonged to the Air Attaché's secretary. 'Groupy's been on the rampage all evening – and I gather he's not the only one. Where were you two at seven o'clock?' There was a faint buzz in the background and she spoke more briskly. 'No, sir, not yet. I'll connect you immediately they get back. I traced them to the Students' Beer Cellar in the Old City – one of the song leaders is seeing them to the Excelsior now.' She drew a deep breath. 'I promised the manager that Mr Fenning would be around in the morning to pay for the damage . . .Oh not much, sir, a few dozen . . . No – glasses, not kroner. It'll be about three hundred kroner I'm afraid – they were specially engraved Orrefors tankards ... Yes, sir,' frostily, 'I am very sorry, but you were tied up with the Minister and the manager already had the police there. I thought the last thing we wanted . . . Thank you, sir. Yes, I'll keep trying.' A sharp click and her voice changed again. 'Come on now – seven o'clock?'

'Gatecrashed a wizard party, sweetheart. But it broke up soon afterwards.'

'It wouldn't have been the official reception at the German Embassy by any chance?'

'Funny you should mention that – there *was* a big red flag

with a swash-swastika hanging over the front door.'

'I gather there wasn't when you left. You're for the chop this time my lad. The Foreign Office summoned the Minister from his dinner for the visiting firemen, and demanded a full explanation – ' The buzzer sounded again. 'Yes, sir, I've got Flight Lieutenant Howard on the line now. You're through.'

'That you Howard? Clinton with you? Both in good order I hope?'

'Yeshir. Bang on.'

'Got good news for you. You're flying to UK at midnight.'

'Tonight? We're flying *tonight*? He flapped his free hand urgently at John who swung his legs to the floor, heaved himself to his feet and rushed into the bathroom.

'Yes indeed. No more pressing engagements I hope?'

'No, sir.' Peter was sobering fast. 'But when we reported at Bromma earlier on they said that two VIPs had priority.'

'Yes – quite right, they *were* going. But the Minister had a word with them, and they're standing down. Saw the point at once, agreed you – er – deserved to go home right away.'

'That's very decent of them.'

'Oh, we're all rallying round – laying on an elk hunt for them tomorrow. Chance to try out m'new rifle.' Abruptly he changed the subject. 'One thing before you go.'

'Sir?'

'The flag. The Minister – ' there were swallowing sounds in Peter's ear. 'That is, I've strict orders that you hand it in at the Legation on your way to the airport.'

'Flag, sir?' He looked down at John who had spread the huge rectangle of red bunting with its central Nazi emblem flat on the carpet and was trying to fold it small enough to pack.

'Don't waste my time, Howard. I assume you've still got it?'

'I'm afraid not, sir.'

'Where the blazes is it?'

A fuddled brain grasped at the word blazes. 'We burned it. Made a bonfire under the Christmas tree outside the King's Palace.'

'You didn't – ' a strangled cry, 'you didn't set fire to the tree?'

'I don't – no, I don't think we did.'

'Howard – I'm sending Squadron Leader Flack over. He'll see you both safely on that plane.'

'No need to bother the Squadron Leader, sir. We'll start out right away. There's more than an hour yet – '

'No! Just stay where you are until he gets there. My driver's gone for him, then he'll take you all out to the airport.'

'Very good of you, sir.'

'Least I can do. And Howard – '

'Sir?'

'Hide it – wrap it round your arse if necessary. But if you let Flack or anyone at Bromma catch a glimpse of it I'll have your balls. Is that understood?'

'Perfectly, sir.'

'Have a good trip. I've signalled the Air Ministry so for God's sake don't get sidetracked on the way.'

'No, sir. Thank you very much – '

'Don't thank me. Thank your lucky stars.' The line went dead.

•   •   •

It was drizzling when they landed at Leuchars aerodrome in the early hours of the morning. They were not expected. After a long wait in an ante-room they were taken before the senior intelligence officer, an army major wearing tartan trews. He did not invite them to sit down while he took their ranks, names and numbers. The German officer who had interrogated Peter when he was captured had been more polite.

'You have to report to the War Office and the Air Ministry,' the major said in dismissal.

'How do we get to London from here?' Peter was hoping that they would fly.

The major was flustered. 'There's – ah – a train for Edinburgh at eight-thirty I think. Then there's the Flying Scotsman. Ah – I'll get my clerk to issue the warrants.'

'Can you lay on a car to the station-'

'Ah – there's a shuttle service. Leaves the main gate on the hour.'

'Can we get a meal first?' John asked.

'Ah – you'll find something in the airmen's mess I think.'

They were given left-over cold bacon and potatoes on enamel plates. The corporal in charge was worried because they had not brought their own knives and forks. There were still two hours to kill before the train; they found empty beds in a crowded dormitory, and fell asleep. Ten minutes later Peter was wakened by a batman.

'The major wants to see you, sir.'

'I've just seen him.'

'He told me to call you, sir.'

Peter climbed out of bed and began to pull on his dressing-gown.

'I should advise you to dress properly, sir. The major's a stickler for proper dress.'

Keep a tight grip, Peter told himself. Don't say what you think. You really are home now.

For a second time he stood in front of the major's desk. There was a captain with him who might have posed as the original for Lancaster's cartoon, *Intelligence has just reached me* . . . He asked Peter's rank, name and number.

'You've just had them.'

The major mumbled something about losing the piece of paper, about needing the details for the travel warrants. He looked too old to be up at that early hour. Peter felt sorry for him. He repeated his rank, name and number.

'How long were you in the bag?' the major asked.

Peter told him.

'What was it like?' He seemed to be making conversation, trying to atone for getting him out of bed.

He could describe the damp barrack blocks at Oflag XXIB, fetid and close from overcrowded living, the rows and rows of two-tier bunks, the scuffing of wooden clogs on damp concrete as the bearded and dirty kriegies queued up for the mid-day ration of cabbage water. He could describe the circuit, the crowd of lonely figures, shoulders hunched, eyes on the mud path, mooching slowly round; self-contained figures, lonely in spite of the proximity of a thousand like them, refusing to acknowledge the existence of the wire. But what could he say of the companionship, of the humour, of the fierce joy of baiting the Hun. What could he say of the home that each man had made of his bed space, the rough shelves above the bunks, the few books, the photographs, the spontaneous gifts when the giver had so little to spare. Of how each man was stripped naked in front of his fellows and was accepted for what he was rather than for what he had. What could he say of the decency and tolerance of the average man. Words could not convey what he felt about that strange, unhappy, glorious, quarrelling, generous, indomitable, scruffy family that he had left behind.

'It wasn't so bad in some ways,' he said. 'The chaps were pretty good.'

'How did the Germans treat you?'

He could tell of Alan, shot through the belly as he climbed the wire; starvation rations, solitary confinement, the stupid petty restrictions. He could tell of the kindly easy-going guards with families at home, and their fear of the Gestapo and the Russian Front. Of the bullying braggart of a Feldwebel who was nothing but a lout and was as likely to have been born in England as in Germany.

'They weren't too bad,' he said. 'There were some decent ones.'

'I hear you had a golf course,' the captain said.

A golf course . . . He looked at the smug non-prisoner face. A golf course. He remembered the earnest ragged kriegies knocking home-made balls round the huts with clubs made from melted-down water jugs. He turned to the major.

'I'd like to get a bath before the train goes.'

'A *bath*?' You would have thought he had never heard of one. 'Ah – I'm afraid – the officers' quarters – there's no hot water.'

Peter gave up the idea. There was probably no heating either. 'Can you let us have some money? We have to cross Edinburgh. Buy meals on the train. Then get from King's Cross to White-hall.'

'You should have been given English money before you left Sweden,' the captain said.

'We've only got Swedish money.'

'There's no – ah – machinery for giving you English money here.' The major was getting flustered again.

263

There was a short silence. The captain asked, 'Do you have a cheque book?'

'Don't be bloody silly.'

The captain saw the red light. He leaned over the major's shoulder. 'I think we can trust them, sir,' he whispered. 'After all, they *are* officers.'